Women in MIDLIFE Crisis

JIM & SALLY CONWAY

LIVING BOOKS

Tyndale House Publishers, Inc.

WHEATON, ILLINOIS

Books by Jim and Sally Conway:

Men in Midlife Crisis, Jim Conway
Your Husband's Midlife Crisis, Sally Conway
Women in Midlife Crisis, Jim and Sally Conway
Maximize Your Midlife Crisis, Jim and Sally Conway
Your Marriage Can Survive Midlife Crisis, Jim and Sally Conway
Making Real Friends in a Phony World, Jim Conway
Trusting God in a Family Crisis, Becki Conway Sanders and Jim and Sally Conway
Menopause, Sally Conway
Adult Children of Legal or Emotional Divorce, Jim Conway
Traits of a Lasting Marriage, Jim and Sally Conway
When a Mate Wants Out, Sally Conway, Jim Conway
Sexual Harassment No More, Jim Conway, Sally Conway
Pure Pleasure: Making Your Marriage a Great Affair, Bill and Pam Farrel and Jim and Sally Conway
Moving On after He Moves Out, Jim Conway, Sally Conway

The Conways have over one million books in print in English and several other languages.

Visit the Conways' Web site at www.midlife.com

ISBN 0-8423-8383-2

Printed in the United States of America

04   03   02   01   00   99   98
8   7   6   5   4   3   2

DEDICATION

To our daughters:

Barbara Conway Schneider
Brenda Conway Russell
Becki Conway Sanders

They have helped us to more fully understand
Life
People
God
and Ourselves

CONTENTS

FOREWORD

Years ago my daughter came home with a stress test from her high school psychology text and gave it to me. I tested out at about 450 points—a healthy recommended average was about 230 points!

It has been another hard year. (I've stopped saying, "Last year was the hardest year of our lives," because I've learned that the middle years of life are often filled with one difficulty after another.) Oh, the normal demands I've learned to juggle: meeting writing deadlines, raising children, and coping with needy people living in our home. But the outward circumstances over which I have no control—such as the death of a parent—often raise my stress quotient. . . .

Mother died on my birthday, my thirty-ninth birthday, and all the next year I knew I would turn forty on the first anniversary of my mother's death.

Unconsciously I began preparing myself for midlife passage when I was twenty-nine years old. I realized then that the woman I would become at forty was the one I decided to be at thirty. I think I would probably have flown through this, my thirty-ninth year, with raised colors and little hesitation . . . but my mother died only two years after my father's death. And the sudden realization that life, *no one's life*, is permanent plunged me into a year of intense personal evaluation.

In some ways, it has been a ruthless evaluation—I am learning not to be sparing when it comes to personal growth. There was fatigue to identify, depression to refuse, healthy work of grief to endure. But deeper, much deeper than this, was the question: What do I want to do with the rest of my life, with the rest of whatever life is remaining to me?

The Lord and I battled that year, not in the adversarial sort of way, but in the co-unioned sort of way; and as all spiritual journeys can become, this turned out to be a sociological journey as well.

I questioned: What gifts have I been given that enabled me to do a job that few others in the kingdom could do? What is the inward calling that is stronger than any other? In what ways was it being diffused into less meaningful activities and commitments?

I discovered that, after ten years of writing, writing is still my deepest calling, but it was becoming a new kind of writing, a writing I have never before done. It had a sharp and different edge.

I discovered a longing for the contemplative life. Though my life is filled with people, I am basically an introvert in that I draw my strength from silence, from quiet, from thought. I began to design a new lifestyle in which prayer and silence were the center, and I refused speaking invitations for the next several years.

As the older children left home to go to college, I discovered areas of neglect in the two younger boys. I had only a few years left for corrective parenting. These were dangerous years for my boys, and I wanted to be near.

Well, the discoveries went on and on, and I would not have missed this inward sociological examination of my soul, this midlife passage. I might have overlooked it or stored it away for a more opportune moment, had Mother not died on my birthday.

In essence, I have reorganized all my intentions, begun scraping away at the gathered barnacles collected while passing through the seas of my thirties. I felt very good about the year forty, even though I would face more difficult questions.

Even more important, I think I'm going to enjoy the woman I will be at sixty because of this habit of inward reflection.

I highly recommend Jim and Sally Conway's book *Women in Midlife Crisis* for every woman (and every man who cares about a woman), whether she is in midlife passage or only looking ahead to one, or wondering what it was that hit her a while back.

This is a book that will stimulate, expose, and explain the inward journey. But it also gives wonderful, healthy, hands-on ways to traverse the inward path and return whole. It forces on us the questions we should all be asking if we are to best fulfill the promise of this life as it is measured in the cadences of decades.

Karen Burton Mains, 1998

PREFACE

How Have Things Changed?

What's the same? In the early eighties we thought midlife crisis was a new issue that would soon disappear as people understood it. But this has not been the case. Current letters to our Midlife Dimensions office carry the same intensity of pain and confusion. Many people even feel as though they are lepers in the Christian community. Husbands tell us their wives were stable, community-involved, church-attending women who suddenly dropped out and ran off with another man.

Husbands describe other changes such as depression, anger, confusion, and a driving desire to catch up on what they feel they have missed. Our office receives thousands of letters, E-mails, and telephone calls every year. The volume is more than twenty times what it was in the early eighties. People seem to reach out to us as their last hope for help with their midlife crisis. A common statistic reported in the 1960s was that six hundred men abandon their homes for every one woman who does. In the nineties an equal number of women and men abandon their homes.

This book has been printed in several other languages as well as English. We hear from people around the world who have read about our books, connected to our Web page, or attended a conference. Midlife crisis is *not going away!*

What's different? The largest segment of the U.S. population, baby boomers, are in midlife. Boomers have grown up expecting it all. But there isn't room for everybody to be company president, drive a Beamer, live in a gated pool community, and have a condo in Palm Springs or Vail. There just isn't enough to go around. There's a deep sense of failure in the lives of many boomers. Now they must make painful choices as they simplify their lives—which often triggers a full-blown midlife crisis.

The media have also changed. In the seventies the computer was a professional tool used only by business and government. The personal computer wasn't on everyone's desk. There was a Web network, but it linked only educational institutions for research. Now home access to the Internet is a reality with all of the benefits—and moral dangers.

Morals in the U.S. are very different. Sexual intercourse was obliquely referred to on TV. But now during prime time you can enter a TV bedroom as actors roll around nude—"making love." On the "Net," it's possible to connect to hundreds of pornographic Internet sites.

But even more seductive for women are the

chat rooms. A woman in California can have an intimate and sexually provocative connection with men on our East Coast or in Australia. This remote sexual experience has been described as the "ultimate safe sex."

TV is not to be left out. It's as if TV is competing with the Internet to see who can be the most sexually explicit. In the spring of 1997, Pamela Anderson Lee, the busty *Baywatch* babe, was the host of *Saturday Night Live*. On live television she took off all of her clothes. Sadly this event was not even noticed as a moral issue. A few weeks later, Ellen Degeneres, in a much promoted episode of *Ellen*, declared she was gay.

How have things changed? In the early eighties midlife crisis was still thought of as unusual, but now it's part of our common experience.

Jim Conway, 1998

PART ONE

Surprised by Midlife Crisis

Collision of Expectations and Reality

I wanted to crawl under the bed. Or better yet, I just wanted to disappear. I didn't want to run away and be somewhere else on the earth. I just wanted to be gone. I didn't want to commit suicide—I just wanted to cease to exist.

I felt so frustrated, and my husband just lay there, falling asleep. I wanted him to talk to me, but I didn't know how to make him talk without making him angry. I finally gave a big sigh and crawled out of bed. In the dark I walked into the living room. Strange emotions were boiling inside me—emotions that had once been unfamiliar but were now all too common. Most of all I wished Jim would be concerned enough to come find me. I wanted to feel loved and comforted; instead I felt terribly alone. I didn't feel openly rejected by him, but he didn't seem to care about my raging internal turmoil.

Of course, I chided myself, I should understand that he was very busy with managing a growing church, and tomorrow was a full day for him—lots of meetings and appointments. He needed his sleep, so I shouldn't expect him to put up with my troubles. Besides, when we did talk, I couldn't seem to help him understand me. I just got more confused and frustrated, and we usually ended up with even more bad feelings toward each other. There wasn't time or emotional energy (or, as I see now, wisdom) to work it all out. It was just better to go to sleep and forget. I also faced a busy day—I always did—but my daily life as a pastor's wife seemed part of another world, foreign and misty and not quite real.

Sure, I would get up as usual and have my devotions ("Please, dear God, today help me die to self, help me not to feel hurt and mad"). Then I'd help Jim and the girls get off to their day's activities, and I'd really dig into my work around the house. I would make several phone calls for a committee meeting later in the week, run errands, get a letter off for someone's birthday, keep appointments with people either in my home or theirs, and have a nice meal ready in the evening.

That evening I'd see that our three girls got off to an evening activity, or I'd help them with homework and piano practice. I would answer the phone several times, do an unplanned load of wash to have one of the girls' gym clothes clean for the next day, let the dog in and out several times, and feel guilty that I hadn't had more time for a sick friend. I'd enjoy hearing the girls tell bits and pieces about their day at school or listen to one of them share some new insight as I tucked them all into bed. After telling them good night, I would get a few more things done before Jim got home from a meeting and we dropped into bed.

And then that gnawing uneasiness I had felt off and on all day would grow stronger and stronger. I wanted to share it with Jim and have him help me get rid of it. He counseled everyone else and received their praise for being so wise and helpful; why wouldn't he help me? Sometimes he did. But too often, I thought, his perception of my need missed the mark. More often, he just didn't seem even to try to understand. He was preoccupied with the church—new programs, plans for spiritual and numerical growth, stimulating meetings with students—great things happening as God worked in other people's lives. I had always shared in his "pastoring"; now I felt left out and unneeded—like a discarded old box. When I looked at the facts, my life wasn't any different from before. I was still active, involved, and included, but I didn't *feel* the same as I felt a few years ago.

A wave of self-pity would wash over me. Then a bigger wave of jealousy would slam into me. And before I could get myself righted from that blow, a third wave of just plain rejection and hurt would hit me. An old box—yes, I felt like a soggy cardboard box, bobbing just offshore. Soon I would be hopelessly saturated and would sink.

But I didn't want to sink! Well, yes, often I did want to vanish from life, but what I really wanted was for my inner confusion to vanish—to get on with the happy life I was supposed to be living. Part of me *was* happy, but a big chunk of me was miserable, and I didn't know why.

Experiences like these were common to me during the last half of my thirties. My frustration and confusion were especially intense from about age thirty-six through thirty-nine. Jim and I thought the problem was simply unique to me—some personal quirks I needed to work out. I struggled desperately with feeling unspiritual, and I went through various spiritual exercises to "die to self" and "crucify the flesh."

Life *Begins* at Forty??

Now we understand that the problem was my transition into midlife. Ever since *Men in Midlife Crisis* (Jim Conway, December 1978) and *You and Your Husband's Midlife Crisis* (Sally Conway, November 1980) were published, we have been contacted by thousands of women from the United States and Canada who also are experiencing a midlife crisis. We have heard heart-wrenching stories from single and married women from all circumstances of life. The severity of the problems varies, but all are seeing age forty on the horizon or have just passed it. They talk about a change in their emotions and their perceptions of life. Many have a strong compulsion to run away—some actually have. Others feel the turmoil less intensely but still are unsettled by it.

We searched to find studies about women at midlife. Although some involved women in their late thirties and early forties, no studies identified women's stress at this era of life as a common pattern among women—a midlife crisis. Many studies and articles did, however, discuss the well-recognized menopausal stress of the late forties or early fifties. We began to ask, If this is such a common experience, what causes it? What can be done to help ease the pressures? We both began to do research and will be reporting what we learned throughout this book.

Colliding Emotions

The midlife transition hits women in many different ways. Take the situation with Ellen, for example.

At a Bible conference, Ellen* had asked to talk to me (Jim) privately. Her lower lip quivered. Her eyes darted back and forth as she scanned my face. She looked desperate. She needed to talk to someone, yet she was afraid because she was a Christian leader in her church.

We went to a quiet place where we could have privacy, and the story began to pour out. The family had spent the summer in a cabin by a mountain lake. Her husband, Fred, stayed in the city to work during the week, but he would come up each weekend. Her oldest son had brought along his friend

*In this illustration and throughout the book, we have changed names and disguised circumstances to protect the privacy of the people involved.

Jeff, age seventeen, to stay with them for the summer. Ellen said that on several occasions when Jeff had been at their house in the city, she had felt that he was watching her. Frequently their eyes had met, and their prolonged gaze had silently communicated a mutual appreciation and stimulation.

"At the time," she said, "I didn't think too much about it, other than that it was flattering to have a good-looking young man look at me with such admiration, especially since my husband seemed too busy even to notice me."

The family had been at the cabin for about two weeks. Fred had joined them for the weekend and had returned to the city on Sunday night. All the kids got up early the next morning to go fishing, except Jeff, who decided to sleep in.

"I had fed them all breakfast and cleaned up the kitchen after they left. Then I decided to wake Jeff. As I pushed open his bedroom door, I saw him sleeping facedown with the top half of his muscular body uncovered. I softly whispered his name, but he didn't respond. So I sat on the edge of the bed and began to gently rub his back to awaken him. He slowly rolled over and said, 'That feels good.' Before I knew what was happening, we were kissing each other, and one thing led to another."

Ellen fidgeted in the chair and kept her eyes down, staring at her hands as she clasped and unclasped her fingers. Slowly, but with great feeling, she said, "I was a very willing partner. Sex with him was not a duty as it was with my husband. It was exhilarating. On that morning I experienced my first orgasm.

"It didn't end with that morning. I found excuses to be alone with him all summer. Now that we are back in the city for the school year, I constantly long to be with him.

"What's happening to me? I'm a Christian. I am a leader in my church. I know this is wrong. I don't want to lose my family. I don't believe in divorce. I know he is only seventeen years old, but the fantasies are running wild in my brain. Someone really loves me and makes me feel like a woman. He has taken away that terrible sense of loneliness and exploitation I feel with my children and my husband. I know I've got to stop seeing him, but I don't want to go back to living the life I had before—a sweet, smiling homemaker, meeting everybody's needs— but not even noticed by my husband."

Even in the Best of Women

We have found that the midlife transition can be difficult for all types of women—married, never married, formerly married; women with or without children; women with previously satisfying careers; and women in a variety of socioeconomic circumstances.

Some single women who always hoped to marry tell us that turning forty seems to be the absolute end to all their hopes. Other single women, who made a choice not to marry so they could throw their energies into education and career, began to have second thoughts when they neared forty.

Some have said, "I see now that I don't want to grow old alone." One single woman confessed, "Until now I felt a husband and kids would just block me from what I wanted to do. Now I wish I had a husband for companionship."

Some women, whether married or unmarried, have a rough, explosive, crisis-type transition into midlife. Others experience only a quiet restlessness and inner confusion without much disruption in their lives or relationships.

Between sessions at a women's retreat where I (Sally) was speaking, I was standing in line at the bookstore, waiting to pay for greeting cards. Although I was not at the retreat to speak on midlife problems, I had been introduced as an author, and wife of an author, of midlife books. As the checkout line moved slowly toward the counter, the pretty, trim woman ahead of me turned and asked, "When are you going to write a book about women's midlife crises?" She then began to pour out her confusion. Her story was very similar to many others we had been hearing in recent months.

"I am thirty-six—but feel as if I'm going on fourteen. I'm struggling with the same feelings I had when I was a young teenager," this composed-looking woman told me. I'm sure others around couldn't detect the disorder she was feeling inside.

"I have a wonderful husband and love him very much. We have two children, and I enjoy being a mother. I have everything that should make me a happy woman, but I feel so torn up and restless inside. I feel empty, and I don't know what's missing. I just want to run away."

She was an active, growing Christian, but her internal confusion was very bewildering. On the one hand, she knew in her mind who she was and what she valued in life, but emotionally everything was scrambled. Her life seemed hollow and vacant. At times, so many responsibilities pressed in and so many strange thoughts bombarded her mind that she felt almost overwhelmed.

No Pat Answers

For about three and a half years we did serious research on women at midlife, not centering so much on the age of menopause and the empty nest, but looking at the era of midthirties and early forties. We've discovered that a number of women go through an emotional trauma of crisis proportion during this time. In this book we'll be referring to this experience as "midlife crisis."

There are no neat conclusions about causes and cures for a woman's midlife crisis. In fact, the actual feelings and events are not alike for any two women. Human behavior and emotions are too complex for cut-and-dried answers. Some *generalizations*, however, can be made from our research data and from the women we have counseled and interviewed. Some or all of the following factors may produce stress or cause a crisis for a woman in the last half of her thirties and early forties:

1. Our cultural view of women as lesser persons
2. An unhappy marital situation or lack of a marriage
3. Her husband's own midlife crisis
4. Demands from children and their growing independence
5. Career priorities related to other life priorities
6. An accumulation of traumatic events, such as death, illnesses, or aging
7. Urgency from her inner clocks to accomplish her life dreams
8. Imperative pressure to review the past and plan the future

Some of these factors are intensified by the mere passing of time. A woman may be forced to realize that some of her expectations are never going to be met. For example, she can put up with a poor marriage for years, thinking "someday soon" it will change. Or she may hope for another child or to become vice president of her company. But by midlife she is faced with the hard reality that not all of her dreams will be realized. There is truly a "collision of expectations and reality."

Every woman will go through the transition from being a young adult to being a midlife adult.

Not all women will have a crisis. Our studies, however, show that more than two-thirds of women do. It is our hope that understanding more about the transition—and potential crisis—will help midlife women, their families, friends, and everyone concerned.

Inner Feelings at Midlife

How do you describe what it feels like when you are in midlife crisis? A Christian midwestern woman who is forty-four and is a frequent speaker at women's clubs described her own midlife crisis in one word: *lonely*. "You feel as if no one understands, and if they do understand, they don't care. You are in it by yourself."

Another woman, age thirty-four, commented, "For the first time in my life I am admitting to myself and everyone around me who I really am and what I want to be. First, I always did what my parents wanted me to do, and then I did what my husband wanted. My parents think I'm acting strangely now, but for the first time in my life I am really acting like myself." This woman had just left her husband and three young children and started working full-time to fulfill her professional dream.

A thirty-eight-year-old East Coast woman declared, "I feel as if I am drowning. Pressures are coming from all sides—caring for my children, making my husband successful, meeting responsibilities at church, PTA, and my part-time job. And now my dad has just had a heart attack. I'm caring for everybody. But who cares for me?"

IN THE PITS

Many women report that they don't know who they are by midlife. These women experience varying degrees of depression. They sense some loss—or many losses. Many feel hopeless and worthless. They often interpret the actions of their husband, children, employers, or fellow workers to mean that they are unneeded, unwanted, and unattractive. They feel burned out and exploited. Their lives seem out of control. They are angry at the telltale signs of aging.

In adolescence a girl struggles to establish an identity and dreams about who she will become. At midlife she is asking, "Who have I become? And do I like who I am?" She has been so busy caring for others that she is not very well acquainted with herself.

Depression is a common feeling of a woman in midlife crisis. Depression incapacitates its victims so they have trouble making decisions and carrying out normal life. They frequently complain of fatigue and experience real or imaginary physical disorders.

Depression almost always involves a deep sense of loss. Many women at midlife feel they have lost their youth, sex appeal, beauty, their chance to do what is most fulfilling—in short, the best years of life. Some may have lost their husbands through death or divorce. Married women with children often feel they've lost the opportunity to grow and use talents other than those needed for keeping house and mothering. Both single and married women without children may feel they are getting past the age when they can give birth to a healthy baby. Unmarried women, whether or not they are single by choice, may want to marry—but the probability of meeting a suitable mate at midlife is slim.

An unmarried career-missionary woman in her late thirties, facing a hysterectomy, writes poignantly of her loss.

For What Might Have Been

It would have been an ecstatic conception.
Then, to know the being under my heart.
Oh, the thrill at the first sense of movement . . .
Possibly there would have been discomfort.
Then the increasing ungainliness of size.
Finally the pains would have come.
(They say it is the pain most easily forgotten.)
Joy and warmth with the nuzzling at breast,
The gift of the life-sustaining flow.
There would have been wonder at that little
* person.*

No ecstasy—empty womb, bare breast.
Lord, channel that love and longing
* which YOU built into me.*
Still my grief, renew my joy.
Fulfill me as Your person.[1]

         —Written on the eve of my hysterectomy

Hopelessness is a common feeling at midlife. How does a woman go back and relive life? How can she return to her youth, with the mature insights she now has about herself, and change the course of her life? She can't go back because life doesn't work that way. Even if she could start over, could she really change the circumstances of her life? If the future seems no better than the past or present—which now looks dreadful—then a desperate hopelessness is only increased.

WHO AM I?

The midlife woman often feels worthless and unnecessary as a person. Oh, she is needed to do the laundry, cook the meals, clean the house, run the errands for her children, be the gracious hostess for her husband's business entertaining, smiling pleasantly at the guests as she stands half a step behind him at his side.

Yes, she is even important at work. She makes all those people successful by her careful attention to detail, writing letters for her boss that make him look like an insightful genius and covering for him with gracious apologies for appointments that he misses. Even the woman who is a successful, effective executive is often treated as if she is working only so she can catch a man, get married, and raise children.

But the real question is whether she is seen as a person or just as a geisha girl, chauffeur, secretary, and scrubwoman.

The Hindus in India used to burn the widow on her husband's funeral pyre. It was a rather frank admission that this woman had lost her usefulness in life and supposedly was being sent on to accompany her husband in the afterlife. We wouldn't think of burning a woman—we just tell the midlife woman who is frustrated and wondering who she is to amuse herself with a hobby or with volunteer service.

WHERE DO I GO FROM HERE?

Taking up a hobby or doing volunteer work, while ignoring the important value questions of "Who am I?" and "What is life all about?" is like allowing someone to put a chloroform-saturated cloth over your nose. "Stop protesting. Just lie back. Breathe deeply." Give up . . . forget about being a person . . . stay detached from reality.

Reality is that God has created you to be a useful person. He has given you specific gifts and talents, and those must be used. God has also given you an identity that is rooted in who you are as a person. Your identity is bigger than your activities of serving your family, people at work, or at church.

Many midlife women feel their lives are out of control. They feel trapped by a lack of experience, lack of self-identity, and lack of encouragement from their husbands (or *lack* of a husband). They may also feel a lack of support from family or employers and a

17

lack of connection with other women that would allow them to verbalize their real feelings.

"Life is moving at warp speed. On average, modern Americans have to make decisions on over 8,000 messages per day. The pager vibrates. You have to decide if and when to respond. The answering machine records a message. Do you screen the call or pick it up? The faxes, the e-mail, the cell phone—more decisions. Your mind is exhausted each night because you've decided so much. Many are little decisions—but there are so many!"[2]

Women are squeezed by too much to do in a day or week. No matter how organized and efficient they are or how fast they run, they are always behind. They often have unsatisfying relationships with their husbands, children, or other people and feel they don't have enough power to improve those relationships. After all, they can't force people to cooperate, give them attention, or love them.

In Spite of Having It All Together . . .

Joan Israel, a psychotherapist from Detroit who has done extensive research on women's issues, thought she would never be troubled by midlife because she was educated, aware of the problems, and a liberated woman. She had little concern about her appearance. She was sure she would age "with confidence, with security, with adventure." She says, "I became a feminist therapist, helping other women explore new facets of themselves so that they would not be dependent on youth and beauty for feeling good about themselves or secure with the men in their lives."[3]

In her chapter "Confessions of a 45-Year-Old Feminist" she continues, "One day, a few weeks after my 45th birthday, I looked into the mirror and said to myself, 'Joan, you look old!' The skin under my chin and neck suddenly sagged and wrinkled. . . . I tried pulling the skin to one side and agreed that this made me look better (younger).

"There I was, face-to-face with me. I did not like what I saw, but I was finding it hard to admit. I had never felt like this before. I had always been happy with me; with my body, my face, my skin.

"After I got over the shock of my neck, I examined my hands. Gee, they looked wrinkled! All of a sudden, there was a lot of gray in my hair. My skin was dryer and flabbier. My breasts drooped.

"But why was I so upset? Was this simply egotism? Would getting older mean I was less attractive as a person? Less attractive to whom? To men in general? This had never been my bag, even when I was younger. Less attractive to my husband? He gave no indication of being turned off. Maybe it was the promise of things to come: aging, illness, death. I still do not know for sure. All I know is I was overwhelmed with concern about getting old."[4]

Sagging and Drooping
Her personal concern with aging threw her even more intensely into research on what women her

age were feeling. She discovered that women in their late thirties are commonly concerned about losing their attractiveness and that most women wrestle with the aging factors in their late thirties or early forties. Perhaps for her the process had been postponed by denial—"I had deluded myself that it wouldn't happen to me."[5]

She goes on to speak of her research: "I was interested to see that most of the women I asked showed generalized concern about wrinkled skin and drooping breasts and buttocks. The dream merchants, advertisers, cosmetics and foundation manufacturers know what they are doing. On the other hand, all of the women felt their sexual organs had improved with age and expected this would continue. Their main fear, like mine, was not that their sexual urge or capacity for enjoying sex would decrease but that their outward appearance would get in the way of finding a partner. They seemed to be saying, 'It doesn't matter who I am, after all, just what I look like.'"[6]

When Does Midlife Crisis Hit?

Midlife is dated not so much by age as by life experiences. Blue-collar workers tend to think of midlife as thirty-five to fifty-five, whereas white-collar workers tend to see it as forty to sixty-five. Women think of midlife in relationship to their family life cycle, linked to when their children enter puberty. Unmarried women define midlife in terms of the family they might have had. But whatever the social status—age forty is a major emotional milestone. In our research we found women experiencing midlife crisis in their late thirties and into their early forties, with the average being 39.2.[7]

It was not until the twentieth century that most people lived through what we now call the middle years. In prehistoric times men lived an average of eighteen years. Fossil remains indicate that only a few lived beyond forty. Even as recently as 1900 life expectancy was about forty-eight for a man and fifty-one for a woman. In 1900 only 10 percent of the population was middle-aged.[8] Today our average adult in the labor force is over forty-five. Our total population has increased almost 100 percent in the last century, but midlifers have increased 200 percent. Today the average woman can expect to live into her middle eighties.

Gail Sheehy points out the significance of age thirty-five as it relates to midlife crisis. She lists the following facts of a woman's life, which all come to focus at about age thirty-five:

> Thirty-four is when the average mother sends her last child off to school.
>
> Thirty-five begins the dangerous age of infidelity.
>
> Thirty-five is when the average married American woman reenters the working world.
>
> Thirty-four is the average age at which the divorced woman takes a new husband.

Thirty-five is the most common age of the
runaway wife.
Thirty-five brings the biological boundary
into sight.[9]

The factors Sheehy lists, along with several
other forces, all converge to bring about the
woman's midlife crisis. These factors will be discussed later in the book.

Reevaluation Time

The midlife woman, for perhaps the first time in
life since adolescence, is becoming reflective. She
is beginning to ask the *why* questions: Why am I in
this career? Why am I serving my children? Why
am I married? Why am I a Christian? Why am I on
the PTA board?

Previously she had thought that merely being
involved in many activities would fulfill the dreams
she had for herself in her late adolescence and early
twenties. She planned to use her talents and abilities to make an impact on the world or to give satisfaction to herself. However, she attempted to
fulfill those dreams through other people: *I'll get
married and help my husband fulfill his dreams. . . . I'll
raise children and help them reach their goals. . . . I'll
take a job and help the company achieve its purposes.*

All of these activities sound very noble and, in
Christian terms, could be viewed as spiritual ministry. In reality, they may have been secondary goals
that leave the midlife woman emotionally and spiri-

tually malnourished. When a person only serves and never receives, she is like a car with the headlights always on. The battery will soon run down, and it will not be able to start the engine. The car will not function—nor will the midlife woman.

Higher Heights

A young woman is concerned with *what* activities she will do. At midlife she asks *why* she does them. There is a value shift in the midlife woman that causes her to think of self-actualization now. Years ago Abraham Maslow outlined a hierarchy of needs. He suggested that basic physical needs have to be met first. Then, he said, we seek security against danger. After those needs are met, then we need love and belonging, followed by self-esteem and respect. Finally, we seek self-actualization.[10]

By midlife most of the lower levels are no longer an issue, and women are ready to look at who they are and what will actually bring about their flowering as a person.

Problems Ignored

A common response of the woman beginning midlife crisis is denial. "I'm just having a bad day today. I'm feeling a little down, but things will be better tomorrow. The problems that I'm having (stale marriage, independent kids, overload of work and commitment, fear of death, and fear of aging) will all pass. Tomorrow is going to be better."

Or, she may claim, "I'm not at the age to have a midlife crisis. If it weren't for my insensitive husband (or unappreciative kids, slave-driving boss, or whatever), my life would be going great. It's not my fault."

It is common for a midlife woman to try to ignore her problems rather than realize that she is facing a major life transition, moving from being a young adult to a midlife adult. She needs to face the transition rather than hide from it with alcohol, TV soaps, mood-altering drugs, romance novels, excessive activities, blaming others, or even chat rooms on the Internet.

Part of the problem is that our youth-oriented society gives a lot of attention to childhood and youth. We also look with fear at old age. But until recently midlife has been ignored. The midlife woman is surprised by what is happening to her, and she is unprepared. Often the result is denial or an attempt to overlook her feelings because she thinks she is alone.

No Models

Where are the older women, especially Christian women, who will talk about what they went through during their thirties? Where are the older role models who will answer the questions of today's midlife woman? "Will I be intellectually competent and have the ability to learn as I get older? Will I shrivel up and lose all interest in sex after menopause? Will I find sex repugnant, painful, or impossible? Will people find me attractive? Will I forget who I am? (Did I ever know?) How do I restore a stale marriage? How can I have it all—be a Christian, have a career, have a happy marriage and children, and be self-actualized?"

Most midlife women have been trained since earliest infancy to be servants. Their status in society, self-worth, and joys in life would come as they served men and children. But what happens if they don't have a man or children to serve? Or what happens if they lose the men or children they are serving?

One midlife woman observes, "Suddenly, with the beginnings of the middle years, we face an identity crisis for which nothing in our past has prepared us and for which nothing in our society can provide guidelines. . . .

"Our expertise, our capabilities and graces in a score of major and minor roles have equipped us for no new place. The years in which we were essential—when we found the 'I' in 'We'—are ended; our worth is no longer to others. . . . We witness the crumbling of all the defenses that society has provided for us—we hurtle off into nothingness."[11]

Jules Henry bluntly stated the problem: "A man validates himself by working and supporting, a woman validates herself by getting a man."[12] He continues to paint the depressing picture of a midlife woman who has centered her energies only on her family and has sought personal fulfillment only through them. He says, "As long as a woman has little to offer other than her physical person, love as obsession and idealization will fade as she gets old and as the daily collisions of marriage make living together difficult or merely routine."[13]

Henry identified the problem of women at midlife back in the sixties—and it is still a problem for women who are crossing the year 2000. Henry believed the midlife melancholia can really be solved only as we train women to live the second half of life. To him, the problem is more than educational. He thought it was partly the midlife woman herself: "Yet, the victims themselves are part of its causation, because so many of them believe that all they should have to offer is youth, beauty, romantic love, and children—and because many of them have entered marriage as an escape from taking responsibility for themselves."[14]

Autonomy with Intimacy

An interviewer talked to a midlife woman named Maureen, whose vivid dream revealed how she felt about herself as a person:

"I was in an apartment, and it was a dingy, dingy place. The living room was narrow and dark. There was only one window, looking out on an airshaft. The whole place was furnished in early mother-in-law hand-me-down furniture. . . . *And I'm working here, and I'm working there, and nothing is showing. I'm getting so very tired.* Off the living room was a windowless room, and inside were *cribs, babies' cribs, lots of them. They were all pulled apart*—headboards, rails, springs, helter-skelter. *I started trying to organize those, too.* I'm working like crazy, when I'm called into an equally dingy kitchen.

"There I see two of my children. I start to clean up—first on top of the refrigerator—when I saw what I took to be a family pet, a little monkey. He had a collar on. He was chained to the door. He sat there, almost mummified. He was so shriveled, skeletal—like those pictures of children starving to death in Bangladesh.

"I looked at the monkey and felt awful. Oh . . . I forgot he was there. I had neglected him. I hadn't fed him. I didn't remember the last time I'd even given him water. I had this horrible, sinking, guilty feeling that I had forgotten. I said to my daughter: 'I didn't feed the monkey! . . .' The poor animal just fell on the food. How could I have forgotten?

"When I awoke, I realized that I was that mummified monkey, and that I was starving, and that it had been going on for twenty years!"

The interviewer asked Maureen what she'd want most if she could be granted any wish in the world. She took a deep breath, stretched her arms toward the sky, and replied: "What I really and truly would like . . . is to have a loving relationship without giving myself up."[15]

The midlife developmental transition is intertwined with all of a woman's life—everything she

27

has done and thought in the past or ever will do or think or become in the future. The passage to mid-life can't be ignored or rejected. The midlife woman is not the same person she was at age twenty or twenty-five, nor are her cultural surroundings the same.

Instead of ignoring or rejecting the midlife transition, it should be viewed as the most exciting growth time in life. We agree with the authors who wrote, "No other decade is more intriguing, complex, interesting, and unsettled. Its characteristics are change, flux, crisis, growth, and intense challenges. Other than childhood, no period has a greater impact on the balance of our lives, for at no other time is anxiety coupled with so great a possibility for fulfillment."[16]

PART TWO

Trapped
by Roles

The Homemaker Runs Dry

"I never thought of being anything else but a wife and mother," Connie said. "The earliest thing I can remember is that someday I would be a mother. Maybe that's because that's all I saw. I never did see much of my father. He was always off at some mysterious place called work. I never went to his office. I never really knew what he did until I became a teenager. My mother never had an outside job after she was married, so I suppose it was easy for me to fall into my mom's role of being a mother and a homemaker.

"Puberty came when I was about twelve and a half, but I was interested in boys before that. Even at twelve I thought like my mom—I would grow up, find this good-looking guy who was going to be successful. We would get married and have kids who would all be bright achievers. We'd have a big house and a couple of cars, a cottage at the lake, and money for trips and vacations. We'd have enough money so that I could have all the clothes I wanted, and we could live the way we wanted to."

Most of Connie's dream had come true. She was married to a very bright, handsome lawyer who was financially successful and well respected in their city. They lived in the best part of town and had three good-looking, well-adjusted children.

She continued, "You know, it's crazy. In a couple of months I'm going to be thirty-seven, and I don't know what's happening to me. All of a sudden the things I seem to have wanted as a girl growing up, and through my college years, don't seem to meet my needs now. It isn't as if I'd grabbed just any guy in college. I was popular, but I never had sex. I wanted to make a clear-thinking choice of the best man I could find who was going to be successful, a good husband, and a good father. I carefully chose Dick so that I could guarantee a good life. I've got all that now, and yet I'm still empty inside. What's wrong?"

Connie shifted in her chair and became more intense. "Please don't start laying all the Christian bit on me. Remember, I became a Christian when I was just a little girl. I've been raised in the church. I've learned all the verses about being submissive, following your husband's leadership, being a good mother and wife. I also know all the verses about trusting God and turning your anxieties over to him. All those things used to work very well in my life. But somehow, they don't seem to carry the impact they did even just a year or two ago. And I'm sick of Christians who play 'Always Victorious' and expect me to do the same!

"Do you want to know what's *really* going on inside of me? I've got everything I ever dreamed of. You know we live in the most expensive area of town. We have two new cars. I've got all the clothes I want. I'm the president or on the cabinet of every women's club in town. I lead a women's Bible study, and I direct the kids' choir at church. I have a husband who will give me anything. I couldn't ask for better kids. But none of them seems to need me very much now. They're in school all day and busy at night—and my husband is so busy succeeding, he can't even see me anymore. Sometimes I'm bored stiff when I have to be around the house alone for very long."

I (Jim) started to make some neutral, empathetic comment, but she kept on pouring out her feelings.

"Do you want to know what I'm thinking inside? It's crazy—but I want to run away! I keep fantasizing about getting in the car and leaving. Or taking a taxi to the airport and flying away!

"I guess my fantasies go in two very different directions. In one of my fantasies, I fly away to the Caribbean islands and spend days lying in the sun, getting golden tan. Then one day I imagine coming in from the beach to get something cool to drink. As I'm sitting on the terrace of the hotel, this good-looking stranger comes up to me and begins to flirt. I respond without being too obvious. I appreciate the hair on his bare chest, his muscular body, his kind, smiling face. I think to myself, *Hey!*

You're a married woman! But I enjoy it as his eyes roll over my body. I like being appreciated. I like being liked for me, not for how clean I keep the house, how well the clothes are cared for, and whether dinner is on time or not.

"My second fantasy goes in the opposite direction. The first romantic fantasy is really a flashback of what I experienced as a college girl. But in this new fantasy, I see myself going back to school, becoming a full-time student, working on a master's degree in psychology.

"When I was a sorority girl in college, we thought working women were really low class. They worked because they couldn't find a man to provide all they needed. Were we snobs! But now here I am, wanting to go to work. Not just work. I want to do something I really care about.

"I suppose it started when I was in high school. There were troubled kids in my class, from dysfunctional homes. They were into drugs, drinking, sex, and petty crime. Part of me reached out to help them. I became a friend to some of those kids. And yet another part of me wanted to stay away from them because they were losers. They weren't going anywhere.

"But now I want to help kids like that. I want to earn a degree and maybe be a school therapist, even a family therapist. Hey, now, that's a joke! I'm not even sure I want to stay with my own family, and now I'm talking about being a family therapist. I told you I was mixed up.

"Where do I go from here? Which direction? All the directions really scare me. If I keep on doing what I'm doing now, I'm going to go crazy. If I hop a plane and go to the beach, I'll lose everything I have. If I go back to school, I may lose part of me, and I still might lose my family. What should I do? What fits me? Who am I? It sounds all jumbled. What I really want to say is, 'Help!'"

Caught Off Guard

This early midlife woman did not understand what was happening to her sexually, in her roles, in her psyche, or with the cultural pressures around her. She couldn't continue playing the happy "Suzy Homemaker" games—using a few of the gifts and abilities God had given her while at the same time avoiding other large segments of her personality.

She had arrived at midlife without looking very far ahead. She always knew her children would grow up and eventually leave home, but she hadn't realized how quickly it would happen. She was beginning to see a foreshadowing of the empty nest. Like many women who have functioned mainly as housewives and mothers without outside careers, she was at a loss to know what to do with herself at midlife.

You may not be struggling as Connie. You may not have children or even be married. In any case, this chapter may help you understand someone else who has spent several years mothering and keeping things running for her husband—but is now experiencing emotional turmoil.

Time to Think

By the late thirties a woman may be hit with a strong need to reevaluate her life. The average woman following the normal family cycle likely has been married fifteen or more years. Her last child has gone off to school for all day. In our book *Men in Midlife Crisis* we called this time the *quiet nest* when everyone is away from home during the day. The *empty nest*, when children move out of the home, will come later. Now she still has plenty of mother jobs, but because the rooms are finally stilled from all the noise and hubbub of preschoolers, she has opportunity to think about the meaning of *her* life.[1]

Quite often the midlife woman who has been exclusively a homemaker and mother will begin to feel that life is passing her by. Her husband generally is consumed with becoming a success in his work, and her children are now launching toward their own worlds. She may feel insignificant. She may wonder if all the work of being a mother has amounted to anything. What does she do for the rest of her life?

What to Do about the Changes

Many midlife women experience a quiet desperation in their desire for more meaning in life but don't know how to make the necessary changes in their thinking and lifestyle to deal with the growing anxieties. Too often the only form of relief is an occasional social diversion. For some of these women, coming to the midlife transition is a jolting experience, much the same as taking hold of a faulty electric appliance cord with wet hands.

Many women have thought they would always have children at home—always be mothering. However, there are many years in a woman's total life span when she is not actively caring for children. In the first ten or twelve years of life, a girl is too young to produce children. In the second ten years she chooses not to have children because she is not married. During her twenties she probably will marry and have all of her children. During her thirties, the average woman raises her children, who will be entering their teens by her late thirties. The woman's forties are the launching years. The children are involved with their teen peer groups, then off to college and into a career or marriage, perhaps making her a grandmother by her late forties. Fifties are the empty nest years, and the sixties retirement.

As you consider an entire lifetime, a woman is really only in the direct mothering process from about age twenty-two through her early forties. Even during these active mothering years, it is important for a woman to shift from being the "mother decision maker" to becoming a confidante and peer as her children become teens.

Mothering: The Passing Phase
When her children leave home for elementary school all day, a woman experiences a deepening sense of losing the mothering role. Until this time

she has thought of herself as a young mother with an important job—caring for her children. Now she begins to realize she is in a different category.

I (Sally) remember when this strange sense of loss hit me. At an early fall meeting of the women's fellowship group at the church we were pastoring in Carol Stream, Illinois, the speaker for the evening wanted to get some idea of the kind of audience she was addressing. She asked us to raise our hands if we had children. I proudly raised my hand with most of the women there. She asked again that we raise our hands if our children still lived at home. I lifted my hand without much thought. Then she asked how many women had preschoolers. I couldn't raise my hand! Many other mothers could. Becki, our youngest, had just started all-day kindergarten a few days earlier, and I was no longer the mother of a "little" girl. For the first time in eleven years, I didn't have at least one child at home all day.

After the matter had been so graphically called to my attention by the hand-raising activity, I couldn't get over it for a long time. I had to tell Jim about it when I got home. In fact, I probably brought it up several times over the next few weeks. Becki's entering kindergarten was definitely a demarcation time in my life.

Many young women enjoy the good, warm feeling when their children call them Mommy. There is something special about being first in a child's vo-cabulary. But as her children grow older and start calling her Mom, she may sense her role is slipping away. With the change of her name, there is the unspoken question of how long it will be before she is called Mother-in-law and Grandmother.

By the time the average midlife woman reaches her late thirties or early forties, she is already becoming painfully aware that her teenagers don't want to be mothered. She realizes that she is losing her grip on the mother career. She must let go and allow her teens to develop independence, or she will have great difficulty in granting freedom to her young adults when she is in her fifties. She likely will be labeled as an interfering mother-in-law and a possessive grandmother.

Midlife Baby

Sometimes the midlife woman who is sensing she is losing her mothering role will decide to have a baby. This may sound very exciting as a dream, but there are many factors to consider, some as simple as energy level. Can she really stand going all night without sleep? One forty-year-old mother put it, "Baby care suits a once-a-week grandmotherly schedule better than every day and every hour."

There also is a higher risk factor to the baby's health. Older mothers "produce a higher percentage of offspring with congenital defects than younger mothers. It is suggested that this has to do with the age of the ovum. Cells in the ovary start producing ova either before or shortly after a baby girl is born. By the time of menopause, an ovum is forty-five to fifty years old, and may well have been subjected to harmful environmental influences such as chemicals, viruses, ionizing radiation, or to spontaneous genetic accidents."[2]

There are some people who suggest that the risk for a midlife baby is not very great because of the procedure called amniocentesis, by which a sample of the amniotic fluid surrounding the fetus is withdrawn and analyzed to determine if the child will be healthy and normal. It is true that you can discover whether or not the child is likely to be normal—but what do you do if you discover the child is abnormal? Do you opt to keep the child or go the abortion route?

There are other problems. If your daughter is born when you are forty, she'll be graduating from college when you are sixty-two. If she delays childbearing as you did, you could be a first-time grandmother at age eighty and never live to see your grandchildren graduate or marry.

The Ideal Family

Since before the 1950s there has been a common fallacy about the composition of the typical American family. We've been told for a long time that the average family is made up of a husband who is working full-time and a wife who is unemployed outside the home. They are both in their first marriage and have 2.5 children. The reality is that only seven out of one hundred families are like this. The more typical American family has a wife who is working at least part-time away from home. There also are vast numbers of single-parent families and blended families (where two previously married people are now remarried, and they, with their children from former marriages, have established a new family unit).

The woman who was solely a homemaker and mother is an image that our nation has commonly accepted, but in reality this image never has been true. In the early days of our country, women labored alongside their men, working in the fields, caring for the animals, or keeping shops. They also had the responsibility of the garden, canning, cooking, making clothes, and all that it took to create a home. They really never were unemployed.

The unemployed homemaker who has been "set free" by a house full of machinery is a rather modern innovation. Today's homemaker has shifted her energies to being a chauffeur, hostess, den mother, PTA board member, and Bible Study Fellowship leader. Some of those activities may really be in line with her personality and talents, and fulfilling to her. But others may be just an accumulated drain on her emotional battery.

Misplaced Meaning

Another common assumption about the woman who chooses to be a homemaker and mother exclusively is that she will find satisfaction in life by living vicariously through the success of her husband and children. A study entitled "Housewives'

Self-Esteem and Their Husbands' Success: The Myth of Vicarious Involvement" revealed that "dependence on her husband for success may reduce a wife's feelings of worth, especially if she is well educated and, presumably, able to earn her own rewards. While a married woman may devise ways of converting her husband's status into her own, her general powerlessness and lack of control over the course of her life may increase her level of psychological disturbance. Non-working housewives with attractive, high-status husbands felt less adequate than married professional women."[3]

Many working women feel their homes are not a place of retreat—but of stress. In an article entitled "No Place Like Work," the author says, "Home life is so frantic and over-scheduled, that the office is now our refuge.

"Family time, for them, has taken on an 'industrial tone'. . . succumbing to a cult of efficiency previously associated with the workplace. Dinner has to take 15 minutes or there's no time to eat before soccer; Jimmy has to bond with Mom and Dad in the half hour before bed, or he's wasting their time.

"The office, by contrast, is where employees get to socialize, feel competent and relax on breaks. Home used to be a refuge from the cold, impersonal world of work. Now work is where the heart is." [4]

If the wife does enter the work world, for whatever reason, she often must take a much lower-level job than her husband because she is untrained. Many women gave up college and career training for marriage—and now may resent being pushed into work as an untrained employee.

Trapped by the Past

Fran wanted to work outside the home, partly to help with the family income while their children were attending college and partly because she "needed to get out of the house." Her husband is a highly respected professional man. Fran took a low-status, minimum-wage clerical job. She is an intelligent, creative woman who is capable of much more, but she doesn't have the education or experience for other positions. She doesn't feel she can go to school at this stage in life, with children still at home. So, although she is adding to the income and finding some outside stimulation, she feels trapped with a job beneath her abilities.

After giving fifteen years or more to homemaking and caring for children, many women find their skills and experiences considered of little value when compared with their husbands' achievements. Some women have felt very happy and considered homemaking the "high calling" that it is. But if a woman is receiving satisfaction and self-esteem *only* from her husband's status and success—she is putting her eggs in a basket with a hole in it. If he dies or they are divorced, suddenly she is not "Dr. Smith's wife"—she has no identity.

Neither will she find happiness in the long run if she lives vicariously through her children's successes. Parents often push their kids to become what they never could be. Sally and I have spent many of our adult years working with students while we pastored churches near college campuses. We have known hundreds of students with confused personal identities because of unreasonable parental expectations. Some of them have desperately tried to please their parents—pressured to do what will bring happiness to the parents, without regard for themselves.

Elizabeth's parents had told her throughout her childhood and adolescence that she was to be a medical doctor. She was encouraged to get high grades so she would be accepted into medical school. At the same time, her parents gave clear signals that she was to get married in her twenties and give them the joy of being grandparents. How would it be possible for this girl to do both full-time jobs simultaneously? When she came for counseling, she was nearly nonfunctional. This A student was now failing her classes.

A mother naturally will find satisfaction if her children are successful in life, but her sole source of happiness cannot depend on them. There may be times when the children will do well, but she can't take all the credit. And when they do not do well, she cannot take all the blame either.

At midlife her mask surely will be ripped off, when her marriage may be stale, her husband doesn't need her as much, and her children are leaving her circle of influence.

An Explosive Resentment

"It hit me quite suddenly—the feeling, I mean, of what my life added up to. I can remember it exactly. I was having a second cup of coffee. The kids had gone off to school; my husband left for work. I tell you, my hands were shaking; I wanted to scream. One more set of breakfast dishes to clean up; one more dinner to worry about; one more bed to make; one more load of laundry. I had had it, I tell you. I wanted to scream. At that moment, if someone had just given me a one-way ticket anywhere, I would have jumped and slammed the door on the whole routine.

"My husband tells me he helps. Who does the cleaning up after supper, he tells me? Well, bully for him. He puts a few dishes in the dishwasher. The kids are supposed to help. Will you tell me why a child fifteen years old won't screw on the top of the ketchup bottle after I remind him one hundred times? I could do without my husband's cleaning up. All it means is I have to go back and throw Ajax into the sink to clean out stains. He won't scrub stains.

"You know what really gets to me? Socks! Will you please tell me why children and one adult male can't stop turning socks inside out and throwing them into the laundry? For eighteen years I have turned socks inside out and matched pairs. Underwear the same. Inside out. Shirts inside out and dumped into the laundry. That's maybe the story of my life—inside out and backwards."[5]

The analytical husband looking in from the out-side probably would say, "Get hold of yourself. Or-ganize your time. You don't have as much pressure on you as I have at work. You don't even have to go out to a job." What he is ignoring and doesn't fully understand is that this woman has sold herself on a dream—the mother/wife dream—and now she finds herself unfulfilled with it. The dirty socks and the stains in the sink are simply the little straws that break the camel's back—or the woman's spirit. It's not that she has too many jobs—but the jobs don't nourish her or match her gifts. Stress is produced by a bad match with her abilities—not by the amount of work.

Escape

The temptation is to run away. The president of a missing persons company described the typical runaway wife as a thirty-five-year-old woman who was married at nineteen and had her first child within eleven months. "Since then, she has de-voted her life to childbearing and housekeeping and is now at an age when she feels she no longer has time to make a meaningful change in her life-style. Often her husband has almost stopped think-ing of her as an individual."[6]

The husband is asked to supply answers about his wife's personal history on a questionnaire given by the person-tracking firm. The common re-sponses are revealing:

Eye Color: Can't remember
Hair Color: Dishwater blonde
Hobby: None
Habits: (blank)
Mental Condition: Emotionally disturbed

It is startling that the runaways are economically well off. The deprivation of "things" is not what drives them to break out. What causes them to leave is the lack of meaning in life—not being valued—not even noticed by their husbands.

Sometimes women do not run away. They simply explode at home. Joanne was doing her normal morning tasks and getting breakfast while the rest of the family was getting dressed. A magazine article tells her story:

"Mom, where're my socks?" shouted Tom from the upstairs hall.

"Mom, who took my blue sweater?" yelled Kevin from his bedroom.

"Mom," wailed David, "I can't find my shoes."

"Honey, did you do the laundry this week? I'm all out of underwear."

"Mom," demanded Sarah from all the way up on the third floor, "make extra coffee—I want to take a thermos to school."

"Mom," cried Jimmy, "my baseball fell in the toilet!"

Joanne McCarty (all names have been changed to protect the privacy of the family) tried to ignore the commotion upstairs as she stirred orange juice and fed bread into the toaster. A dull ache throbbed in her left shoulder.

Five children and their father appeared in the kitchen. Framed by the doorway, their disgruntled faces made an unpleasant family portrait as they raised their voice in a loud chorus: "Mom!"

"Something clicked," Joanne says. "I felt hypnotized—as if I had no control over my body. I took off my apron, poured the orange juice into the sink, dropped the toast in the garbage, and walked out of the kitchen. I remember announcing out loud, 'I quit.'"[7]

Joanne exploded about the time she took her part-time job. She moved into one of the small rooms of their house and did not participate with the family. She simply cared for herself and her new part-time job. She said: "After I went to work, I learned that I had raised a generation of incompetents. They couldn't do anything for themselves; I was mother, wife, housekeeper, cook, bookkeeper— nothing more. I realized that I always told them what to do and when to do it. I thought being in complete command was the only way I could keep order, so I was like a full support system."[8]

When Joanne was asked why she quit the family, she responded, "I couldn't change them . . . and I couldn't go on. I was simply worn out."[9]

Her husband and children wanted her to come back and assume the mothering role. The home was in chaos without her leadership, but she refused to participate in the family. Her husband began to understand what a huge responsibility she was carrying at home and said, "If it's too much . . . I think you should give up the job. We've managed all these years on one paycheck. We still can."

"The problem is, Dan, I don't want to."

The family could not understand that Joanne wanted everyone's needs to be met, *including* her own. The family thought of her only as someone who always met *their* needs—but assumed *she* didn't have needs.

Whose Esteem Powers You?

A study of self-esteem comparing family-oriented and career-oriented women found that "working professional women, whether married or single, by the middle adult years hold themselves in higher regard than equally gifted nonemployed women."[10] The researchers go on to comment, "Given these striking findings, it seems we cannot in good conscience continue to raise girls to seek their *primary* personal fulfillment and self-identity within the family. If bright women seek no other sources of gratification in addition to marriage and maternity, self-esteem eventually drops and loneliness and uncertainty plague them."[11]

Some Christians may argue that God intended women to care for husbands and children—they should be happy doing so. But the Scriptures also urge a husband to care for his wife. Why not split the toilet-scrubbing jobs—so that both partners do part of the low esteem jobs.

We agree that a woman can find great satisfaction in being a wife and mother. But a woman needs to check her motives carefully to determine the source of her identity and self-esteem. This is true whether she is solely a homemaker, a career woman, or a combination of the two. If her occupation as wife and mother suddenly changes—she loses her husband or her children no longer need her as much—she must have a picture of herself based on who God has made her to be as an individual.

No woman, or any person, should live off the identity or accomplishments of another person—her husband, children, employer, work colleagues, or anyone else. She must find God's special uniqueness for her.

The Professional Shifts Dreams

Lois is a single woman who is chairman of her department in a large state university. Her major book, along with her journal writings, has given her national and international status in her field. When we got together to talk about her turmoil, her story poured out as from a little girl who, through tears, was telling of a devastating nightmare.

"I don't know what's happening to me. I just can't do anything—even simple tasks. I don't want to clean my house or make meals. I don't even want to get dressed. Even the little things I used to enjoy doing—like sewing and playing tennis—I don't want to do anymore.

"And my job! I'm supposed to be a teacher, and yet here we are, a month into the semester, and I don't even have an outline prepared for the class. I don't know where I'm going in the course. I'm totally unprepared. I know what I should do, but I just can't do it. What's wrong with me?

"It's as if I'm totally rejecting who I am and what's happening in my life. I keep saying to myself, 'You chose this life.'

"When I was a college woman, I didn't want to get married—I wanted a career. I wanted to be successful, to make a name for myself, to achieve something. I didn't want a marriage or a family to get in the way of my career success. Now, here I am. I have everything I wanted when I was a college woman—knowledge, skills, success, respect. Yet somehow they seem insignificant now.

"Maybe what I'm really saying is that I'm going to be forty—and I wonder if I've been a fool to give up the chance to get married and have children. Yet the idea of such a major life change is scary. I'm not even sure I'd know how to be a good wife and mother if I had the chance. But I really don't want to grow old alone!"

Something Gained, Something Lost

The wrestlings of this midlife woman illustrate that our lives are always changing. We are not static and fixed. Choices we made earlier in life must be continually updated and modified to meet our continually changing value system.

Carl Jung's words in *Modern Man in Search of a Soul* reinforce this idea: "We cannot live the afternoon of life according to the program of life's morning, for what was great in the morning, will be little at evening, and what in the morning was true, will at evening have become a lie. I have given psychological treatment to too many people of advanced years, and have looked into the secret chambers of their souls, not to be moved by this fundamental truth."[1]

There are many women who have chosen the career-only direction, who later struggle with the implications of their choice. They ask, "What have I missed? Or what will I miss?" As we consider the ramifications involved when a woman has made a career the dominant part of her life, we must remember that life changes. Previous choices will be reckoned with, especially during midlife and after.

A third-year Harvard Medical School student said, "I'm going to be a surgeon. I'll never be a trapped housewife like my mother. But I would like to get married and have children, I think. They say we can have it all. But how? I work thirty-six hours in the hospital, twelve hours off. How am I going to have a relationship, much less kids, with hours like that? I'm not sure I can be a super-woman. I'm frightened that I may be kidding myself. Maybe I can't have it all. Either I won't be able to have the kind of marriage I dream of or the kind of medical career I want."[2]

The Time Gamble

A midlife woman in her thirties said, "I'm up against the clock, you might say. If I don't have a child now, it will be too late. But it's an agonizing choice. I've been supporting my husband while he gets his Ph.D. We don't know what kind of job he'll be able to get. There's no pay when you take off to have a baby in my company. They don't guarantee you'll get your job back. If I don't have a baby now, will I somehow miss out on life? Will I really be fulfilled as a woman?"[3]

Because of the absolute biological time limit on a woman's childbearing years, women in their thirties often feel they have to start having their family in spite of where they are with career goals or family economics.

Janet, who is married and in her early thirties, told us she wants to complete her lengthy, demanding education and establish her career (to which she feels a strong call from God) before becoming a mother. She intends to be a good mother when she does have her children, so she wants to be sure she is ready. Janet and her husband both want her career to be self-sustaining so she can devote time and energy to doing a very good job of mothering. But this couple faces the biological time limit. Janet said, "I feel like I'm being forced to choose, and with either choice, I'm losing."

Unsung Heroines

Our society is not very aware that many women in previous centuries chose to remain single—or if married, childless—to devote themselves to service for God and fellow humans. The important work done by these women has not often been included in church history or secular history, but their biographies can be found in libraries. As we have read some of these, we have been stimulated to appreciate their dedication to God's call.

One example is Marcella, a Roman woman who lived in the fourth century. At that time Jerome was translating the Bible into Latin, which was the Bible translation for a thousand years. Marcella persuaded Jerome to teach Bible classes to some of Rome's leading women. At his urging, Marcella studied the Old Testament in the original Hebrew text. She became an excellent scholar of the Bible and established a center for study, prayer, and charity. After Jerome left, he designated Marcella as the one to whom others could go for Bible materials. He also once asked her to settle a dispute over Scripture.

There have been many dedicated women down through the years, including women more familiar to our era, such as Mother Teresa and Corrie ten Boom. *Women at the Crossroads*, by Kari Torjesen Malcolm, gives synopses of the lives of some of the inspiring women in history and also gives the bibliographical information so that you may locate their works.[4] An accurate study of women in Scripture also reveals that God gave women varied gifts and opportunities for service. He called them to do many different kinds of work, and we're impressed by their impact.

The subject of a woman's dedication to a career, whether Christian or secular, is still a matter of motives and perspective. First of all, for a Christ-centered woman, her life's work should not be categorized as either Christian or secular. When we are doing what is right for us, it is Christian—although it may not be funded by a Christian institution. A woman may have a secular employer, but she is in full-time Christian service if her motivation is in line with God's.

Second, a woman's identity and self-worth should not be based solely on what she does. A woman needs a whole-life perspective founded on who she *is*—as a special creation of God, with unique experiences, gifts, and qualities—as well as opportunities for expressing her uniqueness.

At every life stage a woman should evaluate who she is and what she should do so that she doesn't reach midlife needing to make major adjustments. Since life is always changing, a woman must continually fine-tune her goals and motives.

Double Bind

By midlife, the Christian woman may find herself in a double bind. If she has chosen the career-only role, she may find herself unfulfilled as a woman and at the same time criticized by the religious community. If, on the other hand, she chose the housewife/mother-only role, she may find herself out of a job in the middle years and forced to fill empty hours with hobbies or busywork, if she is not to have an outside career.

We are not suggesting that people ought not to work. But the motivation for work should not be an uncontrollable workaholism or an unfulfilled need to justify one's existence. Neither should it be an all-out, I-can-do-it-no-matter-what-you-say effort to prove a point. Rather, we ought to work with an understanding of the abilities God has given us and with his guidance about how these gifts are to be used. When work loses its connection to God and as a ministry to people, then we become inhuman robots.

The Impact of Feminism

The women's movement has had both positive and negative influences on our society—including our Christian subculture. This movement has alerted us to the needs of women and their rights to equal pay, job advancement, and educational opportunities. The movement also has had a positive effect in helping marriages return to a more biblical and egalitarian style.

However, some of the negative effects are that some women, who neither wanted to nor had to work outside their homes, were caused to feel foolish and wrong for finding fulfillment as homemakers and mothers.

Some women also have mistaken equal opportunities and rights to mean that they should act like men. In *The Gift of Feeling*,[5] Paul Tournier, that wise Swiss psychiatrist whose books helped us understand ourselves, reminds us that the world needs both feminine and masculine attributes. Our society needs the sensitivities and perspectives of both sexes. Some feminists have made the error of trying to erase all lines and make one sex. Reading *The Gift of Feeling* makes you glad you were born female and helps you realize that you have important contributions to make to the world.

Feminism Reconsidered

Betty Friedan, author of *The Feminine Mystique* and one of the most important women behind the modern thrust for feminism, did an about-face in her book *The Second Stage:* "I sense something *off*, out of focus, going wrong, in the terms by which these young people [of today] are trying to live the equality we in the women's movement fought for.

"I've begun to sense undertones of pain and puzzlement, a queasiness, and uneasiness, almost a bitterness that they hardly dare admit. Despite all the opportunities we won for them, and for which we envy them, they seem afraid to ask certain questions. And they continue to be troubled by those old needs which shaped our lives and trapped us, those needs against which we rebelled."[6]

Friedan realized that women had exchanged roles. They believed the feminist message and surrendered some of the marriage, mothering, and homemaking roles to accept the career-only role. Now these women are expressing a sense of frustration over being trapped in this newly constructed feminist cage.

Betty Friedan further discussed the fears of the feminist movement to consider the older, important values of motherhood and homemaking. She says: "If we suddenly suggest that old experiences supposedly irrelevant or distracting to new women are, in fact, more important than we wanted to admit—experiences like motherhood, which the old feminine mystique and the new enemies of equality claim are the only important experiences for women—do we thereby deny the importance of the gains won in the women's movement? Would we want to go back?

"That is the fear, of course. That is why we do not want to face new questions, new tests. But if we go on parroting or denouncing or defending the clichés of women's liberation in the same old terms until they harden into a new mystique, denying the realities of our personal experience and the new problems, *then* we are in real danger of going back. *Then* we invite a real backlash of disillusioned, bitter women—and outraged, beleaguered men."[7]

Sometimes Single

Now, more than ever before, women have a choice—to marry at all, to remarry after a divorce or after a husband's death.

In the early 1950s the reasons women gave for being unmarried were "hostility toward marriage or members of the opposite sex, lack of interest in heterosexual partners, emotional involvement with parents, poor health, feelings of physical unattractiveness, unwillingness to assume responsibility, inability to find one's 'true love,' a sense of social inadequacy, the perception of marriage as a threat to career goals, economic problems, and geographic, educational, or occupational isolation that limited the chances of meeting an eligible mate."[8]

By the late nineties, women see other reasons for remaining single. As we've talked with women, we found they enjoy:

- Flexibility
- Travel availability
- Educational opportunities
- Career advancement
- Economic independence
- Personal growth

Being single does provide the opportunity to more easily carry out a career, and the career also provides the capacity to remain single. Lifestyles in earlier times caused women to be dependent upon marriage for support.

Singleness is important for every woman to experience and enjoy because at some point in her adult life every woman is likely to be single for a time if she chooses not to marry or because of death or divorce. The career woman will likely not have to worry about support if she is never married or becomes single after marriage. The woman who has had no work experience, however, may have serious support problems if she becomes single.

Choice for Childlessness

Women are marrying later and are often hesitant to give up their independence. Additionally, marriages seem less stable, and the world in which children are raised seems more frightening.[9] In the early 1960s women wanted four or five children.[10] Today the desired number of children wanted by most couples is two. And a desire to be childless is growing.

According to certain statistics, 15.4 percent of women ages 35 to 39 were childless by choice, or otherwise, in 1984. By 1988, this figure had grown to 17.7 percent; by 1994, it was 19.6 percent. This is a level of childlessness that has not been seen since the Depression, when record numbers of women delayed pregnancy for economic reasons.[11]

The book *For Her Own Good* quotes the *New York* magazine, which presented some self-indulgent arguments against parenthood:

The authors said they didn't have children so they could have "the freedom to pick up and disappear for a weekend or a month or even a year, to sleep odd hours, to breakfast at 3 A.M. or 3 P.M., to hang out the Do Not Disturb sign, to slam a door and be alone, or alone together, to indulge in foolish extravagances, to get out of bed at 7 A.M. and to horseback ride in the park before work . . . to have champagne with dinner for no special reason at all, to tease and love anywhere, any hour, without a nagging guilt that a child is being neglected."[12]

Some women and their husbands are unable to have children, so they have no choice. Others choose not to have children for health reasons or because their careers are such that it would be difficult to care properly for children.

Shifting Values

The decision to enjoy personal freedom or to pursue a career in place of having children may prove to be an unfulfilling decision. As people move into the latter half of midlife, they become "generative," as Erikson has expressed it.[13] (Generativity is a strong urgency to pass something on to another generation, to leave part of yourself behind, to prepare a younger generation for leadership.)

The career-only woman who deliberately chooses childlessness may be setting herself up for a potentially difficult midlife crisis as well as increased stress in later years. Women may fulfill the need for generativity through surrogate children, but many voluntary childless midlife women have reported a deep sadness of being unable to nurture their own children.

Increasing numbers of single women adopt children, and some single midlife women deliberately choose to bear a child outside of marriage in order to have the mothering experience. We do not encourage pregnancy outside of marriage, but it points out a parenting desire that hits most women sooner or later.

Each couple and their circumstances are unique. There can be no pat answer for everyone regarding the choice of children. Each couple need to communicate openly and seek God's guidance about his plan for children in their lives. He is, after all, the only one wise enough to know future circumstances, feelings, and needs.

Career and Marriage

As we think about the working wife, it's important to realize the difference between working for money to pay bills and working in a career. Too many working wives take any available job. They have not considered seriously the match of their gifts with the job. A career not only brings the money but also may bring the satisfaction of "I know who I am. I understand the gifts and abilities that God has given me."

The married career woman needs to think through a whole set of questions as she matches career with marriage. Does she keep her income for herself, put it into the household, or divide it in some way? Will her job require her to be gone from her home during hours when her husband is there? Do her job and the glamour of meeting new people lead her to seek inappropriate experiences that may threaten her marriage? Does her working constitute a threat to her husband's ego and add to his self-doubt?

Each of these factors needs to be evaluated for the careers of both husband and wife. They should look at their overall career goals, keeping them in line with their individual gifts and abilities and making sure that their marriage is not destroyed by their dual careers.

Psychology Today reported the effect if the wife

earns more than her husband: Statistics compiled by the Department of Labor show that, in all, 29 percent of working wives—10.2 million women—make more than their husbands, a figure that has grown by nearly 35 percent since 1988.[14]

Women have mixed feelings about earning more than their husbands do. Working women report that their ability to bring home a paycheck increases feelings of power, improves self-esteem, and gives them fulfillment and independence. But they also sense that society as a whole has yet to embrace female earning power as positive.[15]

Although attitudes are changing, many husbands still feel threatened if their wife earns more money. The male insecurity causes women to downplay their achievements, and frequently the marriage is troubled—or breaks.

It is crucial that both the wife and husband take a serious look at their careers related to their marriage. Later in the book we will explore this in more detail and will make some suggestions from our own experience since we have worked together in rearing a family and in dual careers.

It's OK to Question

A woman needs to carefully evaluate which approach she will follow—career only, no career, or a blend. Be careful not to become isolated from meaningful relationships. As a person ages, quality relationships and personal achievement become more significant.

It is important to listen to those cautions we noted earlier from Betty Friedan—especially if a woman chooses the career-only direction.

A woman would be wise to consider her total personality and, as much as possible, try to understand what needs and feelings she will have as she continues to age.

After working with thousands of women, we have noticed that women who sold themselves to a career-only direction when they were young became disillusioned or resentful at midlife. The career-only lifestyle does not meet important emotional needs as values change.

Wonder Woman
Tries It All

The U.S. Bureau of the Census indicates that in 1960, 79 percent of women with children under the age of six were not in the labor force, compared to 40 percent today.[1] In early 1990, reports the Bureau of Labor Statistics, 73.9 percent of women ages 25 to 34 were working.[2]

Nine out of ten women work outside the home at some time in life. For most it is a necessity—not a choice. Only 40 percent of the jobs in the country pay enough to support a family. Instead of children being the reason for women to stay at home, their expenses were the reason mothers had to go to work. Fifty-five percent of all women over age sixteen are working, including half of the mothers of young children. The number of women will surpass the number of men in the work force.[3]

At some time in life most women marry, and most have children. Until the 1960s, it was exceptional for a woman to combine marriage, family, and a paid career entirely different from her husband's occupation. Since World War II, however, it has not been abnormal for a woman to work at a job to help pay the family bills, and it has never been exceptional for some women to carry out an unpaid mission along with homemaking.

We have said that a woman should not find her identity or life satisfaction solely through a career or only in being a homemaker/mother. Today, however, many women are trying to juggle all three roles—homemaker, mother, and career woman. A new breed of "Superwoman" has evolved. It is just as faulty for a woman to race along in this lifestyle as to choose the career-only or homemaker-only roles. The superwoman lifestyle puts a woman on an exhausting treadmill with little opportunity for reflection or life evaluation. A woman may keep this pace for a while, but when she reaches midlife, she is a prime candidate for a midlife crisis as many forces converge on her.

Three-Thirds Are More than a Whole
Each of the three jobs is more than a one-third-time job. Women who try to handle all three at once often wrestle with massive guilt. Additionally they live with the *actual consequences* of not doing one, or all of them, as well as they could if there were only one role.

Many women are asking if it's worth the stress and small financial gain to work at all. "Although more than half of all women with preschool children hold paid jobs, many of them soon discover that much of their earnings are eaten up by the costs of child care, a professional wardrobe, and other work-related expenses. Ultimately, some women (and many men) argue it doesn't pay for women to work when the kids are small.

"For many women, the decision to work, or not, involves more than money. 'Do I really want someone else raising my child?' asks Denise Larkin. For this 33-year-old former international portfolio trader, the answer was no. Larkin quit shortly after the birth of her first child."[4]

Another problem is how the career is affected by family demands. Usually the mother, not the father, is the one who stays home from work when a child is sick. Schools traditionally call the mother first if a child is injured or becomes sick at school. Many employers who hire mothers are tolerant of this—some even providing day care on the premises.

In trying to meet all the family needs, or what we think they need, some women wear themselves out—and increase family stress. They put a strain on everyone, attempting to prove they are *not* neglecting their family.

Grinding and Gnashing

Eleanor was an efficient but uptight superwoman with lots of guilt about being a working mother. She greatly enjoyed her work, but she also wanted to make sure no one accused her of cheating her family. Her children were in their teen years, and most of their classmates ate lunch at school. Eleanor, however, insisted her children come home so they could be together during lunch. By the time she got home from work at noon and the kids arrived from school, they had twenty-five minutes to make lunch, eat, clean up, and have "togetherness." The kids got back to school feeling they had missed out on all the fun with their friends, and Eleanor raced back to work through traffic—breathless and impatient with her coworkers. In that tense lunch situation, little of value happened.

We have to be realistic about how much we can handle in a day or a week. There are many successful professional women, especially now that the opportunities for women are becoming more prevalent. But there may be a price to pay. The same as successful men must pay when the firm says they must move to another city. For every direction we choose, we have to turn our backs on other options.

Double Duty or Double Pleasure

Dual-career couples have special issues to work out. One is the attitude of the husband toward the wife's outside employment. Many men are still very traditional about providing the income while the wife is to make sure the home front is running smoothly—and his career is unhindered. Additionally, some men are threatened by wives who become too independent in everything from using money to making decisions and having outside stimulation.

The need to strengthen the marriage is always

present, whether both are working or only the husband is. In every situation it takes time to communicate, to have fun together, and to be relaxed for sexual experiences.

To enjoy satisfaction and growth in both the career and marriage, couples must use skills such as conflict resolution, communication, teamwork, preplanning, and setting mutual goals. This is difficult because in marriage there are often emotional triggers that usually are absent in a career setting. People who are normally skilled while on the job often find themselves totally unprofessional when dealing with their partners. Sometimes they feel that "love" will be enough to solve their conflicts, and they fail to recognize the importance of planning to succeed.

Mine, Yours, or Ours

How the wife's income will be used is another issue. Women who go to work to pay the family bills have little choice about how their salaries will be used, but those who work for reasons other than making ends meet often have different uses for their money. Some dual-career couples have specific divisions for their salaries: He pays the mortgage and utilities; she buys the food and clothes. Others use the wife's salary strictly for luxuries they would not otherwise have. Some couples use only the husband's salary for all living expenses, and the wife uses hers totally on herself. However it's done, both mates must agree. Money conflict is a major cause of marital stress.

Probably one of the biggest hassles for the dual-career couple is simply keeping the household running. Household tasks do not carry any prestige—but they still need to be done. In most cases, the woman is the one charged with the responsibility. Even if she can find ways to cut corners and let some things slide, her family may complain. In other cases the family may not mind if things are not done perfectly around the house, but some women insist on perfection because of guilt or the superwoman complex.

Although men seem to be helping more with the housework, they often pick only the jobs they like to do. Some husbands deliberately bungle their jobs to get out of them: "I asked him to vacuum the bedroom, and he did—all around the edges of the furniture, but not under the dresser or the bed!"

We have noticed that men are glad to do special projects, such as barbecuing the meat for guests or making a special dish. Then men count these activities as hours contributed to housework in a month. But the average husband does very little in a month to help with routine jobs—cleaning bathrooms, vacuuming, dusting, laundry, and meal preparation.

If the wife complains about too much to do, she is offered the option of quitting work. Besides, she and her husband keep hearing glorious tales of wonder women who do it all with grace and ease. These imaginary women not only meet every emotional and physical need of their children and husbands, but they also keep the house clean and charmingly decorated, plan and execute gourmet meals *every* day, keep up with the unceasing laundry, carry on the family correspondence, make the runs to doctors and teachers, take adult education classes, stay on a diet-and-exercise program—*and*—sew their own pinch-pleat drapes and their husband's sport coats!

All the while, they are efficiently managing their careers. And let's not forget they keep up with all the community, school, and church activities as well. These wonder women probably also lead a meaningful weekly group Bible study or direct the annual Vacation Bible School program at their local church.

End of the Rope

Many women cope well with running three jobs at once—at least for a few years. However, most women we've met have to make compromises and decide to do less than a magnificent job in several areas. The ones who don't compromise come to some kind of crash.

When the midlife transition time arrives with its many forces of aging, innumerable change events, accumulation of children's and husband's needs, and urgent desire to reevaluate, the superwoman is likely to have a big midlife crisis. Burnout, whether given that label or not, is a common phenomenon of the woman who blindly tries to do it all.

Judy was a well-meaning wife and mother and held a major position in a parachurch organization. She had been so busy that she had not had time to do much reflecting or reorienting of her values for several years. When a family emergency hit, she was unable to be the same strong one who always pulled things through. "I'm burned out. This time I'm not going to carry the load!" She left her husband and children—withdrew from every aspect of her life. At the time we're writing this, no one knows if she will ever return to her ministry, her husband, or her three children.

Whose Drumbeat?

When women try to find fulfillment and meaning in life by meeting financial and family needs, they often get confused by everyone's suggestions. At one extreme, secular, impious advocates propose a woman can have it all (including multiple sex partners and a guilt-free conscience).[5] Just as extreme are those who give scriptural justification for women to only be keepers of home, husband, and children.

Somehow evangelical Christians have come to believe that the "homemaker only" role has always been the norm—God's only will for women. (This pattern was only the norm for a short time before the second world war.) Some Christians believe that in early marriage a woman is to care for her children but that from age thirty-five or so, she is to be content with hobbies or volunteer work. What about the woman who *never* marries? And what about the woman who *must* contribute to the family finances?

We have heard Christian speakers denounce working wives and single moms. Yet sitting in the audience were women who had to work outside the home because of divorce or the husband's physical disability, or his low earning power, or unusual financial needs due to medical or other expenses. These women are not working to provide luxuries or frivolities.

It is true that our standard of living keeps rising and what was once considered an extravagance is now a necessity, but we must be realistic and realize that there are certain minimums for the average American family. Possessing a working refrigerator might be outrageous for a Third-World woman, but it is standard equipment in an American home. As we noted earlier, more than half the jobs in our country do not provide enough income for the family, so many women *must* work. But others choose to work for a variety of reasons, including feeling a calling from God for a particular ministry or profession.

From the Beginning

As we look at Scripture and history, we see that women always have been involved in much more than housework and child care. In the Creation story we read, "God blessed them and told them, 'Multiply and fill the earth and subdue it. Be masters over the fish and birds and all the animals' "

(Genesis 1:28). It is clear from the beginning God was not anticipating a passive role on the part of the woman. Along with helping to multiply, she was also given co-responsibility for managing all aspects of the earth.

Other female examples in Scripture include women who made national impact, such as Deborah, who was the chief executive officer of the nation of Israel (Judges 4:4–5:31), and Esther, whose wisdom and assertiveness saved her people from destruction (Esther 2:5–9:32). In the New Testament there are examples such as Priscilla, who worked alongside her husband in ministry in the early church, contributed to the spiritual development of the apostle Paul and Apollos, and was probably the stronger teacher of the two (Acts 18; Romans 16:3; 1 Corinthians 16:19; 2 Timothy 4:19); and Phoebe, whose leadership Paul placed on a par with his own (Romans 16:1).

Only in recent years have women wondered where they belong. The Industrial Revolution and modern technology have taken over many women's tasks. These jobs have been moved into the marketplace, and at the same time women are told, "Stay home where you belong." The authors of *For Her Own Good* point out that formerly "the skills and work of women [were] indispensable to survival. . . . She could hardly think of herself as a 'misfit' in a world which depended so heavily on her."[6]

In Her Time

When I (Sally) think of models to follow, I think of my own mother. I always loved and appreciated her, but only in recent years, with all the controversy over a "woman's place," have I realized that it was not just because she was my mother that she was an outstanding woman.

As a young woman, my mother was a schoolteacher. She lost her money when the banks failed during the depression, so she did not get to have much college training, but she had more than nearly any other woman—or man, for that matter—in our entire neighborhood ("neighborhood" meaning a ten-mile radius surrounding and including a small rural town of 710 residents). Many had not even finished high school, which was not uncommon in the twenties. My mother continued teaching after marrying my father, who was a farmer. She was probably the only farm woman in that area who had an outside career after marriage.

She was a full-time homemaker and mother for the years my brother and I were home, but that is by no means all she did. She helped with the farm—caring for livestock; milking cows; feeding pigs, lambs, and calves; raising chickens; tending the garden; and preserving food. She helped with special projects in the field, too, such as stacking hay and combining grain. She also did a lot of preparing and serving of huge meals when other farmers came to help with work that neighbors did together in those days.

Mother was also the church treasurer, a Sunday school teacher, an officer in the women's missionary group, school board member, local newspaper columnist, and the one who took the time to solicit funds for every worthy cause. She also cared for the sick and needy of the community. Among many other things, I remember going with her to deliver May baskets filled with canned and baked goodies to elderly friends.

I'm probably forgetting many of the extra things she did, but the point is that when things needed to be done, Mother could do them—and she did them. There was no worry about whether it was her place or not. My dad, brother, and I never felt slighted; in fact, we felt involved in whatever she did. We knew we were first with her anyway.

After my brother and I left home, my parents moved from our Nebraska farm to Denver. In addition to helping manage apartment buildings, my mother went back to her original profession of teaching school. She also continued her unpaid career of people-helping in her new location. When my parents later moved to Texas, Mother began a new profession in the large county library, where she worked for eighteen years until her retirement. After she retired from paid outside employment, she continued ministering to people outside her family—as well as to her husband, children and their mates, grandchildren and their mates, and great-grandchildren.

My mother accomplished so much in her lifetime because she did it according to "seasons." She didn't do everything at one time. When women are young, they tend to think they must get everything done at once. Career choices in one era of life are not binding until death. Not many of us realized when we were young women that we were going to have as many or more years of marriage with the children grown and gone from home as we did when they were in the home.

In general, there is career time for a few years before children are born and then later for many years after they no longer need our care. It is a waste of God-given potential not to plan for the best use of each of your eras of life. It is possible for a woman to have it all—but not all during any one "season" of life.

A Time to Be . . .

Ideally, then, for the wife and mother there appear to be two good seasons for an outside profession— one before children are born and the long period after children leave home. The advantage in the postchild era is that a woman has more life experience, wisdom, and assertiveness than she had as a young woman. But some women have careers they wish to maintain, at least to a certain degree, during the child-rearing years. Others must be employed for economic reasons. Even if a woman is employed or carrying out a ministry during her years of caring for children, the "seasons" concept is a good one to remember.

Eda LeShan, writing during the early years of the women's liberation movement, tells about a highly trained friend of hers who chose to stay home and invest her energies in her children. Eda LeShan chose to combine her career with mothering. During her late midlife years Eda writes:

"Helen was wiser than I: She paid no attention [to predictions that her well-trained mind would be lost by staying at home], stayed home to have three children, enjoyed it thoroughly, and felt she got more out of it than she gave, and then, about ten years ago, when her brood was well on the way to independent lives of their own, she went back to school herself and is now happily fulfilling herself as one of those 'born teachers,' working in one of the toughest and saddest ghettos in the country. I envy her those years at home; I envy the unhurried, contented time of full-time mothering. Not romanticizing it—of course, she had days of despair and disaster, like every other mother—but she also was allowing life to happen, was nourishing the young and savoring it. And I confessed seeing this as profoundly feminine."[7]

Her Seasons

The Proverbs 31 woman is an example of a woman using her gifts and abilities wisely. She has been wrongly accused of being a superwoman, an ideal that none of us can expect to attain—nor would we want to. She has been misunderstood, and we will miss a source of strength if we have tossed out her model. *Nowhere* are we told that she accomplished all those feats in a day or even in a year. She did it in her seasons and according to needs and her gifts and energies. She had herself, her family, her roles, and her spiritual life in balance. Her life is exciting, and I (Sally) have been inspired to pattern mine after hers.

Patricia Gundry's *Complete Woman* is based on the Proverbs woman and will help a woman understand the seasons of life and how to fully utilize all of her gifts. We highly recommend that you read it.[8]

Why Combine Roles?

Many studies show that working women are physically and emotionally healthier than women who are not employed outside the home. They also show that they live longer, have more self-confidence, and enjoy more fun.

"A study led by Donna Kritz-Silverstein of the University of California at San Diego indicates that women with careers are healthier than women who do not work outside the home. Out of a group of 242 women aged 40 to 59, the 129 women who were employed exercised more and smoked and drank less than the homemakers in the group. The employed women also had significantly lower cholesterol and blood sugar levels, which are signs that they may be less likely to develop heart disease or diabetes."[9]

Most people have known for some time that housewives have a high depression rate. But "a number of polls and studies reveal that working mothers derive more rewards from working than just salary and benefits. Self-esteem, intellectual stimulation and a sense of well-being and accomplishment are among the perks cited by working mothers. Seven out of ten working mothers with kids under 18 in a recent Gallup survey said that they work to feel good about themselves. In a study of working couples, three quarters of the women believed that having a career enhanced their relationship with their spouse. Studies have also shown that having a job, particularly an enjoyable one, can protect people from depression and anxiety."[10]

We see evidence that women who are housewives only regress intellectually. One study was done on men and women four years after high school graduation. The women who had married and done only housework for the next four years "scored lower on intellectual measure, . . . were less curious about the world around them, less open-minded, less interested in new experiences, less able to cope with ambiguity, and less autonomous."[11]

Physical and emotional well-being, longer life expectancy, less depression, and intellectual stimulation are a few of the benefits of keeping up with an outside career or ministry. Clearly, homemakers and mothers also have certain advantages, as we have discussed throughout the earlier chapters. Clearly, each woman will need to decide which pattern fits her best. But a blended life of marriage, family, and career at various points in her life seems to be the strongest and most satisfying for most women.

How to Blend

If combining career, homemaking, and mothering is desirable, how do we pull it off? There are no one-size-fits-all patterns. There are too many individual variations to give a pat answer. There are paid and unpaid careers, full-time and part-time careers—and there are just "jobs" to pay the bills. Add to that the many kinds of homemaking and mothering situations, and we can see that one prescription won't work for all.

We can offer some generalized hints, however. *First, evaluate.* Take stock of who you are, your abilities, your interests, and your particular situation related to family needs and career opportunities.

Second, realize that your life has various seasons. Wherever you are on the spectrum, try to adapt your various roles to match your time of life. Whatever you want to do doesn't have to be done all at one time. One woman doesn't have to be on the same time schedule as another woman. Current research shows that between career, child care, and housework, the average working woman works an average of seventy-six to eighty-nine hours a week.[12] Be careful not to be trapped into trying it all at one time.

Third, dream dreams and make plans. Set goals. You don't have to get everything done at once, but neither will you get much done without plans. "[A] wise [woman] think[s] before [she] act[s]. . . . It is pleasant to see dreams come true" (Proverbs 13:16, 19).

A part of goal-setting is realizing your limits. Don't try the wonder-woman stuff. In the long run it will crush you—or the people around you. Be realistic about the number of hours in a day and about your physical and emotional strength.

Fourth, enlist your husband and children to share household tasks. If they can't help, arrange for some paid help. I (Jim) told Sally several years ago that she had scrubbed enough johns in her lifetime, so she didn't need the continued experience to build her character. Her time was worth more in other areas.

Generous Men

There *is* a trend toward husbands helping more with household tasks, although most experts find it usually isn't equal. Kindly and gently start discussions about your needs with your husband. Of course, you'll have more trouble getting him to help if he still thinks housework is "woman's work"—and if he doesn't agree with your working. You'd better work that out too.

Our three sons-in-law are examples of the changing husband. They willingly share in household and parenting tasks. One son-in-law does more ironing than his wife, and Marc has done as much parenting of their five children as our daughter Brenda has. Mike, Marc, and Craig all encourage our daughters to keep developing as the special women God made them to be.

At the writing of this second edition, Barbara has finished her doctorate in clinical psychology. She then stopped her formal practice and is devoting herself full-time to raising her two children. Becki finished her degree in recreational therapy and was a therapist for a few years. She now spends her time raising three daughters as a busy pastor's wife and has a chair-caning business on the side. Brenda has completed her degree in theater arts and is a full-time homemaker who also home-schools all five children and has a bread-baking business on the side. Our daughters' actual homemaking hours vary, depending on their situation. And all three couples spend a great deal of time enriching their marriage.

Your Resources

If your children are still at home, encourage your husband to get more involved with the parenting. He may be getting a late start, but he can do a good job. It's been interesting to see new research that proves that fathers make good nurturers.

If your circumstances don't allow for an outside occupation, look for creative ways to use your gifts and abilities at home. Our daughter Brenda continues to use her degree in communication and theater arts by acting in church drama productions, writing a play, and organizing an improvisational group of other Christian women interested in drama. She also has time to make Christmas and birthday gifts, as well as sell bread she bakes. So she is earning money—as well as saving it.

You are a unique woman, and God has a plan for you. You can help head off a midlife crisis or pull out of it a little faster if you will use your resources and your gifts. And remember that there are seasons for you to produce various kinds of fruit.

My Seasons

We have now lived long enough that we can look back over our many years together and see the different seasons I (Sally) have had. Before we were married, I was a student, an executive secretary, and an elementary schoolteacher. Following our marriage I worked again as a secretary before our first daughter was born. I also audited the first semester of seminary classes the year Jim began his master's degree for pastoral ministry—and I've been forever grateful for that experience. During the seminary years I worked closely with Jim in pastoring a small mountain church and in helping to manage an apartment building in order to pay our rent.

Following our move to our first full-time church, I was a very busy mother of our three daughters—and a pastor's wife. I also was my husband's secretary. The same was true when we moved to our second church six years later. At this time, however, I started to work part-time in order to help with some medical bills and the increased cost of living in the new area. I enjoyed my work with an overseas mission organization. It was a new ministry for me. The job allowed me to be home with our girls before and after school and during vacations.

When we moved to our third church six years later, I thought it would be great to be home all day, keep house exactly as it should be, and attend Christian women's daytime meetings. But that's when I moved into the most difficult time in my personal life—early midlife.

I eventually found ministry-related activities, such as discipling university students and teaching adult Christian education classes in our church, as well as returning to school to complete my B.A. When our oldest daughter started attending a private Christian college, God provided me with a part-time teaching position as a remedial reading specialist. Helping those students improve in language skills was very rewarding to me. Our second daughter also chose the same Christian college, and I continued to teach until I resigned to help Jim through his midlife crisis and with writing projects. By the time our youngest daughter was a senior in high school, I was speaking frequently—locally and away at conferences with Jim.

God gradually increased my opportunities to

write, travel, and speak after our daughters were grown and gone. Since then I have also been an adjunct professor at a seminary, plus Jim and I have traveled extensively in the U.S., Canada, and overseas, had our own daily radio program on two hundred stations, spoken on many, many other radio and TV programs, led hundreds of marriage and family seminars, and written fourteen books and over 150 articles.

My full-time career became possible as my direct mothering responsibilities were reduced and as Jim shared the housework. We not only share many homemaking tasks, but we also enjoy a simpler eating style when we are alone. Neither of us wants big, elaborate meals, so that frees me to use my time elsewhere. And he is as likely to make the meal and to clean up afterward as I am. He has always helped more with the child raising and special household tasks than most men, but as I have moved to a full-time career, our housework has become increasingly egalitarian. He is as busy as he ever was with his professional obligations. As a dual-career couple we help each other to become all that God has planned for us.

So, I have had a full-time career in my early years, then many years of full-time homemaker and mother, followed by most-of-the-time homemaker-mother and part-time career, and gradually moving to less time as a mother and more time in a career. God has allowed me an active participation in a career, mixed with my roles as wife, mother-friend, and grandmother. I am excited about the fruit that God has produced through me, and I am honored that he has made me a part of his plan.

"They [the godly] are like trees planted [transplanted] along the riverbank, bearing fruit *each season* without fail. Their leaves never wither, and in all they do, they prosper" (Psalm 1:3, emphasis added).

PART THREE

Squeezed from the Outside

Culture's Creation

Dianne said, "I don't know why I've become such a mess. I can't understand my emotions or what is going on around me. I feel as if I'm no good to myself or for anyone else. I'm making my family miserable."

Tragically, many women feel guilty for having a midlife crisis, as if they voluntarily brought it on themselves. To make matters worse, critics are jeering on the sidelines, like those in the Roman Coliseum who were glad to see the Christians being devoured by the lions. Antagonists, however, do not remember how our changing culture has created today's midlife woman.

Prior to the Industrial Revolution, before corporations and industry took over a woman's tasks and knowledge in certain areas, she had a position of worth and value alongside her husband. She practiced the skills of sewing, handicrafts, medicine, nursing the sick, raising a garden, canning, smoking meat, cooking meals, and educating her children. She also worked beside her husband in constructing their home or other farm buildings. She helped in the fields and cared for the livestock, or she worked with her husband in their little place of business or small industry. Strangely, in that era, men did not find these co-laborers to be a threat but were glad to have a wife who joined with them. They worked and cared together about their livelihood and family.

Women who were homemakers had a respected position in our culture through the First World War. For example, in a *Ladies' Home Journal* of 1919, the pictures are of midlife women with matronly bodies. They are not skinny, young fashion models poured into Jordache jeans. The fashion sections of the magazine suggest that "the plain country woman finds it absurd to dress up in finery to give the illusion of youth."[1]

In an Ivory soap advertisement in the same magazine, a young mother is giving her baby a bath with her own mother looking over her shoulder. The ad reads, "A quarter-century ago Grandma's mother told her how to bathe a new baby girl. . . . Today she in turn passes on the same instructions to that girl, now a mother herself."[2] That magazine also encouraged women not to send their children to school until they were ten years old and told how mothers could teach their children at home.

The pre-1920s woman not only was devoted to her husband and family, but she also was interested in adventure and in personhood. She read magazine articles about mountain climbing, the first woman born in the West, and about politics and religion. The woman in those early decades seemed to know that she fit into the scheme of life. How very different from the midlife homemaker of today who has had her jobs taken away and is told by some not to go into the marketplace where those jobs are now.

Girl or Woman
During the twenties there started to be a shift in the image of women. The role models were the flappers—young, skinny, dizzy airheads. Women abandoned all of the mature role models that had previously marked them, and they followed a brainless, giddy approach to life.

This change in women coincided with a revolution within the home. Machinery began to take a woman's tasks and skills away from her. Her value would now be found in being a sex symbol without commitment. It was the beginning of woman's struggle to find a new identity after her role at home was diminished.

Other important events took place that made an impact on the role of women. First came the Great Depression, which, interestingly, returned her to her earlier position as a helper. The frivolous flapper girl of the twenties was replaced by the serious woman helping her husband and family to survive the economic chaos of the thirties.

Then, in the forties, we entered the Second World War. "Rosie the Riveter" became the image as women manned the home front in industry and business. Women not only produced the guns, bullets, planes, and tanks, but they were entrusted with the quality of the materials that would protect their men's lives. "For the four years of the war, America was a woman's country, and the woman was a grown-up."[3]

Women had gone to work by the millions, and when their husbands and brothers came home from war, many women continued in jobs outside the home. In the fifties their work was directed toward putting their husbands through school, and later they supported a suburban lifestyle. Only after the sixties and seventies women's movement did women's careers move more toward personal fulfillment. But the women's movement had a positive effect of forcing a more biblical view of women as valued persons with unique gifts that needed to be used to help the community at large.

The Bombs

In 1945 the atomic bomb caused another cultural impact, with universal destruction becoming a frightening possibility. Another bomb, the population bomb, also began to explode after the Second World War. The first members of this large group of people known as "boomers" began to enter midlife as we started the eighties.

Another explosive development of the 1950s and 1960s was the massive involvement in higher education. Knowledge became the avenue for success and upward mobility. Women entered the educational system in record numbers.

Then came the Vietnam War, which created a tremendous division within our country, pitting youth against "The Establishment." We also developed a heightened awareness of civil rights, including equal rights for women, which brought struggles, misunderstandings, and a wide spectrum of beliefs and philosophies about womanhood.

In the fifties and sixties the focus was on childhood; in the late sixties through early eighties the emphasis was on the youth movement. Because of the baby boom population's reaching midlife, the focus of our culture in the late eighties and nineties became midlife. The boomers will continue to control our national thinking as they continue to age.

Roots

Another strong influence on women is that we are now an urban nation rather than a rural one. In 1900 approximately 90 percent of our population lived in rural or small-town settings. Today, less than 10 percent do.[4] That rural setting was marked by a great deal of stability. But since the early 1960s, the average family has moved once every five years.[5]

I (Sally) grew up in a farming community in Nebraska where all of my grandparents, aunts, uncles, and my own parents were known by everyone. These relatives had lived in the community all their lives before I arrived on the scene. When I started attending the one-room Riverside School for my first eight grades, I already had a history because of previous generations. My grandmother and my mother (as well as their brothers and sisters) had been students in my school, and my mother had taught there. Some of my teachers had been my mother's students ten or fifteen years earlier.

My brother and I graduated from the same small Ewing High School that both of our parents and their brothers and sisters had. In fact, when I later attended a summer school session at a teacher's college ninety miles from home, one of my professors had been a high school teacher and principal at Ewing High School during the days of my parents. Her class that summer was highly seasoned with illustrations furnished by my relatives of the earlier generation.

Who Cares

My last name at the time, Christon, gave me immediate identification as coming from a family of hardworking, thrifty, highly moral people. The community knew that my mother's family, the Larsons, were of the same caliber. I grew up knowing that I would never want to bring dishonor to our families. I also knew there were many people in the community who cared for me and to whom I could turn in times of need. Today, mail addressed to me at that location would find me because there is still a network of ties in that community—although my parents and I have moved from there.

When Jim and I, along with our three daughters, two sons-in-law, and one grandson, moved to southern California, we knew the names of our immediate neighbors, but they knew me only as an adjunct instructor at Talbot Seminary, a conference speaker, and writer. They knew nothing of my background.

The problem with mobility is that when a woman needs someone with whom to talk over the crucial issues of life, she finds herself with new friends or impersonal counselors. Often our linkages to other people have been lost. As a nation, we have become a caravan of U-Haul trucks passing in opposite directions on the interstates, stopping only for gas and a Big Mac.

Technology and Knowledge Explosions

Technological advances have done two things to women. One, they have taken away the jobs that they used to do in the home. Two, they have caused them to be quickly outdated if they are out of the workforce for three or four years.

When we were growing up, Monday was always "wash day" at our homes. The clotheslines at Jim's house in Cleveland were strung from the back of the house to several different hooks on the detached garage. On Sally's farm there was room for the clotheslines to be permanently erected. Load after load of clothes would be washed in the tub with the agitator, and hand-fed through the wringer. Jim's mother was more fortunate than Sally's—she had an automatic hot-water heater. Sally's mom had to pump her water, carry it to a "boiler" on a wood cookstove to heat, and then carry it to the washer. In early years she had to hand-crank the agitator and the wringer.

After they were finally washed, the soggy clothes were carried out of the house in baskets and individually pinned to the clothesline. It always seemed strange to Jim that his mom hung the sheets on one side of the yard, the towels on the other side, and the unmentionables in between, where the neighbors could not see them!

What happened in winter? The clothes were hung out anyway. They often were stiff as a board when we took them down—they had frozen before drying. Because of the frequent nasty weather in Cleveland, Jim's mother would hang the clothes in the basement, and then the whole house would feel damp and clammy.

The next day was "ironing day"—all day and all evening—shirts, sheets, tablecloths, dish towels. Sally's grandmother even ironed her husband's and sons' socks. Both of our moms had to cook up buckets of starch into which the clothes were dipped before drying and ironing. Wow! What a mess! Washing and ironing took two full days out of the week.

Remember, there weren't any wash-and-wear materials. How very different to do the laundry now, with automatic washers and dryers as well as permanent-press fabrics that need little or no ironing. Most of Jim's dress shirts are just snatched out of the dryer and given a quick spray of starch and a touch-up on the collars with an iron.

Besides doing laundry, our mothers had to mend and make new clothes. Yes, it was hard work, but at the same time, the women had a sense of identity and purpose. So while technology has taken away some of the drudgery, it also has taken away some of the women's identity.

What's the Internet?

If a woman decides to drop out of her job as a secretary to have a child, she may find when she returns to the office that technology has passed her by. If she quit a secretarial job just a few years ago, she would return now to find that the word-processor systems and computers she used are out of date.

As a woman applies for a new job after being out for just six years, the personnel officer will ask how much experience she has had with new computers. Her response is likely to be, "Little." Yet, in six years fast computers with video telecommunication, satellite feeds, and Internet multiconferencing, and pocket-sized computers with satellite E-mail are standard equipment in offices. She may find herself very intimidated by only a short absence from the working world.

Let's jump to the situation of Carolyn, who decides to drop out of work, raise three children, and then return to work after all three of them are in school full-time. That's about a fifteen-year period. The knowledge in her field would have doubled three times. Suppose that her field was medicine. Let's suppose, when she graduated, fifty books would have contained the core of the information she needed to know. Five years later it would take one hundred books, ten years later it would require two hundred books, and fifteen years down the road she would need to know the information in four hundred books. The reality is that she probably has not even kept up with the original fifty books, so when she steps into the office of a hospital personnel administrator, she feels like a kindergartner going to school for the first time.

Trapped in the Youth Cult

When the Declaration of Independence was written in 1776, half of the nation's population was under sixteen years of age, and three-quarters of the people were under twenty-five. America has been a nation of youth until the boomers start to gray.

When someone asks your age in China, he will likely offer you sympathy if you are young. The older you are, the more enthusiastic will be the congratulations. The Chinese equate age with wisdom, and they esteem both. Americans tend to value what you do more than what you are.

We have a strange situation. No one over forty really enjoys the demands of the youth culture, in terms of the time, energy, and money required to try to stay young. We may hear a woman of forty complain about the youth culture, but at the same time, she wears clothes of the youth culture. Her hair is in a youthful style. She believes the advertisements for younger-looking skin without cellulite, a face free of wrinkles, and no telltale gray in her hair.

In 1993, according to a Bureau of Labor Statistics survey, people ages 35 to 54 accounted for 58 percent of U.S. expenditures on cosmetics and fragrances.[6] The trend that nobody really wants seems to be inexorable, the suction of the whirlpool ever more powerful, drawing midlife women into the vacuum of the youth cult.

If a woman in her late twenties discovers a few strands of gray in her hair, she probably will not be bothered by them. But a few strands of gray hair discovered by the midlife woman who, for the first time, is confronting her aging in the mirror may have an enormously shocking impact. These are not just strands of gray hair. They spell *O-L-D!*

Caught in the Middle

The midlife woman is really caught between two worlds. As a child she was probably brought up to respect older people and to believe they had much wisdom to offer her by their experience. But she is now living in an age that primarily values youth. It used to be that white hair, a lined face, and a bent body earned respect because of a life of hard work.

Today, however, the highest compliment given to someone is, "You don't look your age!"

Some of the fatigue experienced by the midlife woman is from the cultural stress that assaults her. The midlife generation is a tired generation, not only because of pressures, but also because they often don't know who they are or where they are going. "At 20, you can't wait for tomorrow to come. After 40, you never quite finish with the day before yesterday."[7]

New Productive Years

In the early 1900s, families were larger than they are now. A woman also became pregnant more often and was likely to bear children through her thirties.

Normally, her nest would be emptying out when she was in her midfifties. By the time she reached her midforties, however, she was already considered an old woman. To understand a forty-five-year-old woman of the year 1900 we would have to compare her physical condition with the health and vigor of a modern woman in her early eighties.

In 1900, the married woman in midlife often had very young children in the home. Today, however, we recently have had two patterns of childbirth. The first is the childbirth years compressed into the twenties. The mother at thirty-five experiences more freedom than the woman of 1900. By the time the early childbearing mother passes forty, she may have sent her first child off to college or into a career.

A second pattern is emerging. Career women are delaying childbirth until their late thirties or early forties. "The number of new moms aged 35 to 39 grew from 18,200 in 1980 to 82,700 in 1995. During the same period the number of new moms aged 40-44 rose from 2,000 to 13,700. These mothers are disproportionately well-educated and established in their careers, says Stephanie J. Ventura, a demographer with the National Center for Health Statistics in Bethesda, MD."[8] These moms may be looking at early retirement about the time a daughter or son is graduating from college.

Women have a much longer life expectancy and vastly improved physical health. The woman of forty today can easily expect thirty more effective years. This long midlife era has essentially been unknown before in history. It is a phenomenon of our present culture and medical science. With the loss of her traditional jobs, and her extended years of freedom and health, women ask, "Now what do we do with women?"

Marital Dissatisfaction

Marriage expectations have also changed drastically. Before 1900 a suitable wife was one who was able to bear and rear children and was strong enough to help run a farm; grow, preserve, and cook the food; and make the clothing. A desirable husband was ambitious, an able provider, and in good physical condition. Now our expectations of marriage center around psychological elements such as intimacy, companionship, caring, and the capacity to meet each other's needs through verbal sharing and exhilarating sexual experiences.

In a later chapter we will consider in more detail the modern marriage situation and its pressures on the midlife woman. At this point we will simply point out that numerous studies show the midlife years to have the lowest level of satisfaction at any time in a couple's experience together.[9]

In addition to the low level of marriage satisfaction at midlife, we are confronted with strong demands for role redefinition. The inexorable move in our society toward egalitarian marriages is a difficult transition, not only for many husbands, but also for wives.

Insecurity within a marriage often is transmitted to the children, who, realizing that things are not going well with their parents, sometimes begin to look outside the family to other people or to drugs, sex, or early marriage for security.

Sexual Liberation

The new sexual freedom in our culture has allowed the wife to become an active partner in the sexual experience. She can be more than a willing participant. She can be an initiator and stimulator, helping the sexual experience to be creative and fulfilling for both her husband and herself.

Some Christian movements down through history have been antisexual, but God created sexuality, and the Bible encourages sexual relationships in marriage. The dialogue in the Song of Songs is an entrancing picture of a man and a woman as equal partners in a loving physical relationship.

The wife in the account says, "Kiss me again and again, for your love is sweeter than wine. . . . The king is lying on his couch, enchanted by the fragrance of my perfume. My lover is like a sachet of myrrh lying between my breasts" (Song of Songs 1:2, 12-13). This is not the picture of an inactive, passive woman who does not enjoy sex. She is an initiator and an equal with her partner. The woman and man mutually enjoy the physical relationship. There are extensive discussions of sex in marriage in our books *Pure Pleasure* and *Traits of a Lasting Marriage.* [10]

Sexual liberation has had positive benefits by helping us return to a more biblical view of sex, but it also has negative aspects. In some cases it has turned sexual partners into competing contenders in the sexual relationship. Neither seeks to build the other's pleasure, but each exploits the other in order to achieve the full sexual experience that seems due.

When Is Enough Enough?

The distorted images of sex have often been tied to the heavy emphasis on the various vaginal orgasms. Books such as *The G Spot* focus on technique and nerve endings rather than on the psychological and spiritual dimensions of caring, building one another, and providing stability for one another. The sexual revolution has portrayed love as the "sexual experience" instead of *love as a commitment* that results in a sexual experience. Many women experience total marital dissatisfaction because they feel they're being cheated if skyrockets don't go off when they have sex.

A pastor friend of ours tells of a woman in his church (we'll call her Judy) who left her husband, saying she was going to keep on looking until she found a man that "really turned her on, even if he was bad in every other way, because 'I won't go on living with less than a total sex life.'" She left a crushed husband and two young daughters.

The tragedy is that for most of her adult life Judy has envied her sister, who is divorced and who has bounced from bed to bed, from one bad man to another. The sexual liberation movement has created unrealistic expectations that cause many women to become sexual vagabonds, testing their attractiveness and sexual finesse with man after man.

Liberation—From What to What?

As in many other movements, exaggerated extremes have arisen in the women's movement. For example, the women's movement has sometimes confused women's rights with being a woman. An early advocate of the movement, reflecting on this problem, says, "I am convinced that in the process of minimizing differences, women will lose touch with the deepest and most important resources within themselves. We need to differentiate between women's *rights* and women's *liberation*. The first seems just and necessary, but the second seems too often to be associated with the rejection of the enjoyment of being females."[11]

As we have said, women need equal rights, but they should not lose their special feminine insights. If those are lost, all of humanity suffers. Sometimes extreme leaders have pushed for women to be like men. But women sacrifice their unique contributions when they become like men.

Adolescent girls often wear the clothes, hairstyles, and bras-or-no-bras to imitate the look of currently popular female members in the hottest musical groups. The sad thing is that every time one individual duplicates another, the world has lost a person. When women try to duplicate men, simply for the sake of proving they can be like them, they never quite pull off the job, and in the process they lose their own identity and their unique strengths. When we were little kids dressing up in our parents' clothes, the clothes didn't fit—but we really thought we were like our parents because we had their clothes on.

Smell Life's Roses
Some of the price of believing all of the women's movement information is verbalized by Eda Le-Shan, a proponent of women's liberation:

"I think I am eminently qualified to make some

judgments about the price one may pay for liberation. I am delighted that I was encouraged to use whatever capacities I had, and I am deeply grateful for the fact that I *did* live and work in a time when I could fulfill myself as a person. My regrets have to do with what I did *not* do: that in my struggle to achieve, to be an intellectual, I often lost touch with the woman in me.

"When my daughter was a baby, I spent so much time worrying about the possible atrophying of my brilliant mind while changing diapers that I rarely allowed myself the privilege and the joy of *just plain reveling* in motherhood. When we went to the playground, instead of permitting myself to enjoy the wonders of growing, allowing myself to experience the miracle of looking at the world through her eyes, all new and fresh and full of curiosity, I would bury myself in the latest child psychology book. Instead of building sand castles, or walking in puddles or smelling a flower with her, I made notes for my next lecture or article on raising children.

"I was an idiot, and I deeply regret the times I missed out on quiet moments of loving. In recent years I have been discovering that I paid a price for my efficiency, that in the process of directing the traffic of life so well I lost touch with myself and with the people I loved the most."[12]

Missing Morality
Coupled with all of these changes in our culture, there has been a declining morality, dramatized by

Nixon's Watergate of the seventies and Clinton's scandals of the nineties. The difference between the two is that in the nineties, a scandal is so common that people don't seem to care. Every kind of crime is increasing, including armed terror in public schools. In a high school in our community, the students had so vandalized the washrooms that they were unusable—so the school simply refused to repair them.

In a permissive society with declining morality, a woman who is questioning her values at midlife finds it easy to get lost in the fog of shifting values. A woman's morals must be her own. But at a time when she is rethinking her values, it would help if there also were some solid standards to look at.

During the depression of the thirties, American women had a strong female role model in Eleanor Roosevelt, a woman of stability and vision, a tough woman with commitment in spite of her husband's sickness and his infidelity. She was a heroine who, by her manner of living, said, "You can make it, no matter what you're experiencing."

Today the incessant flow of TV soap operas reinforces a permissive morality. The proliferation of cable television, offering optional adult-viewing packages, brings X-rated material directly into a woman's living quarters. Most women wouldn't think of going to an X-rated movie, but many feed on such material in their own homes. In addition, the home computer and the Internet have sucked many women into on-line affairs. The Bible says very simply that as a person "thinks within [herself], so [she] is" (Proverbs 23:7, NASB).

Culture's Impact

Whenever a great number of cultural changes occur in a short time, people will find it difficult to adapt. If a midlife woman is in a personal transition at the same time that culture is also drastically changing, then she will have even more stress.

As a midlife woman, you come to this time in your life comparatively highly educated and self-aware, sometimes assertive, and working toward self-fulfillment. At the same time, everything around you seems to be coming unglued, and you have no models or road maps.

You are a child of the culture. Some voices encourage you to develop yourself. Other voices tell you to be contented to be "barefoot, pregnant, and in the kitchen."

We have found from our national research that women struggle with a great deal of uncertainty that lies just under the surface. This uncertainty comes from cultural confusion—both secular and spiritual—giving women mixed signals. What's a woman to do—and who is believable?

A Stale Marriage

The midlife woman may experience several negative change events at one time, which together may cause a crisis. The events that will cause the most stress are people related. She can put up with the washer breaking down, a leaky bathroom faucet, an old car—but the loss of a close relationship with her husband because of their stale marriage will produce the greatest stress.

How do you tell when a marriage has gone stale? It happens gradually, over many years. At what point do you say, "Yesterday it was fresh—today it is stale"? It's like walking on a country road. After a while you notice a small stone in your shoe. At first you just keep walking because it's not very big and the pain isn't that great. After a while you start tapping your toe, trying to slide the stone to a different position. You keep on walking, moving the stone around from place to place. Finally your foot becomes so painful that you have to sit down and take the stone out. The question is, At what point did the stone become painful? A stale marriage happens over many years, but finally it is painful enough to force you to do something about it.

Lifetime Low

The authors of a journal article, "Marital Satisfaction over the Family Life Cycle: A Reevaluation," summarize several different studies in which events in the family life cycle are correlated with marriage satisfaction. All of the studies showed that the lowest point of marriage satisfaction came at the time when there were teenagers in the home.[1] Having teens in the home usually means that the husband and wife are in their midlife years. Therefore, the lowest marriage satisfaction time in the marriage is at midlife.

Before marriage many forces draw a couple together. When we don't fully understand a person and yet are attracted, we want to know more. During courtship we experience a drawing together for mutual understanding.

We also experience the magnetism of the unexplored sexual relationship. What is this person like sexually? At first the question is, what would it be like to be held in this person's arms? Then, what would it be like to be kissed? Each progressive stage of the relationship has its questions and magnetism that draw the couple toward each other. The wedding, honeymoon, setting up house, and coming of the first child are all forces that draw the couple together.

Centripetal to Centrifugal

After the coming of the first child, life tends to become repetitive and settles down to a routine. At the same time strong forces pull people away from the courtship relationship. The career provides stimulation, adventure, and advancement. The couple find new and challenging people to work with.

For most husbands, and for the career wife, the strong outward pull of the career starts to produce a dullness in the marriage relationship. The centripetal forces that drew them together in the courting relationship have now given way to a centrifugal force that is spinning them away from each other.

That's Enough

Another midlife force that produces a dull marriage is the vast increase in the responsibility caused by children. When you are first pregnant, it's an adventure. Yes, it may be nauseating, but it's an adventure—sure it is! It's going to be fun. When the baby is born, there's a sense of victory. I've done it! I've endured the pain and the pressure! I've become a mother. Hooray for me! But the birth is only the beginning. Ahead lies a whole lifetime of relationships, both positive and negative.

After a couple of years, you begin to say, "Wouldn't it be nice for our child to have a brother or sister?" You think it wouldn't be very much more work or expense. You remember some of the warm, cuddly times. That sort of cuddly reasoning and limited insight causes young couples to make decisions that many midlife women wish they didn't have to put up with twelve or fifteen years later.

Our studies have repeatedly proved the old saying, "I wouldn't take a million dollars for any of my kids, but I wouldn't give a nickel for another one!" Women in our studies love their children, but the agony and stress of raising them has taken a toll on their own personal lives and on their marriages. There was a deep sense of relief, an audible gasp, and a sigh of freedom as the women entered the "launching" and the "empty nest" stages.

Winds of Change

Another pressure on the midlife marriage is the lack of understanding of each other. By midlife they've lived with each other about twelve to fifteen years. They think they have each other all figured out—but they're shocked with the intensity of change at midlife.

The husband becomes a hard-driving, selfishly preoccupied career person who repeatedly puts off everything—except his career. Later in midlife he abruptly changes and becomes angry, frustrated, confused, and disoriented. He may start to verbalize some of his feelings and insecurities that he never before mentioned.

His wife is yo-yoed. At first he seems to be going on in his career without the family. Then, surprisingly, he begins to express "feminine feelings" of tenderness and intimacy.

The wife previously had committed herself to one of several roles—homemaker-only, career-only, or some combination of the two. Now, as she comes to midlife, she becomes more assertive, out-spoken, sometimes almost obnoxious.

She begins to say, "I'm tired of this. It's time for me. It's time for my dreams to be fulfilled." Her husband is shocked by this sudden switch in her personal direction. "What about all of the things we have together?" he asks. What he may be trying to do is keep her quiet, keep things in order, so he can continue his own career. All of these dramatic changes take a toll on the marriage.

The Three Deadly *B*s

Many dull midlife marriages are characterized by *busyness, battering,* or *boredom.*

BUSYNESS

A common response when a couple begins to rec-ognize their marriage is getting dull is to try to keep busy. In the early years their marriage worked fine—children kept them preoccupied. They were able to focus on the things they were buying to-gether—blankets, diapers, tricycles, and the condo.

One of the major problems in a dull midlife mar-riage is a lack of intimacy—lack of understanding and sharing. Intimacy is a quality of life, not the quantity of time a couple spends together. Inti-macy flourishes in a relationship where people share their feelings, encourage each other, serve one another, and intentionally deepen commitment in the marriage.[2]

The dull-marriage/busy-compensation syndrome is illustrated by John and Grace. "At first, things looked better than ever, with extra money and time, Grace and John finally began to make plans to realize their longtime dream of building a country house and leaving the city behind. During the next two years, they seemed busy, happy, excited, and deeply involved in planning, building, and furnishing their house. Finally, the last bedspread was selected, the last painting hung, and they moved in. Two weeks later, Grace packed her bags, took a cab to the train station, and headed for New York. She checked into a hotel and before she even unpacked her bags, contacted the divorce lawyer.

"All of Grace and John's friends were shocked. There had been no clues—or none that we had been able to see, no hints of infidelity, some awful wrong, or any long-standing grievance that had never been resolved. What had happened was not uncommon. Left alone together, without the children and the stimulation of the city, Grace and John had nothing to say to each other, and even worse than that, they seemed constantly to get on each other's nerves. Neither one could make a move that wasn't irritating to the other.

"As Grace told us much later, she and John had never been particularly happy with each other, but they had not come to grips with the problem. At first, they hadn't even been aware of the emptiness of their relationship because they were so distracted by problems of mere survival with very little money and two children to raise. Later, they were both absorbed by and held together by their severe problems with their older child. In addition, their warm interaction with friends and families in the neighborhood kept them socially busy and cheerful most of the time. They weren't even aware of how little time they ever spent alone together.

"When the children grew up and left, and the great silence descended upon them, it was much more agreeable to throw themselves into the dream-house project than to face the truth. For two years, they worked side by side solving the problems of the house—but when the house was finished, they were out of business. They finally saw the sad truth—that they could collaborate only on external problems but could never begin to solve the internal ones of their marital relationship, which was without any emotional or intellectual validity, and no longer had any reason for being. And therefore ended."[3]

BATTERING

An ineffective midlife marriage is one where people are rapidly changing, do not understand each other, and are overloaded with responsibilities. This marriage will quite often turn into a battering relationship in which either the wife or the husband physically or emotionally attacks the other.

"According to national surveys, at least 2 million women suffer abuse at the hands of their partners every year. A study conducted by Anne Flitcraft, codirector of the Domestic Violence Training Project of New Haven, Connecticut, found that women suffer more injuries as a result of domestic violence than from car accidents, rapes, and muggings combined."[4]

"You are more likely to be killed in your own home, and by someone you love, than by a stranger on the street. Your bedroom is the most dangerous place in your world."[5]

The reasons for domestic violence are many, but some believe it is perpetuated when a husband feels he has the authority to punish his wife for any failures as he would punish a child.

We also see a startling correlation between wife beating and child incest. A high incidence of girl/child incest occurs in families where there is violence.

Sociologists also observe frightening overtones to the pattern of being battered or molested as a child. Abuse is likely to change the direction of the child's life. One study found that 70 percent of all young prostitutes and 80 percent of female drug users in the U.S. had been molested by a family member. It was found that in the Los Angeles juvenile hall, 80 percent of the children had been molested.[6]

The pattern seems to be that a child who is battered or molested is more apt to follow an antisocial pattern for his or her life. If that person marries, he or she will likely batter or molest a family member. If a wife is being physically abused, a child is also probably being sexually abused.

If the dull midlife marriage has degenerated into a battering marriage, this indicates more than marital dissatisfaction. Both of the marriage partners are in deep psychological trouble and need therapy so that their problems do not spread to the children and thus cause reverberations for generations to come.

In his short story "A Far Country," Jack London wrote: "Two neophytes entered the Yukon to find their fortune in gold. Undisciplined, they overextended themselves and were forced to winter on the Arctic Coast. Immature, their relationship quickly deteriorated into hatred and violence.

"Each lived alone, refusing to talk, gloating over the marks of death growing upon his adversary as the elements gradually took their toll. While frostbite blackened their faces, scurvy ravished them from within, turning gums, tongue, and lips a creamy white. Each relished in the demise of the other, failing to realize he was staring at his own reflection."[7]

In the battered midlife marriage the combatants fail to see the destruction of themselves as they batter or put up with battering.

BOREDOM

Perhaps the most common expression of the dangerous three *B*s of the stale midlife marriage is being bored. Boredom is as subtle as a husband and wife living together but never being stimulated by the other. They eat together, sleep together, watch TV together, go to movies together, play golf together, attend church together, entertain friends and play bridge together, but the truth is they could do all of these same activities with any of a thousand different people and find it 1,000 percent more stimulating.

It isn't that they hate each other; it isn't that they don't love each other. They are just apathetic. They are bored, bored, bored. They are trapped in roles of marriage by obligations and commitments. They are like two prisoners of war unable to escape, gradually living out their lives while they watch each other age. Their hair grays, but there is not enough stimulation to make life anything more than the deadening, debasing experience of prison life.

The difficulty with boredom is that it creates its own vacuum. The more boring the marriage, the greater the vacuum. Sooner or later something must rush in to fill the vacuum. That something or someone may also cause the breaking of the marriage.

A boring marriage is like the extra pounds you put on year after year. The pounds go on gradually, but one day you think of yourself differently: "I am fat!" You notice that men look at you differently—as if you are no longer an attractive woman. A marriage may get boring slowly, but at some point you realize it has become terribly dull.

A boring marriage causes each partner to think

the other is not worthwhile. The commitment to stay in a boring marriage decreases year by year. Soon there is no commitment to the marriage; there is commitment only to the children, to the church, to other relatives, but not to the person to whom you are married.

Results of the Big Bad Three

We have already alluded to some of the results of a stale marriage—busyness, battering, or boredom. Often other problems, such as a lack of communication, conflict over money, repeated affairs, lack of intimacy, and continual dehumanizing of each other may also contribute to a stale midlife marriage.

One woman in our study said, "I found myself getting angry because I kept thinking, *What about me?* I decided I just don't have it in me any longer to be the loving, supportive wife, and yet I hate to see this marriage go down the drain. We live in such a 'disposable' society—I really don't want this marriage to become a discard. I turned forty this past summer, I work part-time and try to keep up with the family—my faith is weak—and my cup is empty."

Some of the following suggestions may help your tired, stale marriage to recover.

Tips for a Strong Marriage

A journal article entitled "Healthy Family Functioning: What Therapists Say and What Families Want" points out that healthy families have three basic qualities: cohesion, adaptability, and communication.

Cohesion is the bonding or belonging of each family member to the unit and to each other. Some of the aspects of cohesion are emotional attraction, mature dependency, supportiveness, loyalty, psychological safety, reliability, family identification, and physical caretaking.

Adaptability means the family is able to change its rules and change the responsibilities that people carry out during different eras of the family's experience. Some of the qualities of adaptability are being able to be flexible, assertive when necessary, able to negotiate, and willing to give kind feedback.

Communication was viewed by these families and therapists as a means to enable the family to adapt and to be cohesive. Communication skills were divided into three areas: listener, sender, and general skills.

Listener skills included attentive listening, indicating that messages were heard, paraphrasing, and checking out what the listener thought the sender was saying.

Sender skills included speaking for oneself, being specific, and expressing thoughts as well as feelings and intentions.

The *general communication skills* included being spontaneous, providing feedback, and encouraging others to speak.[8]

If you're living in a dull midlife marriage, probably some of these values that family researchers have identified are missing in your relationship or are not functioning properly. To improve a marriage does not require that everything be changed at once. Each small improvement causes your whole relationship to improve.

If you're making stew and have not put in any salt, onion, or bay leaves, the stew will be rather bland, dull, and tasteless. But as you add each of these small ingredients, the meat and all of the vegetables take on a richer taste. Small improvements in your marriage will make the whole marriage taste better.

The Meaning and Functioning of Love

What is love? How can we get it back? Midlife married people repeatedly ask these questions.

Love must function at several different levels to be truly effective. Spouses need an intellectual understanding as well as an emotional understanding of each other's needs. Intellectually, we say, "Yes, I understand you have a need." Emotionally, however, we should begin to *feel* the need of the other person. We must try to see life through the other person's eyes.

Love is also expressed in physical dimensions by touching, hugging, a back rub, a leg massage, or deeply exhilarating sexual intercourse. Love cannot exist as a concept—love must be expressed through intellectual and psychological understanding as well as with physical contact.

Another dimension of love often overlooked is the spiritual caring for each other. In the same way that we reach out physically and touch each other, we also touch each other spiritually, through prayer, by encouraging each other's spiritual gifts, and by reminding each other of the unity that we have because of God's living in our lives. Who else is going to pray for your mate—if you don't? Try combining ways of caring—pray for each other as you give a back rub or while you have sex.

Maturity, Vulnerability, Accountability, Intimacy

Love also must include *maturity*—knowing and accepting our strengths and weaknesses as a gift from God. Maturity also means letting other people care for and teach us. And maturity also is serving other people.

Another characteristic of love is *vulnerability*, or allowing ourselves to be open and exposed to our mates. Through vulnerability we allow our mates to know who we are—our weaknesses as well as our strengths. When you first dated you selectively hid your faults. But in strong marriages, spouses are open to each other.

A quality of love often overlooked is *accountability* to each other. Sometimes it's easier to be accountable *for* someone than *to* someone. It's easier to ask someone to account to you for his actions than it is for you to account to him for your actions. Accountability is closely linked with vulnerability. If we are willing to be open and emotionally exposed to another person, we can usually take the short step toward being accountable.

Flowing out of this will be *intimacy*. One cannot truly be spiritually, intellectually, psychologically intimate with a person without the qualities of maturity, vulnerability, and accountability. Intimacy means you are aware of another person's innermost feelings and attitudes—the core of that person. Intimacy also assumes you both are equally opening up your feelings to each other.

The motivating force that causes all of the rest of these attributes of love to be expressed in a relationship is our will. Somewhere, one makes a choice to be involved with a person—or not to be involved. The dull midlife marriage, tragically, is the repeated choice not to demonstrate the qualities of love. A dull midlife marriage is in reality a nonrelating relationship.

A Mutual Marriage

Marriage styles have changed down through history. There have been sad times when men treated women as possessions, like livestock. In some eras women were viewed as just the carrier of the husband's baby. Not long ago people didn't believe the woman even contributed to the formation of the child. She was just the nest.

But in other periods in history, women have been

highly respected and revered as equal partners in the marriage relationship. Our pioneer forefathers practiced this kind of equality in marriage. It was very different from the European type of marriage they had previously known. The equal marriage in the United States was born out of hardship and necessity. Each person had to pull his or her own weight.

The mutual marriage is built on the scriptural principles that each member of the body of Christ is gifted by Christ (Ephesians 4:7). Each member is to exercise those gifts and abilities on behalf of the whole body so that the entire body grows and becomes complete (Ephesians 4:13, 16).

The concepts of our interrelatedness (mutual dependence on each other and mutual contributions to each other) are clearly foundational stones in the New Testament. The Scriptures teach us that we can't say to each other, "I don't need you" (1 Corinthians 12:21). In fact, the Scriptures say that the weaker, insignificant parts are vital to us (1 Corinthians 12:22-24). The Scriptures also teach that we grow or experience loss as a group—not as individuals (1 Corinthians 12:26).

When people get married, they do not drop out of the body of Christ. Since Scripture teaches us that we are all equal in Christ (Galatians 3:28) and we all have gifts (Ephesians 4:7), we must incorporate the scriptural principles in our marriages. The family should show our equality in Christ. The mutual marriage will be fulfilling for both the husband and the wife as they move through the middle years.

A mutual marriage means that each partner practices mutual submission in the following important areas:

1. *Mutual valuing of each other and ourselves.* If each of us has been given gifts by God that we are obligated to exercise on behalf of the other, then each of us possesses something the other one doesn't have. I then have importance in your life, and you have importance in my life. Both partners value the other's contribution to their lives. We each supply, we are each valuable—no, we are *crucial* to each other!

2. *Mutual responsibility for the growth of the mate.* In marriage, each person is obligated to enrich the other. At times one is stronger than the other and must allow the other to lean on him or her for emotional strength and spiritual direction. We are compared to stones in a building, each one supporting the other and yet resting on the other. Our stones together produce a building that is an honor to God (Ephesians 2:20-22).

3. *Mutual serving and being served.* In the upper room, Jesus clearly set the pattern that we are to serve each other (John 13). I am to let you serve me without bargaining, "OK, first you rub my back; then I'll rub yours." Being served means you allow the other person to contribute to your life without your earning it. Marriage is a grace relationship. Our relationship in the body of

Christ is a grace relationship. We didn't earn it; we don't deserve it; we can never pay it back. Mutual marriage means that we are mutually serving each other. Serving is also a grace expression. It is not something that the other person has earned or for which we expect a return. It is an expression of caring for that other person and wanting the best for that person's life.

4. *Mutual forgiveness.* In the early sixties, Eric Berne wrote *Games People Play.* He pointed out that people relate to each other through predictable patterns, predictable manipulations, predictable leverage. We know how to get what we want. Most marriage relationships are filled with repeated game processes.

Mutual forgiveness means that we give up the game-playing process. We stop the one-upmanship. We are willing, as the Bible teaches, to put up with one another in love (Ephesians 4:2). Forgiveness means I know that my mate may fail—but I dare not manipulate him.

Forgiveness means that I relinquish punishment and correction to God. I yield to God the redirection of my mate's life. Forgiveness means I will no longer hold my mate accountable for something that happened in the past, but I will turn him loose from that bondage. I will allow my mate to straighten the matter out with God; I will allow him to continue to flower under God's leadership.

True Mutual Submission

"True submission does not deny my own value or negate our differences. It *offers* my ideas, opinions, and strengths to you with the motive of adding something to you that only I can give; but this is an *offer*, not a command; a sharing, not a takeover; a giving of myself, not a power play.

"In submitting to you I do not give up my true self; rather I give *out of myself*, not denying who I am but offering who I am as an act of love and trust. True submission cannot take place if I deny my true self because I then have nothing of substance to offer you—not a real person, only an empty shell." [9]

Following is a beautiful statement of a mutual marriage from the book *Choosing to Love* by Jerry and Barbara Cook.

> *If I am the object of your love*
>   *and you are the object of my love,*
>   *then we are each free*
>   *to be ourselves.*
> *When secure in your love*
>   *I need not control you,*
>   *manipulate you,*
>   *compete with you,*
>   *or remake you in my image.*
> *I admire you,*
>   *accept you totally,*
>   *respect and trust you.*
> *But I do not feel I must apologize*
>   *for not being like you,*

for thinking different thoughts,
feeling different emotions,
enjoying something you don't,
or being excited about
something
that bores you.
If I deny who I am,
I have nothing to give you
but a mindless china doll;
an empty shell who is not a
real woman,
but a toy you've outgrown.
When I share what I think,
it is not to coerce—or
demand that you agree.
I offer myself
to persuade—
encourage—
But—
not to dominate.
Whatever I share
is a gift of my love,
an act of trust that you'll accept me
and understand that
I'm making an offer,
an honest disclosure,
not a power play.
Love is not possible between superiors and inferiors
since the superior can only condescend
and the inferior only admire.
Mutual respect means I do not exploit

either your strengths
or your weaknesses,
but enjoy you,
a unique friend.
To believe we can have a marriage of
  sustained mutual respect
  can only mean
  we believe in forgiveness!
So when I ask, in the pattern of Jesus,
  "What do you want?"
  "What are your needs?"
I am not being subservient
  nor am I giving my will to you
  (handing over the lordship of my life . . .
  even God will not take over my will)
I am rather
  making a choice
  a decision to love
  to truly give—for the joy of it
  because of your value to me.[10]

Her Husband's Own Crisis*

We were going out the door to catch a flight to Denver. The phone rang, and we had mixed feelings. Probably someone in trouble was calling. Every day we were receiving about five hours of long-distance phone calls from women whose husbands were in midlife crisis. If we answered this call, we might be late for our plane. I (Jim) picked up the phone anyway.

The crying woman on the other end said, "You don't know me, but I've read your book *Men in Midlife Crisis*, and I need to talk to you about my husband." I asked who she was and where she was calling from, but she said, "I can't give you that information because my husband would be very angry. He doesn't want anyone to know. He is the minister of a large church in our denomination and well known in our state. If he comes into the house, I will have to hang up quickly." The story had barely started to spill out when she abruptly hung up the phone.

*Certain concepts in this chapter can be found in *Men in Midlife Crisis* by Jim Conway (Chariot Victor Publishing Co., 1997) and are used by permission.

During the following days Sally and I prayed often for this unknown woman and her husband. She finally called back about two weeks later, gave me only her first name, and began to tell this story:

"My husband has been acting very differently. He was always very careful of his behavior around women. He would never give women of the church a ride home, even if it were raining and they had no other way, because he wanted to avoid all appearances of sin. But now he has changed drastically.

"Recently, we have been helping a divorced woman," she explained. "We've helped many individuals and families over our years of ministry. This young woman and her children were spending a lot of time with our family as she went through the recovery process following her husband's abandonment.

"One day," the pastor's wife continued, "I came home from work unexpectedly. Her car was at the house, which was not unusual. But when I entered the house, it was strangely quiet. Our two youngest children were playing in their room, but my husband and this woman could not be found anywhere. I went from room to room, looking for them. With a growing dread in the pit of my stomach, I moved toward the last room in the house—our bedroom. I got there to find the door closed and locked. In frantic desperation I beat on the door and called out my husband's name! He came to the door, embarrassed and hurriedly dressing, profusely apologizing for what was happening.

"What would cause my husband, a straight-laced Christian, to make such a radical change? It seems the things he thought were clearly black or white—right or wrong—have become fuzzy gray or have changed colors. The most confusing part is that he doesn't even realize his values have switched."

Why the Change?

On that flight to Denver we picked up the *Flightime* magazine and found a synopsis of Avery Corman's book *The Old Neighborhood*, which describes some of the changes that take place in men as they experience a midlife crisis:

"As a young man, Steve Robbins left his neighborhood to be a success. He has become one of the best advertising copywriters in the field; he has a beautiful, successful wife and two lovely daughters. He has achieved everything he thought he wanted.

"Yet, at forty-five, Steve Robbins finds that the life he had so desperately wanted is meaningless. His relationship with his career-minded wife is less a marriage than a corporation. His children are independent and growing away from him. His career has turned into a monotonous game of being clever. Where once he would have given anything to create an award-winning advertising campaign, he would now trade all his success for an egg cream at Fisher's candy store."[1]

What is it that causes a hard-driving, moral, clearly focused man suddenly to be diverted into a different direction—a direction that is drastically opposite to his previous lifestyle and thinking?

The Last Straw

Martha Lear summarizes some of the stress of a man in midlife crisis: "The hormone-producing levels are dropping, the sexual vigor is diminishing . . . the children are leaving, the parents are dying, the job horizons are narrowing, the friends are having the first heart attacks; the past floods by in a fog of hopes unrealized, opportunities not grasped, potential not fulfilled, and the future is a confrontation with one's own mortality."[2]

Edmond Bergler, a psychoanalyst and author of *The Revolt of the Middle-Aged Man*, calls this time in a man's life an "emotional second adolescence."[3] Author Barbara Fried says this can be a very dangerous time, not only for the one in crisis but for other people as well: "He (or she) has a great deal of social expertise, power, and freedom—considerably more than either an adolescent or an older person; he is old enough to know and young enough to do, so that *his* hostility, *her* rebellion, *their* love affairs are potentially hazardous to others as well as to themselves."[4]

The midlife woman is not only dealing with her role identification as a wife, mother, and career person, but she is also handling the stresses produced from our culture, her children, a marriage that is probably at its lowest level of satisfaction, physical aging, and perhaps other losses in her life. On top of these, her husband may be going through his own midlife crisis.

Anyone who is going through a major developmental life transition, such as passing from young adulthood to midlife, needs to have supportive people around him or her to give perspective and encouragement to make the transition. If both the husband and the wife are going through midlife crises at the same time, they may find themselves unable to help their mate, and they probably will be very critical of each other. Their marriage is likely to experience serious stress—perhaps a break.

A woman in midlife crisis must realize that as the amount of stress increases around her life, she will need an enlarged support group that can provide the emotional and spiritual support she needs. Both she and her husband need friends of their same sex who will help each of them during this hard time when they are less able to help each other.

Frequently Asked Questions

TRANSITION OR CRISIS?
Some people ask, "What's the difference between a midlife transition and a crisis?" A transition means that a person moves from one era or stage of life to another. These transitions take place several times during life—moving from being a child to an adolescent—to a young adult—to a midlife adult—to a mellow adult—to a retiring adult—to an aged

adult. Each of these movements, if properly understood and planned for, can take place without an overwhelming amount of stress. However, if several stresses converge during a transition, then a crisis can be produced.

For example, if your kitchen is like those in many American homes, you probably have too many appliances running off of some of your electrical outlets. If you were to turn all the appliances on at the same time and they were appliances that drew a lot of power, you would probably blow a fuse. The same thing is true of us emotionally.

It's not terribly difficult for most people to handle one or two stresses. If you are a healthy person, you should be able to handle the normal stress of a midlife transition. However, if your children are going through a rough transition from childhood to adolescence or adolescence to young adulthood; if your husband is having a horrible midlife crisis and wants to resign from his job, divorce you, split up the estate, and sail around the world with his secretary; and if your father has just died of a heart attack—then you are likely to have a crisis.

HOW MANY?

Another common question is, "How many people have a midlife crisis?" Our field studies and evaluation show that somewhere around 75 percent of the men and women age thirty-five to fifty-five experience a moderate-to-severe midlife crisis. This means that for a period of time they do not function as usual. They eventually make an extensive evaluation of their life's direction that causes shifts in their values and pursuits.

Daniel Levinson and his Yale research team, who studied forty men from several occupations over a ten-year period, found that 80 percent of the men experienced a midlife crisis.[5]

Other studies show an older trend as the boomers age. "The 1994 General Social Survey (GSS), conducted by Opinion Research Center of the University of Chicago, has statistically documented midlife crisis. GSS interviewers asked a nationally representative sample of Americans whether they had experienced any trauma in the past 12 months. Overall, 40 percent said they had. It is highest among the middle-aged, rising to 49 percent among people in their late 40s and peaking at 53 percent among 50-to-54-year-olds."[6] Our own studies show that a moderate-to-severe midlife crisis will occur in 70-75 percent of men between ages 35 and 55—with the peak in their midforties.[7]

CAN CHRISTIANS AVOID IT?

People often ask, "Will midlife crisis happen if you are a Christian?" Every person will go through the developmental transitions, and, yes, many Christians will experience a crisis at midlife. You do not stop life's processes by being a Christian. You would not say to a ten-year-old, "Look, if you become a Christian, you'll never have to be a teenager. You'll go from childhood to adulthood without the problems of adolescence."

Skipping adolescence is not at all desirable because there are so many things adolescents need to learn as they go through those years, which will prepare them for living the life of a Christian young adult. Being a Christian should help a person sort out values at midlife. And a vital relationship with God will provide stability and perspective. But the midlife issues cannot be avoided. It is not even desirable to skip this midlife time of value redefinition.

WHAT ARE THE SYMPTOMS?

Many wives ask, "If my husband goes into a midlife crisis, how will he act?" Each man is unique, of course, and his reactions to his midlife crisis will be different from any other man's. Some experience a very quiet withdrawal and introspection. Others exhibit drastic outward lifestyle changes.

Some of the early indications of midlife crisis are personality changes. A man may become unusually grumpy and irritable. He will feel that everyone else is wrong and can't do anything right. He is extremely critical of the world around him—he alone is right.

Often there are lifestyle changes. My (Jim's) father, who was a hard-driving workaholic, suddenly bought an airplane and began leaving work in the middle of the day to go flying. Other men become preoccupied with their bodies, take up new hobbies or sports, and perhaps trade in the old, family-style brown Buick for a nice, bright red Lexus coupe.

WILL IT EVER END?

"How long will my husband's midlife crisis last?" The most honest answer is, "Until the transition is completed. Until all of his values can be sorted out and his life reoriented as a midlife person instead of as a young adult." Generally, it takes three to five years. During the first year or so, there probably will be a gradual increase in tension and anxiety, and maybe some lifestyle changes. The middle phase can be quite traumatic, including depression, running away, or a drastic job change. Finally, after many of his values are sorted out and realigned, there is a gradual coming-down from anxiety and a return to a life quite similar to the previous one. However, now his life and values are more refined and effective.

Sometimes the value readjustment at one transition of life is delayed or suppressed, only to bubble up later in life. We have known some men who seemed to have almost no stress at midlife. They deliberately threw themselves heavily into work to forget their aging and to keep from reflecting on their values. They pressed on as if nothing had changed since they were young adults. However, as they came to retirement, they went though a giant internal revolution. They had compressed two transitions into one and experienced a serious crisis.

A difficult factor about the midlife developmental transition is that until recently, our culture did not realize there were changes in the middle years. We believed that after age twenty-one the adult life was very stable until retirement. It was common in education circles to use phrases such as, "You can't teach old dogs new tricks."

In the middle sixties when I (Jim) was working on a master's degree in psychology, it was a common clinical perspective that anybody over thirty-five was essentially hopeless for change. We were to work with them from the viewpoint of making things as tolerable as possible as they lived out the rest of their lives. But now we know that dramatic life changes can happen anywhere in the adult years.

HOW ARE MEN'S AND WOMEN'S MIDLIFE CRISES DIFFERENT?

With regard to midlife crises, men and women are very similar in a number of areas:

1. Both are influenced by the youth culture.
2. Both are aware of their changing bodies.
3. Both are affected by the generations on each side—adolescents and aging parents.
4. Both are influenced by our disposable society, which doesn't seem to need them.
5. Both are experiencing a lowered self-image.
6. Both are aware of their personal aging.
7. Both are feeling unfulfilled in their marriage.

They are, however, distinctly different in a number of areas.

One area is career. The man at midlife is asking, "Why should I work? What have I accomplished? How can I slow down or redirect my energies into meaningful career experiences?" The midlife woman, however, is asking "When can I start a real career? How can I develop my career?" She is wondering about returning to school, finishing a degree. She considers going to seminars. In short, she is really starting to blossom in her career aspirations.

The midlife woman is taking off like a rocket while the man is fizzling like a balloon released by a child. The woman at age forty-one is like a man at age thirty-one. He knew then where he wanted to go, and he committed himself wholly to it. She is just seeing where she wants to go and is willing to put forth great effort to get there, as he did earlier.

A second area of difference is intimacy. The man became intimate in his early adulthood in order to capture a wife and start marriage, but then his concentration shifted toward career. As he enters midlife, however, he thinks about the interpersonal relationships he lost—especially his children. He also wants his wife to be a girlfriend and lover, not just a mother and household manager.

The midlife woman quite often trades intimacy for assertiveness. She sees clearly where she wants to go and sets out to accomplish her goals. Sometimes the goal-oriented midlife woman sacrifices some of her earlier intimacy to accomplish her life goals. She may be back in school as a full-time student. It's catch-up time, and if she is pooped at the end of the day and can't talk—well, then, talking will just have to wait for another day.

A third area of difference is assertiveness. The midlife man who has been a driver and pusher through most of his married life now begins the mellowing-out process. He begins kicking back, putting his feet up, enjoying some of the things he has accomplished. He suggests a few more vacations. "Let's get away for an extended weekend." "Let's slow down."

The midlife woman is going the other direction. She says, "I want to go back to school. I'm eager to get going. Things are finally coming into place so I'm able to get moving." He wants to go out of town for a rest, but she says, "I can't go out of town; I'll miss classes and that special seminar." He says, "Let's spend a quiet evening at home or go to a movie." She says, "I have to work overtime at the office. They're considering me for a new position."

A fourth area of difference is their view of family. Earlier the midlife man ignored his family while he focused on his career. Now he is dealing with remorse and guilt, wishing he could relive some of those years. One man told us, "I'm really a success in business, but in the process I lost my kids."

The midlife woman has spent most of her time with the family. She's ready for a new challenge. It doesn't mean she doesn't care for her family, but now they take a less prominent place in her life. In a sense, he is moving *toward* the family, and she is moving *parallel* to the family but with a focus on her career.

A fifth area of noticeable difference between men and women at midlife is thier view of death. During the forties, there is a sharp rise in the number of men who die suddenly from such problems as heart attacks. A man wonders about life and death—wonders how long he will live—wonders how much time he has to accomplish things—wonders what he should focus on. He is confronting his own mortality.

A twenty-five-year-old sees that twenty-five years have passed since he was born. A forty-five-year-old realizes he may have only twenty-five years left.

The young man does not look at the obituary page; he goes straight to sports. The midlife man, however, takes a glance at the obituary page. And when he reads that someone died at age forty-two, he calls out to his wife, "Hey, honey, did you see this paper? This guy was only forty-two—he died of a heart attack!" He begins to feel his chest, and he wonders about that pain he has been having. But his wife cheerfully responds, "Nah, it's just gas." The midlife man suddenly feels that death isn't far off, especially if he has lost one or more of his parents or close friends. He feels that he is next in line.

The midlife woman, however, is not thinking much about death. Women tend to live longer, and the incidence of sudden death from heart attacks and other diseases usually will not happen until after she passes menopause. So, in a sense, the man is looking at death and wondering when his life will end, while his wife is saying, "Life is just beginning for me."

Jim's Midlife Crisis

Midlife crisis was not supposed to happen to me (Jim). I was aware of the problem and had helped other men work through this era. I had a very secure relationship with my family, who loved me very much. I was soaked with education, with one master's degree in theology, a second in psychology, and a doctoral degree under way. I had a successful ministry at Twin City Bible Church in Urbana, Illinois, and enjoyed a very positive relationship with many people. Each week I received several notes telling of the help my ministry was in individuals' lives. I also had ministered overseas on several occasions, plus had many articles published in national magazines.

I did not anticipate a midlife crisis. But then I turned forty-five; it seemed as if I were stepping off the edge of the world. At the same time, I received word that one of my close friends, Gaston Singh, had died of a massive heart attack at age thirty-six. In a few months Gaston and I were to have gone to India to start an Asian training program.

I began to ask, "What is life all about? What is life, if only to die?" I was experiencing an ever deepening depression. I would ask Sally, "Why did my parents have the right to bring me into the world? Why didn't they just skip over me, wherever I was, and bring somebody else into the world?" I would stare out the living-room window for long hours and say, "You know, living life is the biggest waste of time there is."

As I went through an extended depression, I was angry at society, at life itself, at God for creating life. I had irrational fears of losing my job, that I was useless in life, and that anyone my age was fit only to be buried.

Sections from Psalm 102 expressed my feelings. It helped to see that people from other generations had wrestled with some of my same concerns. The psalmist talked about the breakdown in his physical and emotional life as he experienced midlife stress. He wrestled with the conflict of God's becoming more famous from one generation to another while the psalmist was getting weaker and facing a certain death. I found it helpful to read Psalms 102 and 103 together. Psalm 102 presents the problem; Psalm 103 presents God as ever caring and involved in our life.

Cultural Causes

The focus of this book is the woman's midlife crisis. Yet because women are so relational, when her husband has a midlife crisis, she may be pushed over the edge into her own crisis. Let's look at some of the cultural impacts that intensify the midlife transition and cause it to become a crisis for her husband. Some of these problems are very similar to forces that impact a woman and may also bring on her midlife crisis.

1. *We live in a youth-oriented society.* When we are young adults, we enjoy being "in." However, when we reach midlife, we feel "out."

2. *We live in a throwaway society.* When I (Jim) was at a men's retreat with a number of men who worked for electronic companies, they said their competitive industry has a systematic evaluation program to wash men out as they come to midlife. When they started with the company as young men, they were given lots of affirmation and positive strokes, but when they turned forty, the company started evaluating them more often. These men at the retreat said, "You can always tell the midlife guys who have just been evaluated. They don't show up for work the next couple of days—sometimes they're gone a whole week. They are so devastated." After a while the older men quit. Their leaving makes room for the new, young turkeys coming up the line. Those twenty-seven-year-olds don't realize they are being put on a human conveyor belt that is going to chew them up and spit them out the other end before they are fifty.

3. *We have two other generations to care for.* The middle generation cares for children, and we may begin parenting our parents. Our parents have pro-

vided backup, support, counsel, sometimes even financial assistance. But now it's the other way around. Many parents are needing guidance, emotional support, and perhaps some financial assistance.

4. *Marriage satisfaction is low at midlife.* A man in his thirties is focused toward the single goal of his career—he is willing to sacrifice almost everything else. The marriage in the forties is a target of the husband's midlife crisis—he feels a combination of guilt for neglecting his marriage, and hopelessness because the marriage seems dull and dead. Why should he even try to revive it?

5. *The knowledge explosion is intense.* Actually two forces are working in opposite directions. The one is the explosion of knowledge, and the second is the expanding responsibility at work, demanding more time and energy. Both factors work in opposition to his aging body, which doesn't have the bounce and spring it had at age twenty-five.

6. *The body is aging.* One morning as he is shaving, he looks at his face and sees a really old man. There are wrinkles around his mouth and eyes, graying hair on his temples, a receding hairline, and the growing bald spot on top. Then he looks at where his magnificent chest used to be. He thinks back to his college days when he had muscles there. And then, horror of horrors, he looks at his waist. So, that's where his chest went! Oh, what an ugly glob of fat. That's where all those doughnuts have gone—straight to his middle.

He turns sideways, sucks in his stomach, and sticks out his chest. He almost looks like a man again. He holds his position for a long, glorious moment—but finally he has to breathe. As he breathes, his "chest" flops down over his pajamas again. What a disgusting sight! But then he thinks, "Wow! Am I glad God made belts—otherwise all that fat would keep sliding down, and I'd end up with these giant fat feet."

He mumbles to himself, "I'm not keeping up at work. I'm repeatedly told that youth is the only good age. My marriage is in trouble. My kids think they don't need me. My parents need my help. I'm getting nearer to death. What does it all mean, anyway?"

At this point, we have a man who is entering midlife crisis. He begins to feel his circuit overload. Too many things are keeping him from accomplishing what he wants. He has spent all of the years of his youth, and what has it done for him? His life is disgusting and meaningless!

Enemies

The man in midlife crisis decides he has strong enemies against him. If he could get rid of these destructive forces, then life might be better.*

The first enemy is his body—this sagging blob of

---

*These enemies were first identified by Jim Conway in 1977 as he worked with other men in midlife crisis and after going through his own crisis. He discusses them in more detail in his newly revised book *Men in Midlife Crisis 1997*.[8] These ideas have since been used by several other writers.

flesh standing before the mirror. If he could get it back in shape, he'd feel better about himself. He remembers recently when he was playing racquetball with a younger guy from the office. His mind said to his arm, "Go get that ball! Stretch! Reach!" But his body just stood there and said, "You've gotta be kidding!" He has to do something about this body that opposes his mind.

A second enemy is his work. He feels trapped—he needs the dollars to pay for piano lessons, karate lessons, orthodontic braces, new computers for the kids, and college educations. He also knows if he drops out of work now or tries to shift to a job he might like better, he'll not only take a cut in salary, but he'd also lose other benefits. And he might not even find another job. He wonders what he could do for work that would give him satisfaction and meet his obligations.

His wife and family are the third enemy. He sees them as the reason he is trapped at work and kept from doing what he really wants to do. During the midlife years a family needs the biggest house and the greatest number of cars—they have their highest expenses. He has too many family obligations to just drop out, walk along the beach, pick up odd jobs, paint pictures, or sail.

God is identified as the fourth enemy. God is the ultimate culprit. He pictures God grinning fiendishly over the banister of heaven and pointing a long, bony finger saying, "You despicable, disgraceful Christian! You are the worst possible example of a mature man. You're selfish. You're filled with lust. You're lazy. You're so disgusting that I want to spew you out of my mouth!"[9]

The midlife man sees God as an unfair accuser. The man says to God, "You are the one that made me this way. You gave me these drives for achievement. You gave me strong sexual urges. You designed me as a disposable human being who would grow old and die. Now, God, you come along and say, 'Adjust to it. Live with it. If you step out of line or think bad thoughts, I'm going to squash you like a bug.' That's unfair!"

Reactions

The man in midlife crisis becomes engaged in what is called projection. He is not owning his problems—whether his body, his work, his wife and family, or his relationship with God. He is projecting all of the internal value struggles onto other people, situations, or objects. This process is a dead-end road and will only cause him to be more angry and feel like a victim. He must take charge, think through his values, and reorder his life according to midlife values.

The average midlife man will try a few short-range solutions by which he hopes to escape these enemies. Unfortunately, they are not the real answers.

WITHDRAWAL

A midlife man may try to relieve his stress by withdrawing. It may take the form of alcohol:

"Just a couple of beers after work to take the edge off—so I don't have to think." Or he may escape by sleeping: "When I'm asleep, I'm not thinking about my problems." Endless hours of TV may also provide diversion. He has a personal pity party. He becomes a martyr: "Perhaps if I'm seen in a desperate situation, someone will love me." Depression, along with alcohol, TV, sleep, and other escape mechanisms, may appear to provide relief, but it is false, temporary relief.

ANGER
A midlife man may think he'll feel better if he can punch something. His anger is aimless. He is not sure what he is angry at; it's everything—himself, society, individual people, and God. He has a chip on his shoulder. He's grumpy and irritable. He can't stand the imperfections and the distractions of life. He's in turmoil, and the slightest incident may trigger a massive explosion.

NEW IMAGE
Another escape a midlife man quite often tries is the new look. Suddenly he wants to be the macho man with a suntanned body. He works out regularly at the local fitness center. When he's around women, he tends to stand so he can show off his muscles. He wears tight shirts or shirts that can be unbuttoned down to his belt. A chain finishes off the image. But what can he do about the clump of gray chest hair showing out of his open shirt? There's always hair color.

A man with a brand-new yellow Toyota Celica picked me (Jim) up in front of my hotel to take me to a speaking engagement. As I got into the car, I noticed a well-worn copy of *Men in Midlife Crisis* on the console between our two seats. He put the car into first gear and nearly snapped my head off as we took off from the curb. We came to the first corner—he downshifted—*vroom, vroom, vroom!* Three different gears. We whipped around the corner, and he went up through the shifting process again. We came to another corner—and the same thing. He hardly stepped on the brakes. He downshifted all the way. I thought for a while that I was in a Grand Prix race. Finally, after we had gone around every corner in the whole city—or so it seemed—we were out on the freeway. When he finally got it into fifth gear, he looked sheepishly at me and said, "I really wanted to buy a Porsche, but I couldn't afford it!"

The midlife man in the old brown Buick gets a small, sexy sports car and tells his friends it's because it gets good gas mileage. The truth is, it's the image. *If I can change my lifestyle*, he thinks, *maybe it'll calm this turmoil.*

DROP OUT

Many men try dropping out of work. Retiring at age forty-three sounds funny, but the thought occurs to many men. One of our friends in his late thirties wants to retire to a small farm where he and his family can be totally self-sufficient. They want to raise their own animals and vegetables—grow a corn crop to convert into gasohol to provide the fuel for vehicles and electricity. They are designing an energy-efficient house, and they will drill their own well. But all of these dreams are really escape dreams. He actually is saying, "Life is too much to handle. Stop the world, I want to get off for a while." The problem is—and this is what's so frustrating at midlife—you can't stop the world! You can't get off for a while!

NEW LOVE

Of all the possible escape solutions the midlife man may try, the affair is the most disturbing to his wife—and the most played up by the media. A wife can probably handle job changes, a different car, his working out at the gym, and his new wardrobe. She can even handle his withdrawal and anger—but the specter of the other woman cuts deep into the wife's self-image. She feels rejected. "I have been evaluated, compared with another woman, and I've been given low marks by my husband." The sanctity and specialness between the two of them—the sacredness of something given by God—is broken by the affair.

If your husband has been or is in an affair, you may be pushed into your own midlife crisis. It is important to remember not to moralize at this point but to understand the dynamics inside your husband and in your marriage. Focus your thoughts and energy on understanding each other, meeting each other's needs, and restoring your marriage.

Questions always come. Will the affair last? Will he marry the younger woman? We've observed that very few midlife men actually marry the younger woman with whom they had an affair. The younger woman quite often sees the older man as a father figure, and the relationship can be very rewarding at first. But sooner or later most young women want more than a father figure—and most midlife men want more than a daughter. Remember, the problem is not the other woman, it's your husband and his feeling of dissatisfaction with himself—and your marriage.

Healing from the Midlife Affair

As dreadful as your husband's affair might be and as damaging to your self-image as it has been, perhaps you can turn it into new growth and insight for your life. Following is one woman's story:

"That image of the other woman sliced [me] and became a nagging obsession. What did she look like? Was she tall? Slender? Young? [I] imagined her as someone he worked with at the college—someone intelligent, informed, and involved in the world. Saturday afternoons were probably the only times she was free so they could meet.

"Where did they go? To a motel? [I] tried to picture them together—how they made love. Did he *love* her? What were the things they talked about? Science? World affairs? How long had they known each other? Were they *still* together? What really were his plans for the future? . . .

"Suddenly, [I] knew no fear. I exist too. I think I've earned the right. . . . I know this must sound funny, but the woman my husband was involved with changed my image of myself—of what a woman should be. That old image of me was pretty much destroyed. I felt worthless; my pride hurt, and my ego sagged. I went out and bought a completely new wardrobe. Don't misunderstand. I don't mean that as a surface thing. I *suddenly cared enough about myself* to want to take care of myself. No more skimping. No more tattered sweaters. I'd lost fifteen pounds because I'd been upset, but it was becoming. I didn't want to be a gray-haired lady anymore either. So I went red!

"I got shocked out of my complacency in many ways. She did me a service. I wanted to be the woman I imagined him with. An involved, independent woman. Maybe it was the kind of woman I wanted to be all along, but never dared to be."[10]

Try to keep your perspective and calm. You have history on your side. If you have done some growing and eliminating of friction areas, your husband may find it a pleasure to be with you once again and to continue what he has had with you for all these years.[11]

Dr. Bernice Neugarten, professor of human development at the University of Chicago, has said, "Intimacy can be quickly attained, but it somehow doesn't suffice if it is without length. . . . You can go to bed with someone, but that somehow doesn't dismiss the need for the long-standing relationship; you *still* want to go home to someone who has known you for twenty-five years."[12]

Helping the Man through His Midlife Crisis

Your husband's midlife crisis is one of those additional loads on your circuit that may cause your transition to become more difficult or perhaps push you into your own midlife crisis. If you know how to reduce your husband's crisis and help him through this time, it will lessen the pressure on both of you and your marriage.

First, understand midlife crisis. You have accomplished some of that by reading through this chapter. Perhaps you need to extend your reading a bit further by reading other books suggested in the chapter notes at the end of this book.

Second, listen to him. Listen as a friend—nonjudgmentally. Yes, there may be some things he is doing or thinking that are wrong, but let him sort out those values. If you impose your values on him at this point, the crisis will be prolonged. He needs to evaluate and establish his own values.

Also, listen to him without yielding to the urge to set him straight. He may be thinking about irrational or impetuous moves in his career or marriage. Gently caution him, and provide him the courage to investigate, to explore what these options might mean—but don't tell him which one is right unless he asks you.

Draw him out. Encourage him to talk about his wishes, hopes, and dreams. What are the things he's always wanted to accomplish but is afraid he's not going to do before he dies? Your willingness to participate will help him as he wrestles with his heavy problems.

As our friend Dale came to midlife, he decided to quit his secure position in a state job and start his own business. This would mean reduced income and longer work hours for a time. It would require his wife's assistance in the work. When Dale shared his dream with his wife, Evelyn, they discussed it cautiously. Evelyn told Dale she was willing to make the necessary sacrifices to see Dale's dream come true. She was a good sounding board as he weighed the advantages and disadvantages of his dream. She got caught up in the dream too, so that it was not just Dale's dream but also hers. Today they have a happy marriage and a shared career.

Third, be with him. Don't hover and mother— but be available. When I (Jim) was going through my midlife crisis, Sally was teaching school Monday through Friday. My day off was Monday. In order to be available to be with me, Sally took personal leave, and her principal graciously gave her sick days so that we could get away more frequently for the recuperation and reflection time I needed.

There will be crucial times when you need to be with him. At other times he needs to be alone. Be sensitive to the times when he is lonely or would like to yell, "Help!"

Fourth, commit yourself to be his friend. What your

husband needs is a girlfriend—not a mother. Think of the two words: *girl*, carrying the idea of spontaneity and freedom; and *friend*, someone who is willing to be a peer, a companion.

Think back to when you were dating. How did you act then? What were the things you did to attract him? Do you remember how you made a study of him? Do that now. Friendship grows through understanding each other and meeting each other's needs.

Commit yourself to being his friend no matter what—even when his values are not your values and when he does things you don't like. Commit yourself to him with unconditional love. "I'll love you no matter what. I'll be your friend no matter what."

Fifth, be reflective when he is ready. Be a mirror to him. A time will come in your relationship when he begins to ask, "What do you think?" Reflect—don't be direct. A mirror does not show anything of itself; it only reflects the images that are presented to it. He is asking what you think, but he doesn't want a domineering opinion. He wants more of a discussion.

Your response should be, "Well, what have you been thinking? What are some of the options? Let's talk about it." After the discussion progresses, perhaps you can insert comments, such as, "Seems to me there's another option" or "Maybe this is a spin-off of what you suggested earlier."

Ask questions in response to his questions. If he says, "I've been thinking about quitting work," your response might be, "What does that mean to you?" He can go on to explain his feelings, his anxieties and frustrations. When he comes to a stopping point, he is stopping to see how you react. He is deciding whether to keep talking because you are listening and understanding—or whether he should shut up because you are being threatened.

When he stops, pick up on his last ideas and reflect them back to him. "John, what I hear you saying is that you've worked for twenty years for Widget, Inc., and now you want to go on your own. But you have a mixture of fear and enthusiasm." When you respond this way, you give him the permission to continue to talk and share his feelings with you.

When all the feelings get out on the table, along with all the options, give him a chance to verbalize the direction he's leaning. At this point, because you have been a good listener, he probably will want more input from you. When he asks, then begin to share your thoughts, feelings, reasons, anxieties, or joys.

Together you have begun to solve a major problem. Instead of your husband handling his problems in isolation, or with another woman, you have worked on it together. The process will reduce tension and will draw you closer together.

The Pain of Parenting

It's no secret that children add stress to our lives. Along with the joys, fun, and fulfillment, they produce problems we wouldn't otherwise have. Many studies show that women who have children will have a lower life satisfaction and a lower marriage satisfaction.[1] Yet most women experience a strong urge to have children, and those who haven't had children feel they've missed something. Apparently, it's the years of living with children after they're born that takes away the joy!

It's strange, isn't it, that children seem to cause more dissatisfaction for the present midlife generation than for earlier generations, yet boomers have concentrated more on their children. One authority observes, "We were the first crop of parents to take our children's failures and limitations as an indication of *our* inadequacy, not theirs; the first to believe, even briefly, that one could aspire to being a perfect parent. We were the first parents in the era of the child-centered family."[2]

Mothers at All Ages

Midlife mothers could have children whose ages range from newborn to college. Some women in our survey started families while they were yet in their teens, with their childbearing completed by age twenty-three. Other women delayed having children, choosing to have a career first, so childbearing didn't start until their midthirties.

In recent decades the standard childbearing era was during a woman's twenties, but that is no longer true. Not many years ago if a woman had a child in her midthirties, everyone was convinced something went wrong. Quite often there was a nosy person around who would ask what everyone else was wondering: "What happened?" Today a midlife pregnancy is often planned.

"In the U.S., between 1970 and 1987, the number of women who waited until their thirties to have their first child [increased nearly 400 percent]. According to a recent Census Bureau survey, more than half of all women in their early thirties who don't have a child yet are still planning to someday."[3]

"Relatively few female executives or CEOs [in the U.S.] identify 'commitment to family responsibilities' as among the top obstacles to women's advancement. . . . 64 percent are mothers, but 20 percent say they decided not to have children as a means to manage their career and personal lives. Twenty-six percent postponed childbearing as part of their career/life balancing strategy."[4]

As we evaluate the impact of children on the midlife woman, we must notice not only that career women are delaying childbirth but also that people are getting married later. "The median age at marriage has risen from a low of 20.3 for women and 22.8 for men in 1960, to 24.5 for women and 26.7 for men in 1994. The proportion of women never married by their late 20s tripled from a historical low of 11 percent in 1960 to a high of 33 percent in 1993."[5]

Mutual Shaping

Most women who want to have children plan to raise them in an atmosphere of love and marital strength. But ready or not, the coming of children causes a redefinition of your life as a woman at each step along your way.

The apartment, condo, or house you live in is not only an expression of you, but your home also tends to form you. The same is true with the coming of a child. Building a nest and filling it with a child says something about you as a person and the things you value.

When you were married, you surrendered some of your independence, but you looked at your gains in intimacy and companionship as more than equal to your losses. The same reshaping of you by gains and losses happens with the coming of children. You form your life around them, and, in effect, they mold you.

Sometimes the younger woman experiences her

special life dream being put on hold when her first child comes. She begins to wait, biding her time until her children become independent—then she can pick up her dream. The unthoughtful woman, who quickly lays aside her career dream or has her dream shoved aside by an unwanted pregnancy, may at midlife find herself ventilating years of suppressed anger. Her innocent child may then be the focus of this woman's anger because she feels unfulfilled.

From Pampers to Puberty

When our oldest daughter went off to kindergarten, we realized we were no longer newlyweds, even though we had three children by that time. Jim had graduated from seminary, and we were pastoring a church. Yet, in our minds, we thought of ourselves as just beginning married life. At each milestone for our daughters, we were forced to update ourselves.

Do you remember the first time you saw pubic hair on your children? Did it make you feel old? One woman told about taking her son to the hospital emergency room. They stripped off his clothes to attend to him, and she said, "It was a shock to me to find out he already had pubic hair. I felt about a hundred years old."[6]

If a mother has found her identity and self-fulfillment only in her children, she will lose part of herself when they grow up and leave. If, on the other hand, she has raised her children from the beginning to become gradually independent, then adolescence and young adulthood are simply the next stage with her children.

New Friends

As a couple, we are enjoying our daughters and their husbands relating to us as equals, friends, peers. We have three daughters—Barbara, Brenda, and Becki. Barbara and her husband, Michael, spent two years in Switzerland, working with high school kids under the auspices of Youth for Christ and doing postgraduate work in architecture. We were in frequent contact, but we were surprised by one call from Switzerland. When we asked if everything was all right, they said, "Yes, we just wanted to call and tell you that we really love you, and of all the people in the world, you are our closest mature friends."

We were excited as we watched the three young couples launch into the world to take various challenges from God. And we find it very pleasant to have a growing, trusting, open, true friendship with each of these couples and their children.

Even Grandchildren Shape Us

We also noticed our self-images were changed by the coming of our first grandson, Nathan. Except for Barbara and Mike in Switzerland, we were all at the mobile home during the last day of Brenda's pregnancy. She had been in labor several hours, and Marc was caring for all of us, including his parents, as we waited for the birth of this child.

But there were identity questions. For Sally, the

transition to being a grandmother was easy, joyful, and fun. But for me (Jim), it was different. I didn't want to be called Grandpa because the media characterize grandfathers as gray-haired, deaf, senile old codgers who smilingly rock in their chairs. I didn't feel like that kind of man. I felt as if I were thirty-two years old, in the prime of life, with a world of ministry ahead of me that I wanted to accomplish for God.

The family kept pressing me, "What should Nathan call you?" I said, "Have him call me Jim; that's my name." They all laughed and said, "No, we can't do that! You've got to have a different name." After a lot of family discussion, it was finally decided I would be called "Jimpa"! Isn't that wonderful! I'm not really Grandpa. I'm "Jimpa," with my own unique identity. Nathan's arrival forever changed my name—I'm known as Jimpa to all ten of our grandchildren.

As the life cycle progresses, our children will continue to define us. By midlife this can be both negative and positive. Knowing how to raise your children and lead them to maturity will help make your midlife transition go more smoothly as well as help them define themselves.

Adolescence—A Recent Identification

The devoted focus toward children is a recent development. "In the twelfth century, there was no concept of childhood. It is difficult, in this child-adoring world, to think what it might mean never to have been a child, but in the society of the Middle Ages an infant was nursed in his swaddling clothes until the age of six or seven and then became a small adult, living the same life as his elders, gaming, eating, dressing as they did, marrying at twelve or fourteen. When Jesus suffers little children to come unto Him, the Medieval painter portrays Christ surrounded by eight little men."[7]

Only in the sixteenth and seventeenth centuries did children begin to acquire special clothes that set them apart from adults. In the eighteenth century, pressure from the church for child education helped to define childhood more clearly. Not until the twentieth century did the adolescent era become one of the ages of man. Previously, children were considered miniature adults who stepped right into full adulthood. Now we have further refined life development stages so that we clearly see stages and substages for children, adolescents, young adults, midlife adults, and aging adults.

Maturity the Goal

We get older without trying. The task is to mature in each stage. As we've indicated, a midlife woman may be at a crucial time in her own development at the same time she needs to help her children mature.

ACCEPTANCE AND APPRECIATION

Maturity has many dimensions, but one of the qualities we definitely want to help our children attain is an acceptance and appreciation of themselves as special persons. Your role is to help your children define who they are. What are the insights you have of your child? What gifts and abilities do you see God has given your child? What are his or her strengths and weaknesses? Almost all of the definition of self in the early years of life comes from family members—especially Mom and Dad. As a mother, you have the most strategic input because of your closeness and the amount of time that you spend with your child.

Here's the catch. If you don't think much of yourself, you will probably pass a low sense of worth to your children. The Bible says the sins of the parents will be visited on the third and the fourth generations (Exodus 34:7). In self-image terms, that means if a mother has a low self-image, she influences her children to have low self-images. They then influence their children, and the cycle keeps on going until something intervenes. Reading and working on the projects in this book will help you to grow and be a better mom.

LOVE

Help your children learn to love other people. Loving is a two-way street. One side of love is to understand people—to give energy from our lives to enrich others.

The other side of love is learning to accept love from others—not earning it but receiving it as a gift. Sometimes children are "good" or do kind things to *earn* our love. They need to feel that they are loved unconditionally—whether they are good or bad—whether they do kind things or not. Genuine love is *not* something we earn but is offered unconditionally.

Loving your children unconditionally helps them to understand that God loves them in the same way. If they are caught in the trap of thinking God loves them *only* when they are good, they may end up with a "works" religion and think they must earn their salvation by doing more good than bad.

VALUES

Help your children establish their own values. Have you ever said to your children, "We don't do that in our family"? That's an appropriate way to teach children values and how your family is different from other families. But unless those values become their own, they may not follow your definitions and values when they become adolescents.

When our daughters moved into their teenage years, we realized we could not control all of their lives—all of the time. We couldn't go with them to school and make sure they didn't cheat, tell dirty jokes, or get involved in drugs, alcohol, or sex. Nor could we force them to become witnesses for Christ. All of these values had to be their values, or they would never live them out all their lives.

Help children wrestle with *why*. What are the reasons behind the statement "Our family doesn't do that"? When they get to school, someone is going to ask them the *why* questions.

Suppose your child says to another child, "Our family doesn't drink."

But your child's peer group will ask, "Why not?"

"Well, I don't know; my parents just don't drink."

"Well, why don't you?"

"My parents told me I shouldn't."

"What's wrong with drinking? Have you ever tried it? How do you know it's not OK? Who says your parents are right when all the rest of our parents say it's all right? Maybe you just have odd parents. How many parents do you know who don't drink?"

Unless the *why* questions have been handled so your children have a chance to reflect thoughtfully and make them their own values, they'll never be able to stand the pressure during the teen years.

The teen years are characterized by a necessary separation from the parental home and an alignment with the teen peers. If children have been living off of parental or church values—which are not their own—then they will reject those values as they connect with peers.

HOW TO DEVELOP A VALUE SYSTEM
To develop your children's own value system, let us suggest that you think about ways to accomplish some of the following:

Your children need to be confronted with authority-based information. The source of values is the Bible. Your children need to have value concepts to work with. What are the scriptural bases for deciding such issues as lying, stealing, and sexual sin? What are the Scriptures you would suggest?

Your children also need alone times to think about those concepts. Encourage your children to have down times. It's OK to sit on the roof or behind a tree. Maybe those are good places for them to sit and listen to a bird, watch a sunset, count the clouds. Hold up the value of meditating. Let them see you spending quiet, reflective times.

Create times of open discussions with lots of give and take where they can verbalize their questions and doubts. Don't shut them up with the famous old line "Just do it because I said so!" You may be able temporarily to silence your children and make them do or think what you want them to—but that old line certainly won't work during the teen years or beyond.

Your children need life experience to establish their own values. Use incidents around them as learning experiences to develop their value system. Talk about the kids who are cheating in school. They are getting ahead and are getting better grades than they deserve now—but what does the Bible say? (Read Proverbs for coaching.) Cheating is only a short-term gain. Help them think about what happens to people who keep on cheating. Point out some of the examples of white-collar crime. Life experience, coupled with the other three factors of value information—meditation time, and free discussion—will help bring value development in your children.

Also, avoid protecting your children from all the results of their own wrongdoing. For example, if one of your children is caught cheating in school, let the child experience the natural consequences so the life experience can bring their change and growth. But don't carry that to an extreme. Protect them from destroying themselves or their future—that's part of being a parent.

SERVING

Another quality of maturity is learning to serve other people. Jesus did not come "to be served but to serve" (Matthew 20:28). When he was with his disciples in the upper room during the last hours before his crucifixion, he took the role of a servant boy. If you have read the account in John 13, you know that the disciples were humbled to have Christ take off his outer robe, wrap a towel around his waist, and wash their feet. Jesus was Master and Lord. He was their leader, and yet he was down on his knees as a servant. Peter finally exclaimed, "You will never wash my feet!" (John 13:8). (Peter had not yet learned how to receive love.) Jesus said, "But if I don't wash you, you won't belong to me."

Jesus' act made an indelible impression on their minds—an impression they would never forget. He reinforced his action by saying, "You call me 'Teacher' and 'Lord'. . . because it is true. And since I, the Lord and Teacher, have washed your feet, you ought to wash each other's feet. I have given you an example to follow" (John 13:13-15).

Your children need to learn to serve other people, including their family—not for an allowance or for your convenience—but for their growth. They need to understand serving as their special ministry to people. Without helping people, we become self-centered, and we buy into the "me-ism" that has grossly distorted our culture.

LIVING WITH LIMITATIONS

An additional quality of maturity for your child is to learn to live with the imperfections of life. Nothing in life is perfect, or lasts forever—other than our relationship with God.

Our youngest daughter, Becki, has written a book about limitations. Becki knows from experience. She was only a sixteen-year-old high school junior, winning track meets, when she had to have her left leg amputated above midthigh because of cancer. [8]

Becki shared how it is to live life with a twenty-four-hour-a-day reminder that life is imperfect. Help your children learn that losses hurt—but life has both gains and losses. When disappointments come, remind them that God loves them and stress helps them to become mature.

Those Terrific and Trying Teens

The majority of women in their late thirties and early forties have children who are teens. Adolescence generally is not a quiet, smooth period of development! Emotional upheavals are frequent as the teen leaps toward adulthood and/or acts as a child. The teen years can be painful, filled with stressful inconsistencies and a testing of limits. It's a time of frustration, conflict, and growth. Even under the best of circumstances, with the best integrated parents and children, it can be a time of major family strain.

During the teen years *both* the mother and the child are going through very important developmental times. The teen is emerging from childhood and moving into young adulthood. The mother is emerging from young adulthood into midlife. Usually there is a lot of misunderstanding. In a sense, they both need each other—but each is preoccupied with his or her own needs and may not be able to help.

Famed psychiatrist Anna Freud described what happens in the adolescent. But her description also pictures what is happening in the mother of the adolescent:

> It is normal for an adolescent to behave in an inconsistent and unpredictable manner, to fight his impulses, and to accept them; to love his parents and to hate them; to be deeply ashamed to acknowledge his mother before others, and unexpectedly to desire heart-to-heart talks with her; to thrive on imitation and identify with others, while searching unceasingly for his identity; to be more idealistic, ar-

tistic, generous, and unselfish than he ever will be again, but also the opposite: self-centered, egotistic, calculating.[9]

Catch Up! Time for Two Generations

Sometimes the problems in your teens will create tension within you because you find yourself reexperiencing some of the same issues that were not fully resolved when you were an adolescent. These old problems, revisiting your personality, may make your midlife transition more difficult and cause you to project your anger toward your teens when you see the same issues in them.

You may feel a great urgency to take advantage of these last years of training as your teen is rapidly moving away from your authority. You may feel very rejected and hopelessly cut out of his or her life. And you may feel a deep sense of guilt: "Look what's happening! I've failed as a mother." During this era you are probably wrestling with your own self-identity, and the conflict with your teen may reinforce your low self-image. It's common for a mother either to put down her teens—or to live through them.

Dorothy would visibly light up when her daughters had teenage boys around the house. She would stand straighter and freshen her hair with a quick comb. She tended to wear tighter clothes and was constantly pulling her sweater down tighter. She became noticeably more witty, positive, and outgoing around these young males.

Dorothy had no idea what she was doing, but

unconsciously she was living through her teenage daughters. If she were confronted, she would deny she was trying to win the approval of these young males. But her actions clearly indicated there were needs being filled by these experiences.

We have also watched mothers who belittle their children in front of friends or constantly harass them. These actions will diminish your teens' self-image and drive them to other people for understanding and love.

Both of these expressions—living vicariously or putting your teen down—indicate some incompleteness in you that you should process as you make your midlife transition.

Both Need Love

A family can be very tense if both the adolescents and one or more of the midlife parents are going through a transition at the same time. Each needs to help and love the other—but neither can muster the energy to do so.

People need to know they are unconditionally loved as they go through life transitions. A grabbing line from the play *A Woman of No Importance* says, "Children begin by loving their parents; after a time they judge them; rarely, if ever, do [children] forgive [parents]."[10]

Bertrand Russell, in *The Conquest of Happiness*, says: "The value of parental affection lies largely in the fact that it is more reliable than any other affection. Friends like one for one's merits; lovers for one's charms. If the merits or the charms diminish, the friends and lovers may vanish. . . . Our parents love us because we are their children, and this is unalterable fact."[11]

Providing your teens with unconditional love, which they don't have to earn, will reduce tension in the home and make your own midlife transition easier. Sally and I have learned a simple plan from a book by Ross Campbell—*How to Really Love Your Children.* He suggests a parent do the following three things:

- Touch your child—hand on shoulder, or arm over their shoulder.
- Look directly into his or her face.
- Speak words of affirmation—"I think you're great. I love you. You are becoming a great person. I'm proud of you."

The combination of all three acts has a powerful effect on building the self-esteem of your child or young adult—and lessens tensions between you.[12]

Leaving the Nest

Mothers report mixed feelings in the child-launching era of life. On the one hand, they are glad to have the young adult move out, go to college, get into a career, or get married. It means a reduction in tension, space to breathe, perhaps even an opportunity for mom to launch her career. More time can be spent on the marriage or on re-establishing friendships.

On the other hand, women report a strong

desire to replay some of the earlier childhood years. Mothers aren't saying, "Give me the present time with you." They are saying, "Give me the past with you." But it can't be done.

Sometimes there is a deep sense of loss. She may experience an intense desire to replay those early childhood years—to make changes for growth, to lessen tension, and to reduce this gnawing sense of guilt and failure.

One parent said, "For years I've been in mourning and not for my dead; it's for this boy, or for whatever corner in my heart died when his childhood slid out of my arms."[13]

This is a hard time in your life. Your husband may be moving away from you as he madly dashes to use his last few years to achieve all his career goals. Your children are also moving away from you, trying to establish their independence. You know they have to—but you feel very lonely and isolated.

You may feel a desperate need to be needed—a need that is frustrated by your husband's career and your children's independence. A woman "offers love, support, guidance, help to others—and the significant people in her life counter with hostility and desire to escape from her nurturing."[14]

Your marriage may be at a low ebb. You may be questioning your worth as a person because you feel less needed. If you are caught in this vise grip of life, you may find yourself almost dependently clutching your children.

No Chance to Grow Up

Years ago we surveyed University of Illinois students whose parents had divorced within the last five years, and we heard a repeated story. Parents who were unsuccessful in their marriage or were separated or divorced became dependent on their children. One girl stated that she would hold her mother in her arms and rock her while the mother wept. Another graduate student reported that he was the intermediary between his first family and the second. He was the messenger and mediator between his father and his mother even though they were divorced and each had remarried. Another girl, who told us incident after incident of parental dependency, said, "You know, I need parents too!"

When your young adults come to the point of leaving home, you must let them leave, physically and emotionally. They should not be given the responsibility of parenting you at this age in their lives. Later on, when you have reached old age, they will parent you. But at this stage they need to establish their own independence and identity.

New Roles

A rather new phenomenon is taking place now as young adults leave the nest to start careers, get married, or go for higher education. They are returning to the nest in great numbers because of financial need—and sometimes because they need emotional support. When they reenter the nest as adults, the emotional boundaries between parent and child must be different. This takes loving communication, understanding, and flexibility by everyone.

The midlife woman must search for a new identity in relationship to her grown children. You cannot be a dictator or a domineering mother. You must not be a meddling mother-in-law, but you can have an extremely fulfilling role as a counselor, mentor, and friend.

In these roles, you can continue to have an intimate relationship with your young adults. They will welcome your input when it is offered—rather than imposed. These roles as counselor, mentor, and friend also allow you to put your experience to good use. Your relationship with your young adults is not ended when they leave home—it is just changed to a new level of relationship. You will not always be "mothering"—but you will always be a mother.

Too Much Too Fast

❧

The four Bradleys were having a normal breakfast. The two kids were partially dressed for school. As they ate their breakfast, they read the cereal boxes and exchanged their usual competitive verbal jabs. Mom was playing her role of referee; Dad was scanning the morning paper. Just the evening before, he had returned from a week of leading seminars at a Christian retreat center.

Mom finally hustled the kids away from the table, supervised their last preparations for school, and sent them out the door. She returned to the table, where she and her husband, David, leisurely enjoyed another cup of coffee.

Without warning, David suddenly fell off his chair, grabbed his chest, and cried out in pain. He had great trouble breathing. Everything in his throat seemed to have closed off. His body jerked and convulsed. Donna didn't know what to do. She felt a sense of frustration, terror, and panic. She kept calling his name, asking if he was all right. Then he gave a shudder and his body lay still.

It was only then that she thought to get help.

She frantically called 911, and they immediately sent a paramedic ambulance team. It was a full eight minutes before the team arrived. No, it wasn't eight minutes—it was a lifetime—an eternity of feeling helpless, of praying desperately, *Please, God, don't let this happen*—of thinking this nightmare would be over shortly and she would awaken to find David alive and well.

But it was no dream. The rescue team rushed through the front door, began to pound on David's chest, and inserted IVs. They ripped open his shirt and applied the heart defibrillator while Donna watched helplessly. David's body convulsed repeatedly. Miracle of miracles, his heart started to beat! David was alive. He was going to be OK.

Quickly he was put on a stretcher. But before they could get him out the door, his heart stopped again. Again the team jumped into action. Again the heart responded. In moments the ambulance was screaming down the quiet little residential street toward the hospital. The hospital emergency team had been alerted. In five minutes David would be in the cardiac unit, but during those five minutes his heart would stop two more times.

He was wheeled into the emergency room, and people in green gowns swarmed all around him. Orders were snapped by specialists. Machines sprang to life, monitoring David's vital signs. Tubes were running everywhere. The urgent work to control his condition went on for more than an hour.

Finally he was stabilized. He was under an oxygen tent and listed as extremely critical. The head physician came to the waiting room and talked to Donna. He explained that David's brain had been without oxygen for probably more than ten minutes. The likelihood of his surviving was extremely remote. If he did survive, he would be nothing more than a vegetable.

What does a woman with two children do when her husband is gravely ill? In a few short minutes, she went from being the wife of a successful Christian leader to becoming either a widow—or even more dreadful—a wife with a living husband who was really dead.

A woman in midlife may be experiencing the normal routine of life, coping with the transition from young adulthood to being a midlife adult without any great stress. If, however, an unexpected or traumatic loss occurs, everything in her life may become too much to handle. She may experience the domino effect—an overload of her circuitry—too many straws on the camel's back.

Many things can happen at midlife that can become traumatic:

- The early death of her husband, parents, children, or a friend
- The unplanned birth of a child
- An early empty nest or early grand-parenthood
- Forced retirement

- Major illness or injury
- Financial loss
- A relocation that causes loss of friends

Change Events

Each incident that happens to us is called a change event. Every change event has some effect on us. Obviously, the more major the event, the more significant it is in our lives. Some of these major change events cause us to spring into action. Perhaps we will seek more education, the counsel of a friend, a spiritual-growth activity, or some other positive adjustment.

A study by Aslanian and Brickell, reported in *Americans in Transition*, found that adults do not learn or grow simply because they have the opportunity—a life event triggers their action. Eighty-three percent of those learning experiences are related to family and/or career change events.[1] A traumatic event in your life may become part of the impetus that will bring about a great deal of growth.

Major change events can also bring negative directions to your life. This generally happens when the event is so large and so significant that it overwhelms you, or when it causes a chain reaction of disasters in your life. The death of one of your parents at the same time your teen gets into trouble with the law may cause you to go into deep depression. You may be unable to function at work—you could lose your job.

In our research studies we found many women

who had experienced traumatic losses, such as death, divorce, illness, or financial loss, at midlife. The women felt that these jarring events were a crucial part of their personal midlife crisis.

The Domino Effect

Gail's divorce was so shattering to her that she was unable to cope. As a result, she was hospitalized under psychiatric care. She lost her job, and her husband was given custody of their children. The event of divorce started the toppling of the dominoes. After losing her ability to function, then losing her job and her children, she was severely depressed. Her self-image previously had been built on her relationship to her husband and her children. When these were gone, she said, "I feel as if I don't exist."

You will experience hundreds of major change events, such as an illness, death, family stress, financial loss, or a number of other traumatic events. But when a large number of change events happen in a short period of time, you experience a greater stress—even if all the change events are not negative. In addition there are predictable times in life when change events will come at you as a landslide—and therefore massive stress.

In the Beginning

One crucial time with many changes is during the transition from adolescence to young adulthood. Adolescents are trying to develop their own identity and independence. They are learning how to relate to other people and how to give and receive love appropriately. They are trying to establish career directions and to decide if they should marry, and whom.

During a five-year period, late teens and early twenties, the average young adult moves from their parental home to their own home. They probably will finish college and/or will choose a career direction, will establish friendships, probably will choose their marital partner, and perhaps start a family. In that five-year span they go from being inexperienced adolescents to responsible young adults—we hope.

From their midtwenties to midthirties, people usually experience career advancement and move to a larger house or apartment. If they are married, the last of their children usually are born during this time, and those children start school. At this time adults get settled into life. Their change events are spread out over a longer period of time compared to the late-teen/early-twenties era.

At retirement a large number of change events also accumulate rapidly. Many of the events relate to the career change of the husband and/or wife. Retirement from the job that controlled daily routine often is accompanied by a loss of self-image and identity. They may also experience reduced income and loss of benefits such as medical plans, paid vacations, use of a company car and company facilities, and free continuing education. The home life and schedule will be readjusted. Often they must take a part-time job with all the associated anxieties of starting a new job. Sometimes they move to smaller housing and perhaps a smaller car. They may even relocate to a totally different part of the country.

The change events in moving from adolescence to young adulthood are viewed by most people as positive even though they may be stressful. But change events at retirement are generally viewed as losses and carry stress with them.

In the Middle

Change events for midlife people are both negative and positive—but mostly negative. The positive change events are usually enjoyed by midlife women. They feel they have earned the benefits of success, and it's time to collect. But the negative change events are what really throw the midlife woman for a loss.

At midlife you have a huge number of change events. Your children are probably moving into adolescence, with all their urges to break free. Your husband is making his last wild dash to make it big in his career. You may want to reenter school or go back to work or begin thinking of work as a career instead of just a job.

Added to all of these change events, you are also involved with the change events of your parents and parents-in-law who are retiring and coping with aging. At midlife you are impacted by the change events of a younger generation, your own midlife transition, and the adjustments of the older generation. These three different developmental ages contain dozens of potentially traumatic events that could cause your own midlife transition to become a midlife crisis.

On Time/Off Time

Bernice Neugarten suggests that predictable, "on time" events are not unsettling when they arrive because "the events are anticipated and rehearsed, the grief work completed, the reconciliation accomplished without shattering the sense of continuity to the life cycle."[2] Her point is that major stress is caused when events in our lives do not arrive "on time." She says that when the rhythm of life is broken—such as by the early death of a parent, a child born too early or too late, the unforeseen empty nest, unexpected grandparenthood, untimely retirement, major illness, or widowhood coming at an unexpected time—a major crisis is produced. She does not believe that the ordinary problems of living through change events produce crisis.

Other researchers, such as Roger Gould, would disagree. In his article "Phases of Adult Life," Gould shows eighteen sample curves portraying degrees of satisfaction associated with the major, normal experiences of the adult life span. Fifteen of these research items show that men and women experience discomfort and stress during the midlife years.[3]

From our observations during more than thirty-five years of counseling, stress is not caused simply by the events of the midlife years happening outside of sequence or "off time" but by the change events themselves—whether on schedule or unanticipated. For example, the mid-life woman knows her body is aging, but simply knowing it will happen does not eliminate the stress since our society places so much value on being young.

The midlife woman also may know her husband is going to experience his own midlife transition. Having that process appear on time does not reduce the trauma of his failing leadership in the home, personal depression, criticism and rejection of her as a mate—or any other actions or attitudes he displays during his midlife transition. The empty nest may appear on schedule, but even if the woman has not placed all of her energies and inter-est in her children, she still will experience trauma. The timing of the event is not the most important element, although it does bear impact.

Another factor is the sheer number of events taking place at one time—in her life and in the lives of significant people around her. But perhaps the most important factor that will determine the degree of stress is the importance she assigns to each of the change events.

Growth or Collapse

One woman may look at the independence of her children as very exciting and the fulfillment of all that she has been trying to accomplish. She may view the event as providing additional time for her to pursue her own career and educational direc-tions. Another woman may look at the same event and feel that she has lost some essential part of her self-identity.

Some women have rebounded positively from a husband's involvement in an affair and have gone back to school, become engrossed in a career, taken up hobbies, and lost weight. Even though their husbands' affairs were traumatic experiences initially, they would say their deepened marriage that resulted was, overall, positive.

Other women we have known have gone into deep and prolonged depression that caused them to become nonfunctional. Women who had personal worth apart from their husbands were able to stand on their own. But other women, whose life values were centered in their husbands, lost everything.

Why is it that some women seem to be able to handle more stress than others? We think, in addition to the importance they assign to each problem, it has something to do with the personal worth and security they feel within themselves.

Some women who place little value on themselves tend to assign great importance to events that take place around their lives. A few stressful events can then produce a high cumulative stress level. Other women feel quite secure within themselves. The world can be swirling around them, but their stress levels will be much lower. These women are able to go through a torrent of trouble and still not get sucked under.

Internal Worth

What causes you to think of yourself as worthwhile? Do you personally appreciate yourself, or do you have worth only as you feel significant to other people? If you feel you are worthwhile *only* because your parents, husband, and children love you—what will you do if this support is missing?

Children do become increasingly independent, and you may interpret that as rejection. If one or both of your parents die, you may lose not only a parent but also a part of your own self-image. If your husband has a traumatic midlife transition and begins to criticize and reject you, you may find you have lost more than a deep relationship—you have lost some of your identity.

It is true that our worth is initially established by significant others, such as our parents. As we mature, we need to shift to value ourselves apart from what others think. Otherwise, we are vulnerable to being manipulated by others' opinions of us—or to living through others.

Midlife Pepperoni

From our research, women experience midlife stress from many sources. Some stress came from husbands and their attitudes or lifestyle changes. Unhappy situations with children, family illnesses or injuries, death of a loved one, or divorce greatly compounded the midlife issues.

Husband stress was a major factor. For example, if the husband decides to reduce work, take more vacations, and start slowing down, his wife may view this as a personal threat to her goals. If her husband does change his work patterns, how is she going to expand her career? She may want to go back to school, but that would require they be in town most of the time. Or she may have full-time employment and be trying to climb the employment ladder by putting in extra time and energy. Her husband has made a decision, and he assumes either that his wife wants the same thing or that she doesn't care.

At midlife Ron decided to change careers. Instead of staying in his position with a pharmaceutical firm where he was making about seventy-five thousand dollars a year, he decided to open a pizza parlor. This meant he had to invest all the family savings, mortgage their home, and start working from dawn until midnight. The business was not a success. They suffered heavy financial losses.

Ron's wife, Millie, had wanted to go back to college to pick up her degree in special education but was forced to take a mundane job just to earn money. She had to support the family while her husband muddled along through the collapse and chaos of his decision. "It wasn't just that the business failed," she said, "but I realized now I was never going to be able to accomplish the things I had hoped to achieve."

Skim or Whole Milk

A midlife mother can experience traumatic loss if a child leaves home under messy circumstances.

Carol had assumed there would be the normal chain of events with their son, Rich—childhood, adolescence, college, getting married, starting his own family—and always close ties.

But when Rich turned fifteen, he had a strong urge for independence. At the same time, John, his father, was in the depths of his own midlife crisis. Everything seemed to irritate John. One evening the three of them were shopping for a few items at the grocery store. Carol put two different kinds of milk in the cart, skim milk for the parents and whole milk for Rich. The aisle was jammed with people, but to John it was as if they were alone. In a loud, angry voice he roared, "What are you doing—buying two kinds of milk?"

"One for you and me, and the other one for Rich," Carol answered.

Then there gushed forth a surge of anger and obscenities. "Why do we have to spend extra money on that kid? Why is he a privileged character?"

Rich quickly disappeared and went to the car. Carol tried to slink out of the store, but all the way through the checkout John was talking in a loud, angry voice. It wasn't the ten-cents-a-gallon difference in price. John was struggling with a deep-seated dissatisfaction with himself—and an unresolved relationship with his son.

When they reached home, John was still angry. Dinner had just barely started when John and Rich were at it again. John's eruption of anger was even more violent than in the store. Rich fought back. Finally his father said, "Pack your stuff and get out!"

The fifteen-year-old boy pushed past his mother as he left the room. Her mouth was open in disbelief. She followed him to his room. Rich jammed some clothes and personal belongings into a duffel bag. He grabbed his sleeping bag, and in spite of his mother's protests and pleadings, he pushed her aside, slammed out the door, hopped on his bike, and was gone into the night.

All of the dreams she had of gradual growth and transition from childhood to manhood were gone. What would happen now? Maybe it would blow over. Maybe there would be forgiveness and reconciliation between John and Rich.

Two days went by. There was no softening or bending on either side. Two weeks, two months passed.

More than two years passed since Rich moved out. He lived with a friend for a while and took a part-time job. He finally moved into an apartment with other guys and has been living an independent life. His mother never planned on this sudden, tragic emptying of the nest. The sorrow and loss have left her depressed even when she speaks of it now—years later.

Life Rains on Everybody

We know that bad things happen to good people. The Bible says the rain falls on the just and the unjust. But somehow we never really believe that bad things are going to happen to us—or to our family. For some reason we're never really prepared to handle the unexplained—the unexpected tragedies of life.

At age fifteen our daughter Becki had recurring pains in her left knee. Doctors assured us her problem was just growing pains and stress from being a cheerleader and gymnast.

One Friday as she was being treated for the displacement of her tailbone, a new doctor noticed she was limping. He was concerned when she told him her knee had frequently troubled her for a couple of years and sometimes caused her to stay at home and keep it elevated. When he x-rayed her knee, he discovered a massive enlargement of the bone just above the knee. "I want you to see an orthopedic surgeon immediately," he announced.

We had an emergency appointment with an orthopedist, a Christian who attended our church. His x-rays also showed the enlargement in the bone, and he began to explain how serious this problem might be. A biopsy would be performed to take samples, which would be sent to several labs around the United States. There might be nothing to worry about—or perhaps the six-inch bone section would need to be replaced. Becki might, however, need an amputation—and there is the possibility of death.

Within days the biopsy was performed, and samples of the growth were sent to labs specializing in rare tumors. The reports indicated an uncertainty about the type of tumor, but doctors decided it was benign and we should just watch it. The eight-inch incision on the outer side of Becki's leg healed, and she went back to running hurdles in track. The incident was pushed to the back of our minds as life continued and as my (Jim's) midlife crisis really heated up.

But the leg began to swell again. The bone definitely was enlarging. After another biopsy a year later, the specialists decided the growth was malignant and the best solution was amputation. Becki was now sixteen, and I was just coming out of my midlife crisis.

I wanted to vomit as I saw Becki being wheeled on a gurney back to her hospital room after surgery. At first I saw her face framed by her pretty blond hair. The sheet was pulled up tightly under her chin. My eyes followed the contour of her body from her neck down. I could see her right leg supporting the sheet all the way out to her toes. Then my eyes followed the sheet where her left leg should have been. The sheet was raised for about six inches and then fell off in a sickening, flat manner all the rest of the way down the bed. There was no strong, muscular leg. There were no toes pointing up and holding the sheet in line with her other toes. That leg was gone.

What would happen to her now? Would she be able to finish school? What would she do for her life's work? Would any man ever want to marry her?

Suddenly I found myself again at the bottom of

my midlife crisis pit. The last time I was down, I had known God was in the pit with me. This time I wasn't sure that he existed—or if he did, that he cared. [Note: Becki, Jim, and Sally have written about Becki's amputation and other life losses in their books *What God Gives When Life Takes* and *Trusting God in a Family Crisis*.[4]]

Only Other People Die

We all know that death is a reality. Remember when you were twenty-three? You knew about death, but it always happened to older people. Until midlife we keep living with the illusion that death happens to someone else—in some other distant place. When you were a little girl, a whole line of people ahead of you had to die before you did. Those people, in a sense, protected you from dying. By the time you get to midlife, some of those protective people have been snatched away. You become aware that you are more vulnerable. In fact, you may already have been startled by the death of somebody in your peer group. Gradually you begin to realize that you are no longer young—you are not immortal.

When you looked in the mirror this morning, did you notice how your face had changed since yesterday? Probably not. You may notice a difference from a year ago. More likely, you notice only the change that takes place over several years as you compare old photographs. Aging is like that—gradual, almost unnoticed.

Yesterday you were in college. Today you might be a midlife woman with children who are moving toward independence and a husband nearing the peak of his career. Crazy as it seems, you still think of yourself as a young woman. Aging is tricky. It sneaks up and catches you when you're not looking. You don't notice you are aging until you go to your high school reunion and wonder why they let all those old people come to the meeting.

"Death and aging are different, though they may be intimately intertwined: death is absolute, aging is forever relative."[5]

Death isn't gradual. An illness may lead gradually to death, but the moment of death is definite. Death is traumatic at midlife because it's not supposed to happen then.

The death of a significant person at any time in your life can be traumatic for you. The death of an important person, along with the other pressures of midlife, could trigger or accentuate your midlife crisis.

The Nightmare

If a wife loses her husband in midlife, she will experience many feelings. One of these could be anger directed at several different people.

Harry had a history of heart problems. Each time he had an attack, Suzanne was afraid. One night when Harry got up to go to the bathroom, he felt a stabbing pain in his chest. Instead of waking his wife, he went downstairs to get his medicine. Before he could take the medicine, he collapsed and died on the kitchen floor. Suzanne punished herself. "Why didn't I wake him up?" "Why wasn't I more thoughtful and have his medicine in several places in the house?" "How could I have been so irresponsible?" Her anger was mixed with guilt—she felt she could have kept him from dying.

Strangely, anger quite often is directed at the person who died. The remaining mate says in the midst of sobbing, "Now why did you go and die on me? You've left me in a terrible situation. I don't know how to do all of the stuff you did. Now what am I going to do?" Anger directed at the person who has died is sometimes a way of saying, "I can't get along without you. You're crucial to the support of my life." In some cases the anger means, "You lucky duck, you got out of this mess, but I'm left holding the bag." The problem with leftover death anger is that you can't sit down and work it out with the one who has died.

Too Busy—Except to Die

A midlife woman who loses her husband also experiences guilt. Guilt for her actions, thoughts, and words that were wrong and unkind. "Why did we have that dumb fight just the day before he died? Why did I insist on my own way?"

She also feels guilty because of things she never got to say or do. Midlife is a very busy time of life, and it's easy to put things on the back shelf. She confesses, "We had always planned to. . . . We talked about. . . . We enjoyed so much, but we never had a chance." Only the blank moments are left. She keeps feeling responsible for not filling those empty spots, for allowing their lives to be pushed by the tyranny of the urgent. "Why didn't we live life by our priorities? Why is it now, after you're dead, that I think about changing my values?"

His Affair

The mail this morning brought the usual flow of hurts from midlife women whose husbands are involved in an affair or who have decided to end the marriage through divorce. Part of one letter, typical of hundreds, read like this:

"I know you don't know me, but I've read two of your books, and they describe my husband very accurately. We've been married for seventeen years. He has been a loving, kind husband who has been thoughtful and gentle. He is a good provider. He loves the kids and is a good father. He's been a strong Christian and has been a highly respected leader in our church.

"One morning he announced he can't stand me. Just my presence in the room disturbs him, even if I only sit and read quietly, even when I don't say a thing. Just my walking through the room drives him crazy. He told me that our marriage has always been bad, and probably we never should have married. He's involved with another woman. He wants a divorce.

"My life has been so complete and happy up to this time. Now I'm shattered. I don't know which way to turn. Even the Christians in our church have turned their backs on me. I almost feel as if I don't exist, or I wish I didn't. Where do I go from here? Please—I need help."

If your husband is involved in an affair, you certainly will feel a loss of self-esteem, a sense of inadequacy, or failure. "I didn't please him—somehow I didn't meet his needs." You realize your communication broke down. You probably feel wronged and betrayed. You may feel guilty. "I could have changed, but I just didn't do it." Perhaps you feel shame, and you're trying to carry your burden in secret. You can't just tell your small Bible study group, "Well, Tom isn't here tonight because he's having an affair with his secretary. I'd appreciate your praying about that." Most women tend to carry these feelings inside, too embarrassed to share this problem or ask for help.

A man involved in an affair causes great devastation to his wife—but there is hope. Many marriages *are* restored after an affair, but your husband's despicable affair may push you over the edge into a deep midlife crisis.

The Divorce Boom

People call our office, write, or send E-mail from all over the United States and Canada as well as overseas, to receive counseling. Again and again we are startled when callers say their local pastors and/or Christian counselors have advised them to get a divorce because of an affair.

According to the U.S. Census Bureau, divorce has increased over 900 percent since 1900 for women ages forty-five to sixty-four.[6] "It takes most divorced women and children at least five years to regain their pre-divorce standard of living (if they ever do). Such divorce-driven dislocation ripples throughout children's lives. Compared with kids in two-parent marriages, they are one-third more likely to move (and they tend to move more often), [and] they are three times as likely to be in poverty."[7]

With the sharp rise in divorce, we would like to think there would be a corresponding sharp rise in the commitment among pastors and counselors to keep marriages together—and to help couples work through their problems. Unfortunately, some pastors and counselors display a growing sense of futility about midlife marriages.

We believe that pastors and counselors give up on troubled midlife marriages because they don't understand midlife crisis. They don't see it as a temporary problem of working through the midlife transition. They think the situation is a hopeless pond of quicksand, sucking people down to permanent destruction.

If you are going through a midlife marital breakup, it is *not* hopeless. Don't believe all that you hear from pessimistic leaders or friends. And don't believe your life will be better if you get out of this marriage.

One woman told us, "I went to my evangelical pastor when my husband asked for a divorce. He said, 'Just give up on the bum.' I went to a well-known Christian counselor in our community, and his observation was that my husband was too old to change and our marriage could not be restored. He said the wisest decision was for me to face reality and prepare for the divorce."

Each time this woman called us, she asked, "Does that sound right? Isn't there any hope at all? Where is God in this whole situation? Can't he make a difference?"

We encouraged her not to give up. There is hope. God does make a difference! Some marriages do end in divorce, but we have seen many restored when each mate worked on the relationship. In most cases one mate started the working before the other was willing. And because she or he didn't rush into agreeing to the divorce request, they have their marriage today.

The Children

Midlife women have a difficult time adjusting to marital separation. In a report by David Chiriboga, women in their thirties showed more stress than women in their twenties or forties. They also had more health problems and visits to the doctor than women of other ages.[8] Perhaps the increased stress reported by women in their thirties is directly linked to the responsibility they bear for their children during a marital breakup.

Children in divorce situations have a difficult time of recovery and often bear lifelong scars. In a book entitled *Surviving the Breakup: How Children and Parents Cope with Divorce*, it is reported, "Five years after the breakup, 34 percent of the kids are happy and thriving, 29 percent are doing reasonably well, but 37 percent are depressed."[9] Other studies confirm these findings by reporting that children of divorce often experience fear, anger, depression, and guilt that carry into adulthood so that they continue to be classified as less happy, more prone to anxiety, and experiencing a lower self-esteem.[10]

To verify the effects of divorce on older children, we carried out a study with University of Illinois students whose parents had been divorced within the previous five years. We found a great number of troubled students who were not able to function at full capacity in school or other activities. They struggled with self-worth, were afraid of close relationships, and were fearful of the future—especially marriage.

Death Would Be Easier

In the book *A Guide to Divorce Counseling* there is a graphic and gruesome description of the divorce process: "Divorce is the death of the marriage: The husband and the wife together with the children are the mourners, the lawyers are the undertakers, the court is the cemetery where the coffin is sealed and the dead marriage is buried."[11] Unfortunately, divorce does not really bring death to the marriage relationship. It usually only separates the combatants, who go on feeling antagonism and anger.

In most death situations, the bad is forgotten, and the good is remembered. In most divorce situations, the good is forgotten, and only the bad is remembered. The legal process often makes the situation worse as each mate must be shown to be defective.

As human beings we are inescapably connected to our roles in life. When one or more of these is lost, part of us is gone. The midlife woman facing divorce is experiencing the loss of one of her roles along with loss of identity. Depression is very normal, and it may be enough to push a midlife woman into midlife crisis.

God Is Always There

We need to be reminded that even though we experience many traumatic changes and losses at midlife, God does not intend those events to overwhelm us. He doesn't promise to eliminate problems—but he does promise to be with us: "When you go through deep waters and great trouble, I will be with you" (Isaiah 43:2).

We can use the difficulties to produce growth and beauty in our life, such as Shirley reveals in her letter to us:

"I wanted to get in touch with you again to bring you up-to-date. Roy finally did file for a divorce and it has been final for a year now. [She wrote about additional things she had done to try to restore her marriage since we had talked.]

"Once I worked through my anger and disappointment, I have been able to move on. I have really changed and grown through all this. I do like much about the 'new me.' I have taken classes and obtained my Realtor's license. I love selling, although the market isn't so great right now.

"I have had an exciting trip to visit my missionary sister overseas and stopped in several countries in Europe and Asia. I've taken up some exciting new hobbies—things Roy wouldn't believe I would ever do. I go sailing quite often and have become quite an able sailor. I've started scuba diving lessons and want to continue.

"Even though things didn't turn out as I planned and especially after I worked so hard at it, I'm glad I now have a better sense of who I am. I've learned there's a lot I can do. I also know God more intimately. I wish growth didn't hurt, but I'm glad that since I had to go through the pain, I can feel that now I'm a more complete, more interesting person."

The Marks of Time

There are four stages for women—childhood, adolescence, young adulthood, and "you look wonderful." Ever since the beginning of time, people have had a deep desire to prevent death or its foreshadows. Fighting the aging process seems to be inborn. Resisting aging isn't just a social conspiracy pushed by advertisers, but people have a deep-seated dread of losing what they now have. The only way to beat the game is to make youth last a lifetime.

"Someone your age should expect such trouble," was one of the lines my gynecologist said to me (Sally) as I sat draped in a sheet on the cold, hard table. I vividly remember what happened that day when I went for my annual gynecological exam. I always accumulated a list of the little medical problems to ask about during my yearly visits. Every year my doctor would politely try to give medical solutions for each of my rather insignificant troubles.

Then one year he seemed to give little thought to any of the problems on my list but answered with remarks such as, "Well, at your age your body doesn't . . ." or "Now that you're older, you have to expect that. . . ." I laughed and said to him, "You're going to have me walking out of here as an old woman!" He didn't say a thing in reply! As I walked out the door, wondering about his changed attitude, I realized he had deduced by my birth date that I was forty years old.

Two or three years later I wanted to know more about menopause so I could be adequately prepared and be able to go through the time as positively as possible. The doctor brusquely said, "When it happens, you'll know!" I asked if he had some materials I could read on the subject. He thought a minute and excused himself from the room. While I waited for him, I noticed folders in his display boxes containing booklets on family planning, natural childbirth, breast-feeding, and other topics for *young women*. After about ten minutes he returned with a rather worn-out little pamphlet on menopause. "Here, take this. We don't seem to have much," he mumbled. This was at a large clinic with six or eight gynecologists on staff!

I felt very much as if I had crossed some line into the land of the undesirables. One of the nurses, who is my personal friend, bluntly told me: "These doctors are men, and men are *not* interested in older women. They'd rather spend their time looking at younger women's bodies. You should hear them joke about the 'old crocks' over forty—they'd rather have a young woman for a patient than look at an old, worn-out woman."

An "Age-Old" Battle

Over the years I have had opportunity to see younger and older women in various stages of undress (this is still Sally writing!) in women's locker rooms and in our daughters' college dorms. The comparison between the old and young bodies is shocking. Even though some young girls may be overweight, most of them have good muscle tone, with their breasts in full form, thighs thin, and buttocks and stomachs tight.

Midlife and older women may be thin, but they have flabby abdominal muscles and thicker waists. They may have been skinny in their twenties, but it's hard to say that about most women after thirty-five. They may have varicose veins, and many have scars from surgeries. They look as if they have dozens of marbles tucked away just under the skin of their thighs. (It's strange that when we buy a side of beef for the freezer, we like it well marbled with fat—we call it prime beef. But when a woman gets well marbled with fat, we just call her fat and old.)

That frightening battle against "old" is what gives the hucksters an opportunity to push all their magical potions on us. The benefits are mostly for the people who sell them. Women in midlife wildly go after "fad diets, lotions, sunlamps, wrinkle-removers, vitamins, plastic surgery, beauty preparations from exotic insect ingredients, exercise salons, machines guaranteed to restore youthful tone to age-slackened skin and muscles, and books on techniques for 'sex after forty.' It reassures us that everything is not yet lost, and there's still a magical chance that we might, like middle-aged Cinderellas, be restored to our youthful glory in the nick of time. Lots of luck."[1]

The Prime of Life

Unfortunately, our society has a crazy double standard. When we were pastoring a college church, Sally would say to me (Jim), "The way some of the girls fall all over you isn't fair. They want to see you in your office, and they offer to do projects for you, anything around the church—just to be near you." Yet, my sideburns were turning gray, and my face had lots of wrinkles.

You see, a man with gray sideburns seems to be wise. And wrinkles are just laugh lines that show he has lots of character. Sally is a very pretty woman, but the young guys who sought her out were genuinely wanting her counsel, her motherly advice, and insights as a woman. They were not flirting.

We live in a funny world. At that same time, Barbara, our oldest, at age twenty-seven was saying she would be glad when she got into her thirties so she would get more respect as a counselor.

What exactly *is* the right age? For a woman, it seems to be somewhere between thirty-four-and-a-half, when you're still young enough to be admired, and thirty-five, when you fear being put out to pasture.

The Bitter Fight

Biologically speaking, from the very beginning of life we're dying. Cells do increase faster than they die until about age twenty-one, but the last three-quarters of our lives cells die faster than they are created.

During midlife, physical changes occur more rapidly. After age thirty-three, hand and finger movements are progressively more clumsy. By age fifty, most adults have at least one pair of glasses. There's not much change in taste sensitivity until after about age fifty. Sensitivity to smell decreases slightly about age forty, and sensitivity to touch after about age forty-five. Hearing is best at age twenty, and then there is a gradual loss of the high tones. Balance, interestingly, is at its best between ages forty and fifty. The voice also begins to change, and by midlife many singers have retired, but it isn't until old age that the voice will lose its lower ranges and become more high pitched.[2]

But these areas are not really where the sting is. Changes in appearance are the most devastating to midlife women. Susan Sontag, a poet, writes passionately about a woman's loss of beauty at midlife: "Beauty, women's business in this society, is the theater of their enslavement. Only one standard of female beauty is sanctioned: the girl. The standard of beauty in a woman of any age is how far she retains or how she manages to simulate the appearance of youth. . . . Most of the women who successfully delay the appearance of age are rich."[3]

Does She or Doesn't She?

The three big appearance issues for midlife women are hair, skin, and weight. But the hair begins to thin by age forty, and by fifty most women have some gray hair—although only your hairdresser and L'Oréal really know for sure. Before 1938 the *New York Times* would not accept advertisements for hair coloring,[4] but when you look at the women around you now, you realize what an impact Miss Clairol has made. Since gray is usually judged as not beautiful in our society, that leaves a lot of gray-haired people with a problem.

Psychologist Joyce Brothers reminds us that we believe "beautiful people have beautiful personalities. . . . We may not be aware of our bias, but we consistently judge them to be more sensitive, kind, intelligent, interesting, sociable, and exciting than less attractive people."[5]

A New Wrinkle

The skin, the second battleground of appearance, begins to show more wrinkles because the fatty tissue just under the skin on the face and arms begins to disappear as one ages. The skin then sags over the bone structures. No face creams can really restore the fatty tissue under the skin to give a youthful, full-face look.

One author's description is grim but accurate: "The skin loses elasticity. It becomes coarser and darker on the face, neck, arms, and hands, and wrinkles appear. Some of these skin-associated changes result from muscle flabbiness underlying the skin. For example, bags and dark circles form under the eyes. These are particularly noticeable because the rest of the skin pales."[6]

The battle against aging is so often fought at the skin level because a woman's skin shows her real age. A good bra, control-top pantyhose, and a lightweight girdle can pull a lot of things into shape. But it's difficult to cover up the crow's feet around her eyes and those little wrinkles at the corners of her mouth. If she didn't have to move her eyes or mouth, then maybe makeup would cover the lines. On a man, wrinkles say he's "experienced"—on a woman they say "old."

Cosmetic surgery is one solution women try to tighten the skin and remove the bags under the eyes and chin. It's important to investigate this kind of surgery thoroughly before proceeding. There are risks involved—nerve and muscle damage and even permanent deformity. In spite of the risks, it is estimated that forty-five to fifty-five thousand people a year submit to having their faces lifted.[7]

Perhaps columnist Nancy Stahl sums it up best: "When I was 15, I [spent] half an hour in front of the bathroom mirror, experimenting with makeup in any effort to look 21. I do the same thing at 39."[8]

The War on Weight
The third big enemy in the physical war game is weight. Once you decide that "fat is old" and you

don't want to look that way, you probably will start losing weight. However, some forces work against you. Apart from how much you eat or exercise, body fat is redistributed, and muscle is gradually converted to fat. Body fat makes up only 10 percent of total weight in adolescence, but it is at least 20 percent by middle age, and most of it settles around the waist. The bust becomes smaller and, unfortunately, the abdomen and hips become larger.[9]

Perhaps at this point you're saying, "That's me! I'm not what I used to be." Your ideal weight is what you weighed after you attained your full stature and you were in your early twenties—assuming you were not overweight then. Given the normal conditions of life in our society and the change in body metabolism as you grow older, you will have to deliberately work at keeping off excess weight. Not only is fat ugly and old, but it produces stress on the rest of your body systems.

The Protective Layer

Keeping weight off is more than watching calories and exercising—it is also a mental attitude. Many midlife women struggle with feelings of personal inadequacy and sometimes a deep-seated hatred of themselves. Frequently an overweight woman has an unhappy past, present, or both.

Doris was an early midlife woman who had all of the potential for being a very attractive woman, but she was about seventy pounds overweight. Her hair was not cared for, and she seemed to have no understanding of how makeup could be used to enhance her natural beauty. As she talked to me (Jim), she eventually poured out a history of sexual exploitation. First, her father sexually molested her, and later an uncle did. When she was a teenager, she had a pretty face and sexy body and was in several beauty contests. But her contacts with boys tended to be very physical. She thought in her mind, *I'm a dirty person already; what difference does one more make?*

While she was a college student, God brought her to himself in a beautiful way and began to change many of her directions in life. But since she was still under the influence of her negative self-image, her weight did not respond immediately.

When she was in her late twenties, God led a caring Christian man into her life who wanted her to reach her full potential in Christ. She had experienced much growth in her life in her early years of marriage, but she continued wrestling with her self-image and weight problem as she entered mid-life. Again and again she had tried diets, only to fail.

After we talked for a few sessions and worked a bit on her self-image, she came to see that her accumulation of weight really had become a protection against the sexual approaches of men. Only as she confronted the distorted sexual area of her life was she finally able to make headway in the weight battle. She had to go back in her mind and forgive all the men who had exploited her. She accepted God's forgiveness and realized that she was a clean and forgiven person. She came to a new understanding of God's intention for sex and also was able to lose her excess weight.

It may be that the weight you're struggling with has more to do with emotional and spiritual battles than with liking chocolate brownies and hot fudge sundaes. Perhaps a counselor can help you resolve the real issues that cause your weight problem.

Never Say, "Diet"

Dozens of fad diets and quick-weight-loss schemes are available. The fad diets may burn off fat, but they tend to put the body under stress and, at the same time, may destroy muscle tissue. Some of the severe low-calorie diets, below five hundred calories per day, have been demonstrated to be harmful to the body's overall health.

In fast weight loss, your skin has to adjust to cover less territory, and it cannot adjust as rapidly as it could when you were a teenager. So, if you go on a crash diet, you may lose a lot of weight, but you may lose some of the smooth appearance you had with extra weight. Bluntly speaking, you may become saggy and creepy looking. Joyce Brothers puts it this way: "No woman really looks sexy no matter how great her figure when her shape is slip-covered in prune skin."[10]

Eating less is only part of losing weight. We also need to eat the right kinds of food in a balanced diet—and get good exercise. For many years Sally and I walked together every day. It did several things for us. It was a break from our heavy workload, and an opportunity to talk with each other. Exercise also improves mental attitude. On top of that, if you walk thirty minutes a day at a brisk pace, over a year's time you will burn off about sixteen pounds.

Too Old for Sex?

Two outside forces work on an early midlife woman regarding her sexuality. One is culture, which fosters the notion that older people do not have sexual relationships. There is, however, considerable research that shows that sexual interest and activity can exist into the ninth decade and beyond.[11]

Another author points out, "Our society is basically anti-old. . . . Sex in our society is not for older adults. You are supposed to have outgrown sex a long time ago! If you listen long enough to this kind of attitude, you start believing it, and before you know it, you are living it. You are too old for sex, you are too old for your job, and just too old to be around."[12]

The second force against a midlife woman's sexuality comes from her children's thinking. As they learn about sexuality, they think of it in terms of sexual fun and games—and babies. It logically follows that "since my parents are no longer interested in babies and they are not having any fun in life, certainly they must not be having sex."

A study in *Psychology Today* reported that 646

Illinois State University students felt their parents "had intercourse once a month or less, never had intercourse before they were married, [and] never had oral genital sex."

The students had great trouble accepting the reality of their parents' sex life. "Ninety percent of students who felt their parents were happily married and still in love believed they maintained this happy state without the help of sex, or at least not much of it."

Some students reacted very negatively, apparently not wanting to even think about their parents' sex life: "'This questionnaire stinks.' 'Whoever thinks about their parents' sexual relations, except perverts?' 'What stupid person made up these questions?'"[13]

Some Things Improve with Age

But an opposite force is at work in the midlife woman—an increased sexual drive. Most midlife women tend to become more assertive, have a greater frequency of orgasm, and can experience repeated orgasms with little time lag. In other words, the midlife woman is really coming into her sexual prime.

Because most sexual literature has been written by men, studies of the sexual development of adults tend to follow male thinking and ignore the reality of women's experiences. Males often have a slowing down sexually, but their wives are just reaching their peak.

Turned On at Thirty-Nine

Arnie was struggling with the difference in sexual interest between himself and his wife. "I've never talked with anyone about this before," he said to me (Jim), "but I'm beginning to pick up from other guys that I'm not the only one with the problem. You see, it wasn't until we'd been married for a long time that Pat seemed to like having sex. Oh, sure, we had sex often when we were first married, but I think she didn't enjoy it very much. She just pretended she did—to make me feel good. Then she would go for long spells where she would put me off with headaches—or being too tired.

"Of course, she was tired with three kids all over the place. I wanted to be considerate, so if she didn't want sex, I'd forget it for a few nights. After a while, though, it would build up—I really needed it, and she'd give in.

"Eventually this got old. Besides, Pat's figure kind of went to pot, and she started letting herself get fat. She wanted me to touch her more before we had sex, but I didn't find myself turned on by her body as much anymore. In fact, I was beginning to find the whole thing wasn't very great.

"Then, whammy! When she was about thirty-nine, she started wanting more sex. She would make moves on me as soon as I'd get home. I'd be tired, but I'd try to go along with her. In fact, I was glad for the change for a while, but she seemed inexhaustible, with an urge I couldn't quench. After a while I couldn't keep up with her.

"Then one time, it happened. I couldn't get an erection—I'm embarrassed to even say this. I felt crummy. And she felt I didn't love her anymore. I felt like I'd just lost my manhood, and she was sure I had somebody else. That made me mad, so we had a big fight.

"I can't understand why she's so turned on now when she wasn't earlier. She gets excited before I ever get home. I get tired just thinking about it. Even when we do have sex, she never gets enough."

The Secret Is Out

Often the woman who has an increased sexual interest at midlife wonders if she is out of line. Society, her husband, and her kids think she ought to be slowing down. Instead she wants to have more sex with her husband, and she's also interested in variety and experimentation. How does she handle all of that in the context of being a Christian woman—and not think of herself as a dirty old woman?

A midlife woman needs to understand that her changes are normal and she's likely to have a high sexual interest through the rest of her midyears. In fact, the decrease of sexual activity in older women has less to do with their interest or drive than with their opportunities. Most sex is still initiated by the male, and women in the later years are often widowed, frequently do not remarry, and in a sense, voluntarily surrender their sexual interest.

Mirror, Mirror

Some of the midlife woman's increased interest in sexual contact is because of the physical changes she sees in the mirror. Ever since she was a young woman and became aware of her sexuality, she realized her sexuality was connected with her physical body. Now as she sees her body begin to change shape, sag, show a few wrinkles and gray hairs, she asks, "Am I still sexually interesting to males—to my husband?"

This sexual insecurity can cause a midlife woman to question herself and may even force her into a panic to prove herself. She may become increasingly flirtatious with her body, her eyes, her walk, her conversation. It's almost as if she is saying, "Time is really running out for me. In the past I've always known I was worthwhile because men were sexually attracted to me. Now I'm not sure anymore. If I lose sexual appeal, maybe I've lost myself."

I (Jim) was on a Hollywood location where an advertisement was being filmed. The group included a number of extras who were hired just for the day. One of them was a midlife woman, about age forty, who was quite attractive. She apparently had a need for men to be attracted to her—to make her feel good about herself.

She made several passes at me with her eyes. She complimented me on how fit and trim I was. Then she moved in really close. While we were moving along the buffet table during the lunch break, she reached ahead of me several times for an item of food. Her movements were strategically planned so that her breast would rub against my arm. She obviously was looking for a response.

Part of me was flattered that this attractive woman was coming on to me. Yet on the way home I thought, *Isn't it tragic that this woman seems only to be able to develop relationships through her body. She doesn't feel she can make it with her personality or mind.*

Let me put it to you bluntly. There comes a time in all our lives when we have to learn to live on something other than our physical bodies. Midlife is the time when you *must* learn to love and to be loved for other qualities—not only for your sexual being.

Emphasizing your other attributes doesn't mean you can't have good sexual times with your husband. But the physical aging of your body should cause you to redirect your energies so that you are also attractive because you are a loving, caring person who has intellectual and spiritual contributions to make.

The Meno Monster

Sometimes midlife women panic sexually because they dread the thought of menopause. The cessation of menstruation usually takes place in the late forties or early fifties. Changes do take place, but you will hear a lot of old wives' tales about menopause.

Menopause does not mean you're going to become sexless. Instead, you have a new freedom because you don't have to bother with contraception or worry about pregnancy. This freedom may cause a rise in your sexual interest and activity. Perhaps for the first time in your life, you will be instantly available for sex with your husband. Maybe the *hunted* will now become the *hunter*. Remember, you don't become a senior citizen or sexless merely because your ovaries cease functioning.

Perhaps you've heard that menopause brings on emotional instability with rapid mood shifts, hot flashes, nervousness, irritability, insomnia, and fatigue. You also may have heard that vaginal lubricating fluids diminish and cause intercourse to be painful, and sometimes there is itching, burning, and bleeding. All of these are potentially true, but if a woman is experiencing some of these symptoms, she needs to get help from her doctor.

Many of these physical and emotional changes can be eliminated or minimized by the replacement of the estrogen hormone. After menopause, less estrogen is produced by the body. Doctors have a running debate about the use of estrogen therapy. Opponents argue it causes an increase in the incidence of uterine cancer, especially if large doses are used. Smaller doses do not seem to carry the same risk.

The opposite side of the argument is that, in addition to stabilizing emotions, hormone therapy reduces the loss of calcium from the bones, preventing a condition called osteoporosis. Estrogen therapy also combats loss of muscle tone and loss of elasticity in the skin. Also, strong evidence shows that estrogen treatment protects women against the incidence of heart attack that rises after menopause.

We recommend that you consult a doctor who works with hormone imbalance at midlife and ask about estrogen therapy. If estrogen cannot be used, a concerned doctor will see that you get help by way of vitamins and other medications. (Ask about B vitamins to lessen depression.) You may have to hunt to find a doctor who cares about women at midlife, but the effort will be worthwhile. (Sally has written an entire book on this subject entitled *Menopause: Help and Hope for This Passage.)*[14]

A Cutting Experience

Midlife is when many women have a hysterectomy. Some medical professionals have the attitude that "when a woman is finished with child-bearing, her uterus is expendable." Dr. William A. Nolen, chief of the Department of Surgery at Meeker County Hospital, Litchfield, Minnesota, castigates this "male chauvinism." "A patient's ovaries," he adds, "are another favorite target of both gynecologists and general surgeons. There's a saying in surgical circles that if ovaries were testicles, there'd be a lot fewer of them removed. I know that's true."[15]

Sometimes a woman herself is convinced that her "uterus is expendable" and that monthly periods are distasteful. She should realize, however, that a hysterectomy often results in hormone imbalance, which can cause emotional stress.

Another common operation for early midlife women is a mastectomy caused by breast cancer. Breast cancer accounts for over 20 percent of all female malignancies of American women each year. In the early eighties, approximately one woman in fourteen got breast cancer.[16] In 1997 one out of nine got breast cancer nationwide, while one out of seven got breast cancer in Orange County, California.[17]

Mind over Body

If you're troubled by the impact of aging, menopause, and midlife surgeries, let us suggest that the problems may not be only physical but also psychological. Unresolved problems from the past are usually carried into the next era.

Suppose as a teenager you were disgusted with your physical body. You may have thought your arms and legs were too skinny, your hips too big, your breasts not big enough. If you didn't settle that problem in adolescence, it was probably carried over into young adulthood. If you still didn't accept it, you probably are going to deal with it again in midlife, especially as your torso picks up more weight, your limbs get thinner, and everything, including your breasts, begins to sag a little.

You see, we're dealing with self-image and perfectionism. Raquel Welch is reported not to have liked the proportions of her body. She said she isn't well balanced. Really! When is enough enough?

Self-acceptance is crucial at midlife. Lack of self-acceptance can start a domino effect. When you don't like the way you look or you're afraid of getting older, or of losing your shape and figure, or of being rejected by your husband, or of losing your sex drive, then you might act out those fears. You may begin to lose the sparkle of your smile or conversation—that which makes you attractive in the first place. Then when people are not attracted to you, the feeling that you are unattractive is reinforced. Somewhere you have to break the cycle—or the physical aging process will destroy you.

Women—The Worst Enemies

A study done by Carol A. Nowak concludes: "While middle-aged men with 'touches of gray' look 'distinguished,' women who haven't 'colored away the gray' look drab. While middle-aged men with 'lines' and 'furrows' have 'character,' middle-aged women with 'wrinkles' and 'crow's feet' look ugly. While middle-aged men are generally taken for a handsome lot, middle-aged women are typically judged as 'over the hill.' And middle-aged women themselves are most guilty of perpetuating these expectations. They are their own worst critics."

In this study, Nowak wanted to see how different age groups and different sexes would respond to pictures of people's faces. Would they judge them as attractive, plain, or unattractive? How would they rate them as to youthfulness? She sums up her study of 240 men and women by saying, "As I'd expected, middle-aged women judged the most 'attractive' models, regardless of their age, to be most youthful."[18] The tragedy is that these midlife women were judging themselves as being unattractive because they internally believed the most attractive women were young adults.

Another author comments, "It is perfectly true that the cosmetic industry has terrorized us about what it means to be sexy and attractive to men, and that if they have their way we would all be Barbie dolls. It surely is high time that we insisted on what we know, somewhere deep down, below the TV-level of consciousness, that beautiful, sensuous, feminine women come in all shapes, sizes, ages, hair color, and skin tones, and that what makes them that way is not false eyelashes, dyed hair, corsets, lanolized skin, but something deep inside which exults in being female."[19]

What Are You Worth?

The woman who comes to midlife with a low sense of her self-worth and little or no purpose for living is like a sailboat in a storm, with a broken rudder and the sails in shreds. The sailboat is at the mercy of the wind and the waves. It probably will be battered apart on some shore.

If you're a woman at midlife without internal

spiritual direction and you're listening only to voices on the outside, you probably will view your midlife physical aging as very negative. Growing older may be the force that causes you to enter into a deep midlife crisis.

PART FOUR

Discouraged on the Inside

Defeated by a Sagging Self-Esteem

MaryAnn is a deeply committed Christian with strong leadership abilities and a deep love for her three children and her husband. She recently wrote cryptically, "The past two years haven't been nice." She went on to explain how her self-image was smashed through a series of experiences related to the loss of her job, friends, physical appearance—and then her husband moved out.

"I had been an administrative supervisor for a health department for several years. I supervised several women. I also ran a clinic for pregnant teens. Generally, I had a lot of responsibility and respect from fellow workers and patients. I enjoyed my job.

"Then, cuts in funding caused my department to close down all clinic activities except immunizations. I was kept on as a secretary at my normal salary. I enjoyed the quiet for a time but gradually began missing the previous responsibilities and challenges. I felt I had been demoted, and my self-esteem began to plummet. My secretarial skills deteriorated and generally I began to feel worthless.

"In January I learned that a girlhood friend had

died of cancer. I think that more than anything else threw me off center. She was a year younger than I, and while we were not close at the time of her death, we had maintained our friendship over the years through letters.

"In February I turned forty, in March I got bifocals (a silly thing to cause so much trauma), and in April I wondered who I was—what is my reason for living—had I ever been happy in my whole life—if I died tomorrow, what would I leave behind that was worthwhile? I wasn't sure I loved anyone—actually, I wasn't sure I was capable of loving anyone. I felt cold, uncaring, and dull. I didn't think my children cared for me because they never listened to my 'wise counsel.' And I was sure my husband didn't love me."

The Conformers

Many midlife women experience a sagging self-esteem because of the many losses at midlife—and because of early life training. Girls are socialized quite differently from boys. Boys are encouraged to give up childish ways, to be tough and hard, to be independent, and to prove themselves. Girls, however, are encouraged to be conformists, to be compliant, to be "good girls."

In Her Time gives the results of a study in which "mothers of four-year-olds were asked at what age they thought parents should permit their children to cross the street alone, use a sharp knife without supervision, or be permitted to play away from home for long periods without first telling their parents where they would be. Consistently, the mothers of boys gave younger ages than the mothers of girls—despite the fact that girls mature earlier and are less impulsive."[1]

The ways in which girls are socialized causes a delay in their search for identity, development of autonomy, and establishment of their internal standards for self-esteem. Socialization toward a low self-esteem continues in adulthood. College men and women were asked to read and evaluate several articles. One group was told the articles were written by women. The second group was told the same articles were written by men. Both sexes rated the articles written by men as more valuable.[2]

In his book *Dark Clouds, Silver Linings*, Dr. Archibald Hart puts his finger on why women are more depressed. "The connection between diminished self-esteem and depression has long been known. Depression not only causes low self-esteem, but anyone whose esteem has been eroded is likely to be more prone to depression as well. In our culture, women clearly tend to experience lower self-esteem than men.

"Partly it's due to the lower social status of women, who tend to earn less money for equivalent types of work. But largely it's due to being female in a male-dominated culture. Maleness is preferred over femaleness in many sectors of our society, and this bias is even greater against women of color."[3]

In spite of this societal prejudice, women must clearly understand that they are special in God's sight and that they make a crucial contribution to the world. In fact, the world would be a blighted place of male competitiveness and unfeeling arrogance without God's gift of women.

Denise Mann, in an article entitled "Women Must Become More Involved in Treating Midlife Depression," quotes Dr. Diana L. Dell, from Duke University Medical Center, as saying, "Midlife is a vulnerable period for recurrence of depression. Warning signs of depression among middle-aged women may include current alcohol and drug abuse, a past history of sexual abuse, severe premenstrual syndrome, post-partum depression and a family history of depression. Women need to be heavily involved in the diagnosis process, which can include writing a list of physical and emotional complaints to show the doctor."[4]

What Is Self-Esteem?

Many times the words *self-esteem*, *self-love*, *self-image*, *self-worth*, and *self-acceptance* are used interchangeably. There are some distinctions in the words, which could help you to understand yourself better, especially the differences between self-image and self-esteem.

Self-image is how we think of ourselves. *Self-esteem* is how we appreciate ourselves. Often these concepts are linked—if a woman has a low self-image, she also will not appreciate herself. The reverse is also true. A woman who does not appreciate herself tends to have a limited understanding of her positive traits.

In discussions of self-image and self-esteem, Christians often raise questions about pride and humility. Pride is claiming that all we are is the result of our own effort and strength. Humility means that we accurately assess who we are—with both strengths and weaknesses—and see God at work in us. "Be honest in your estimate of yourselves." (Romans 12:3).

How the Self Develops

Before we are born and throughout our lives, we receive impressions about ourselves from other people and the environment. We interact with those impressions and decide how much we will allow those impressions to affect us. Those impressions and how we accept them become our self-image.

When people grow up, they will, as psychologist James Dobson in his book *Hide or Seek* says, either hide from life or seek life.[5] Archibald Hart, in *Feeling Free*, shows that people will think of themselves either as giants or midgets.[6]

We have found it helpful to think of the development of the self-image in terms of "love dollars" and "love debits." When you were a child, your mother and father, brothers, sisters, grandparents, other relatives, friends, schoolteachers, and even the dog, had input into your life. Each interaction helped form your self-image. You accumulated both self-image love dollars (pluses) and self-image love debits (minuses). (See the chart below.)

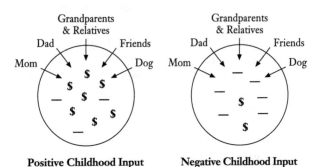

Positive Childhood Input **Negative Childhood Input**

Figure 1

If you grew up having a lot of "love dollars" put into your personality, you'll be a person who is outgoing, trusting, eager for life, willing to take risks, and willing to give love to other people. If, on the other hand, you accumulate a lot of self-image "debits," you'll be afraid of people, unwilling to give love, afraid to try new things, and you may tend to be critical, intolerant, angry, and easily defeated by life.

The tragedy is that the woman who needs love the most is the one with the most debits and is often the least lovable. This woman builds a strong wall of protection so no one can come in and steal any of her few remaining love dollars. The woman with many love dollars doesn't need as much love, yet she is the one most open to being loved—the most lovable. Later we'll show how you can break the vicious circle of low self-image, or love debits.

Culture's Five *B*s

Our culture has defined several ingredients that are supposed to make you a worthwhile person.

Beauty is the first. All through life, much of a woman's value and self-esteem are linked to her "looking good." It's not only hair and skin care, but physical fitness has also become a goal for women.

Brains are the second worthwhile female commodity. Intelligence is important, but she is taught not to compete in "boys' subjects," such as math and business. She is to stay in "girls' subjects," such as English and poetry. As an adult she is to be bright—but not aggressive.

Bank account also defines a person. What kind of clothes do you wear? Where do you live? What kind of car do you drive? Are those real diamond earrings? Is that heavy gold necklace you're wearing real or only gold-filled? Culture evaluates you by your net worth, implying that a high dollar worth equals a good person.

Busyness is the fourth cultural standard. You are to produce. How high is your productivity? What are you accomplishing in the world? If you're not beautiful, don't have brains, or aren't wealthy—at least produce something.

Belonging is the fifth *B*. Do you belong? Are you an insider? The conformity yardstick is used frequently by Christians who say you've got to act and think as we do, or you cannot belong to our group. Conformity sticks out when certain issues come up—to have or not have a career, divorce and remarriage, abortion, women's roles in the church. If you don't believe what "the group" believes, you're less of a person.

A midlife woman could be devalued in several of the above areas. She may experience a loss of beauty as well as a loss in intellectual confidence because she has been out of her career for a long time. She also may feel she has no access to financial resources because she doesn't work. Her productivity could be despised if she is "just a housewife." At the same time, she may be experiencing shifting values as she rethinks life's major issues out of step with her religious subculture. In short, she may find herself with a sagging self-esteem.

Results of a Low Self-Image

A person with a low self-image tends to have several of the following traits:

She becomes a *person pleaser*. Her self-image has been so severely damaged that she doesn't want to cross anybody. She's afraid to take risks, afraid to speak up—because she might get more hurt.

Strangely, a person with a low self-image also tends to become a *leg chopper*. If it's safe, a person with a low self-image cuts other people down. She feels that if she can make other people look smaller, she will look bigger.

A woman with a low self-image is very *protective*. She keeps things to herself—generally is not outgoing or generous unless she is people-pleasing.

Low self-image causes one to be *external*. She looks outside herself for value and worth. She is vulnerable to every situation around her. She is continually being inflated or deflated. She needs but rejects positive input because she is convinced she's not worth it. She accepts the negative because that's how she has come to see herself.

Another common characteristic is *perfectionism*. A person with a low self-image is constantly trying to be better. Yet her low self-image is also partially created by perfectionism. It is her low self-image that keeps her striving toward perfection. Dr. David Seamands says the three favorite phrases of the perfectionist are "could have, should have, and would have." He says that the perfectionist is "always standing on tiptoe."[7]

The woman with a low self-image never really knows who she is—and neither do people around her. The following poem depicts such a person.

The Mask

Always a mask
Held in the slim hand,
Whitely;

Always she had a mask
Before her face—
Smiling and sprightly,
The Mask.

Truly the wrist
Holding it lightly
Fitted the task:
Sometimes however
Was there a shiver,
Fingertip quiver,
Ever so slightly—
Holding the mask?

For years and years and
Years I wondered
But dared not ask.

And then—
I blundered,
I looked behind,
Behind the mask,
To find
Nothing—She had no face.

She had become
Merely a hand

Holding a mask
With grace.

—Helen Haiman Joseph[8]

How to Build a Positive Self-Image

A woman's self-image can be improved as she works on simple but *specific physical projects*—diet, exercise, and proper rest. In *Better Than Ever*, Dr. Joyce Brothers tells of her own experience of looking at herself at midlife and how working on appearance factors improved her self-image.[9]

Building a strong self-image also means you are "willing to devote time to *unstructured solitude* . . . be willing to daydream and speculate . . . be willing to be reflective, to consider strengths and weaknesses, along with problems . . . opportunity . . . a sense of direction . . . be willing to express . . . feelings. Allow the mind to freely associate with such phrases as 'I'd like to,' 'I choose to,' 'I have to,' 'I'm afraid to,' or 'I can't.'"[10]

Other activities can improve your self-image. *Give up self-condemnation*—honestly accept the strengths God has placed in you. A practical way is to pay compliments to other people and appreciate their strengths and values. Affirming others helps you to think positively of human beings in general—and accept yourself. As you begin speaking positively about others, you will respond positively to people who, in turn, will help build your self-image.

You also need to *forgive yourself*. Some things *might* have been different—mistakes *were* made, but those are in the past. After asking God and others to forgive you, it is time to forgive yourself. (See Philippians 3:12-14.)

Listen to yourself. Imagine your body is hooked to a polygraph machine. Be sensitive to when the stress level is increased or reduced. Listening will enable you to modify and restructure your life toward less stress.

Cecil Osborne, in *The Art of Learning to Love Yourself,* suggests these practical ways of building a self-image: Give love and understanding to others, learn to receive love as well as to give it, join a sharing group, share your guilt with other people, distinguish between neurotic fantasies and realistic goals, choose goals well within your reach, and do the things that make you like yourself better.[11]

Developing a positive self-image means you are willing to *become your unique person.* "When Albert Schweitzer, the great missionary doctor, was a boy, his friend proposed that they go up in the hills and kill birds. Albert was reluctant, but, afraid of being laughed at, he went along. They arrived at a tree in which a flock of birds was singing; the boys put stones in their catapults. Then the church bells began to ring, mingling music with the bird song. For Albert, it was a voice from heaven. He shooed the birds away and went home. From that day on, reverence for life was more important to him than the fear of being laughed at. His priorities were clear."[12]

Building a positive self-image includes taking a look at what you do, what you think, the people with whom you relate, and all the information you store or dismiss that comes to your life. We are also convinced, after working with people for many years, that a vital, personal *relationship with God* will assist this internal integration producing a strong self-image.

A certain level of self-esteem in every woman's personality cannot be improved by what other human beings think. Even if they encourage you— you can still feel empty. Human affirmation does not touch the very deepest level of self-worth. A vital, personal relationship with God will provide nourishment and build your self-image so you can handle the stress with confidence.

The apostle Paul speaks of this confidence God gives: "If God is for us, who can ever be against us? . . . Who dares accuse us whom God has chosen for his own? Will God? No! He is the one who has given us right standing with himself. Who then will condemn us? Will Christ Jesus? No, for he is the one who died for us and was raised to life for us and is sitting at the place of highest honor next to God, pleading for us. . . . Does it mean he no longer loves us if we have trouble or calamity, or are persecuted, or are hungry or cold or in danger or threatened with death? . . . And I am convinced that nothing can ever separate us from his love. . . Our fears for today, our worries about tomorrow . . . nothing in all creation will ever be able to separate us from the love of God that is revealed in Christ Jesus our Lord" (Romans 8:31-39).

Source of Confidence

How do we get this confidence? First, invite Jesus Christ to come into your life to forgive your sins. Mentally exchange your weaknesses for Christ's life and his strength. Receive his righteousness as he takes your guilt upon himself (2 Corinthians 5:21).

Second, this confidence comes from a knowledge that God genuinely cares for you and is working the best for you in all events of your life. Romans 8:28 says, "And we know that God causes everything to work together for the good of those who love God and are called according to his purpose for them."

The third concept for a positive self-esteem is to remember that God is moving you toward growth. You have a future. God is not finished with you. You are still under construction. Amazing things are yet to be accomplished.

Spiritual commitment to God comes as you spend more time thinking about what God has said in the Bible and talking over these ideas in prayer with him. You *will become* like the ideas you take into your personality. That is why the Scriptures encourage us to "fix [our] thoughts on what is true and honorable and right . . . and the God of peace will be with you" (Philippians 4:8-9).

Always Perfect

To develop a positive self-image, you may have to deal with your perfectionism. Perfectionism is the all-or-nothing, feast-or-famine type of thinking.

"One dieting physician ate a tablespoon of ice cream and scolded herself by saying, 'I shouldn't have done that! I'm a pig.' These ideas so upset her that she went on to eat an entire quart of ice cream."[13] Dr. David Burns from the University of Pennsylvania School of Medicine suggests several work projects to help perfectionists correct their distortions:

"We urge them to make a list of the advantages and disadvantages of attempting to be perfect."[14] (Take a situation in your life, and make a specific list.)

Dr. Burns tells us about one of his clients: "Jennifer was able to list only one advantage of perfectionism: 'It can produce fine work. I'll try hard to come up with an excellent result.' She listed six disadvantages: 'One, it makes me so tight and nervous I can't produce fine work or even adequate work at times. Two, I am often unwilling to risk the mistakes necessary to come up with a creative piece of work. Three, my perfectionism inhibits me from trying new things and making discoveries because I am so preoccupied with being 'safe.' Thus, my work becomes narrow and somewhat boring, and I lose out on the opportunity for new challenges. Four, it makes me self-critical and takes the joy out of life. Five, I can't ever relax because I'll always find something that isn't perfect. Six, it makes me intolerant of others because I am constantly aware of the errors people make, and I end up being perceived as a fault-finder.'"[15]

Obviously, the disadvantages of being a perfectionist were very strong in Jennifer's mind but had never been put out on paper where she could look at them.

Totally, Completely Perfect?

A second suggestion from Dr. Burns is to "ask perfectionists to spend a day investigating whether or not the world can be evaluated in a meaningful way using all-or-nothing categories. As they notice people and things, they are to ask themselves, 'Are the walls in this room totally clean, or do they have at least some dirt?' They might also ask, 'Is that person totally handsome? Or totally ugly? Or somewhere in between?' The exercise usually demonstrates the irrationality of dichotomous thinking. As one client reported, 'I found out that the universe simply does not divide itself into two categories, all good versus all bad.'"[16]

Another technique that Burns uses is to confront the perfectionist's thoughts with reality: "If I don't do a good job and have the house absolutely clean, what will happen? Well, then my husband will think less of me." The confrontation then involves asking those people, "Do you think less of me because my house is not absolutely clean?" And the reality comes back, "No, we don't."[17]

Another suggestion is to think of setting different goals in your life. The perfectionist always takes the ultimate goal as the standard. Perfectionists set standards so high that they find it difficult ever to get started and often don't produce anything.

One writer shared with Dr. Burns that he would say to himself, "'This has to be outstanding.' Then he would daydream or obsess over the first sentence and eventually give up in disgust. When, instead, he told himself, 'I'll just crank out a below-average draft and have it typed up,' he found his resistance to writing diminished, and he was able to improve his output substantially.

"It struck him as odd that as he began to aim to make his writing increasingly 'average,' other people seemed increasingly impressed. Eventually, he gave up his perfectionism entirely and became addicted, he said, to the idea of being average."[18]

Loved but Vulnerable

Perfectionism ultimately is an attempt to win approval because of personal insecurity. This insecurity can be changed by realizing how deeply God loves you. The Scriptures teach that before the world ever began, God the Father loved you. His Son, Jesus Christ, came into the world in order to die for you, to exchange places with you, and—if you have accepted his work for you—the Holy Spirit lives in you to shepherd, guide, and enable you. When you wonder whether you're worth anything—when you think about having to earn people's love—remember that God loves you with an unconditional love demonstrated by all three members of the Godhead.

Midlife is a dangerous time for the self-image because it can be smashed by many different negative events. This can also be a positive time for the self-image because it gives the person an opportunity to grow. Midlife is something like the time when the lobster must shed its shell in order to grow larger. For a time after it has shed its shell, it is naked and vulnerable. It is in danger from a number of predators of the sea. But without the shedding of the shell, it cannot grow any larger.

So it is at midlife. You are shedding the old shell, the old, limited, self-image. You are now becoming a different person. Yes, you are vulnerable now. You may experience damage to your self-image. But God is there and says, "I will not fail you or abandon you" (Joshua 1:5).

Dietrich Bonhoeffer, in his poem entitled "A Poem," said:

> *Who am I? This or the other?*
> *Am I one person today and tomorrow another?*
> *Am I both at once? A hypocrite before others, and*
> *before myself a contemptibly woebegone weakling?*
> *Or is something within me still like a beaten*
> *army,*
> *fleeing in disorder from victory already achieved?*
> *Who am I? They mock me, these lonely questions*
> *of mine.*
> *Whoever I am, thou knowest, O God, I am*
> *thine.*[19]

CHAPTER TWELVE

Trapped by Depression

As a young pastor and wife, we had very little experience with helping depressed people. We had been through normal seminary training, which didn't include any practical help for working with depressed people.

So it was a rather startling moment for us when Anna appeared at the church-study door. She was a midlife church member whom we had visited while she was hospitalized. We did not know she had been released. She obviously was in deep distress. She walked slightly hunched over, shuffled to one of the study chairs, and dropped into it with her head down, her hands just lying loosely in her lap. Her puffy cheeks, disheveled hair, and red eyes added to the total picture of dejection and hopelessness.

After some minutes of silence, broken only by quiet crying, she said simply, "My psychiatrist says he has done all that he can do for me—he sent me to you." Her problem was depression, which had started months before and had kept building. She had been depressed for several months and thought the only way to solve the problem was to take her life. Repeatedly, in fits of anguish and torment, she attempted suicide.

Sometimes in despair she would run out of the house and into an open field—running, running, without any purpose or direction, trying to escape from herself and the terrible depression.

Her husband loved her very much and was continually frightened by what she might do next. Would he come home and find her dead because she had sliced her wrists with a butcher knife? Would she just disappear, driven by her depression?

He finally decided to take her to a psychiatrist even though his religious convictions and his culture had a deep suspicion of psychiatrists. Somehow, he thought, God ought to be able to help without these men. They might even be ambassadors of Satan.

But he was desperate, so in spite of his strong negative feelings, he sought professional help. Anna was admitted to a local psychiatric hospital and was involved in prolonged psychotherapy. She got no better, and the medical staff displayed a growing sense of desperation. She was shifted from doctor to doctor and finally moved to another medical facility where she underwent approximately fifteen shock treatments.

This was a whole new world to Sally and me. When we walked into these hospitals and into the locked wards, we felt very alien and inadequate.

We visited Anna often and were stunned to see only the shell of a human being. She gave no response to us at all. The medication and shock treatments designed to block her depression seemed instead to be creating a nonperson.

Anna went through endless months of individual and group therapy, as well as physical and occupational therapy. Finally she was released, with little change in her feelings or behavior. Her psychiatrist gave her the news, "We've done all that we can for you. The best thing I can suggest is that you visit a clergyman."

As I (Jim) sat in my office and listened to her repeat her psychiatrist's suggestion, I wanted to punch him in the nose. There he was with millions of dollars of equipment, scores of trained professionals, and a vast accumulation of expertise—yet he had the audacity to dump this poor, depressed soul into my study chair with my skimpy resources and zero experience at age twenty-seven.

While I looked at Anna, I spoke to God silently. *Lord, I'd like to punch that psychiatrist. You know I don't know what to do with Anna. I don't know how to help depressed people, but for some reason you've dropped her in my lap, and I can only trust you to work this thing through.*

Description or Depression

"The woman who is depressed is weighed down with a pervading sadness, a sense of hopelessness and despair. She loses interest in her family and friends and even doubts that she still loves them. Along with a loss of self-esteem, she also loses interest in herself and can become ridden with self-hate, guilt, and a feeling of worthlessness. With a loss of zest for life there is a loss of the will to live. She may want to run away, to hide, to curl up and die. To help deaden the pain, the body seems to deaden itself; there can be a slowing down of body functions—lack of energy, inability to sleep, loss of appetite and of interest in sex.

"Sometimes she finds that her activities become agitated, but most often she finds it difficult and well nigh impossible to get through the ordinary daily tasks which she used to perform with ease. Perhaps the worst part of this bleak condition is that she feels there is no hope for the future and that these unhappy circumstances will continue indefinitely. Depression has been called a woman's disease with symptoms that express harsh, self-critical, self-depriving, and often self-destructive attitudes."[1]

A Woman's Cross

Depression is a significant problem in our country. "Depression is epidemic. One of every 18 adults—about 10 million of us—suffers from depression, a problem that seems to be on the rise. As a culture, we may well have entered our own emotional 'Great Depression.'"[2]

More women than men seem to be affected. When Maggie Scarf was doing some work for another subject, she encountered the statistics on women and depression: "The figures seemed strange—strange almost to the point of absurdity. If they *were* accurate, though the evidence was clear and overwhelming: women, from adolescence onward—and throughout every subsequent phase of the life cycle—are far more vulnerable to depression than are men. . . .

"The same results or findings—more depressed females than males—turned up . . . in *every* study, carried out anywhere and everywhere. More women were in treatment for depression. It was so, in every institution—inpatient and outpatient—across the country. It was true in state and county facilities. It was the case in community mental health centers. It was simply true, across the board. And, when the figures were adjusted for age, or phase of life, or social class and economic circumstances . . . the outcome was still the same."[3]

"A recent survey of 20 major medical and psychiatric journals by a California newspaper found every advertisement for antidepressants targeted women. A report to the Psychological Association, entitled, 'A Woman's Mental Agenda,' noted that 73 percent of all psychiatric drugs, including antidepressants, are prescribed to females. This takes on the color of an impending national disaster in light of an April 1996 article in the *American Journal of Psychiatry*, which links psychiatric drugs, particularly antidepressants, to breast cancer."[4]

"A study of a random sample of 9,000 people in

the community showed that 33 percent of women, as against 25 percent of men, had psychiatric symptoms of anxiety and depression worldwide. . . . On the whole, one quarter of the world's population is estimated to be affected at any one time."[5]

Margaret Crockett, speaking of her work with depressed women in a state mental hospital, says that at the nurses' station a poster hung on the wall to remind them of the stress these patients were experiencing. "It pictured the barely visible face of an unhappy woman floating in space and darkness and surrounded by the printed categories of torments that described her condition: LACK OF ESTEEM, NEGATIVISM, INSOMNIA, ANXIETY, CRYING, GASTROINTESTINAL DISTRESS, GUILT FEELINGS, HOPELESSNESS, FATIGUE, LACK OF INTEREST, INDECISIVENESS."[6]

Depressed Saints

Depression is not a modern phenomenon, nor does depression happen only to bad people or to people who aren't well adjusted. The Bible shares the accounts of several of God's chosen being depressed.

The prophet Jonah in the Old Testament said, "Just kill me now, Lord! I'd rather be dead than alive because nothing I predicted is going to happen" (Jonah 4:3). Elijah, following a great victory over paganism in his country, ran away in fear and experienced an emotional breakdown. In his depressed state, he said, "I have had enough. . . . Take my life, for I am no better than my ancestors" (1 Kings 19:4).

Jeremiah, a major prophet of the Old Testament, is sometimes called the weeping prophet. He experienced depression. He said, "What sadness is mine. . . . Oh, that I had died at birth! Lord, you know I am suffering for your sake" (Jeremiah 15:10-15).

When Moses was leading the nation of Israel away from Egypt and into the Promised Land, he felt extreme discouragement and depression at times. He complained, "Why are you treating me, your servant, so miserably? What did I do to deserve the burden of a people like this? . . . The load is far too heavy! I'd rather you killed me than treat me like this" (Numbers 11:11, 14-15).

A spiritual woman, Naomi, had lost her husband and her two sons: "Don't call me Naomi [pleasant]," she said. "Instead, call me Mara, for the Almighty has made life very bitter for me. I went away full, but the Lord has brought me home empty" (Ruth 1:20-21).

Perhaps the most classic example in the Old Testament is that of Job—the richest man in the world. But almost overnight his entire wealth was taken away. He received word that all of his children were killed in a freak accident. On top of that he was afflicted with boils from his head to his feet, his wife despised him, and her advice was to curse God and die.

Job's response was one of deep depression:

"Why didn't I die at birth as I came from the womb? Why did my mother let me live? . . . Why was I not buried like a stillborn child, like a baby who never lives to see the light?" (Job 3:11-12, 16).

You're in Good Company

Depression is not just an Old Testament experience—it's also seen in New Testament people, such as Peter, who was disillusioned and depressed after his denial of Christ before Christ's crucifixion. After denouncing Christ, "he went away, crying bitterly" (Matthew 26:75).

We detect a note of depression in Paul as he speaks of his physical problem: "Three different times I begged the Lord to take it away" (2 Corinthians 12:8).

Sometimes we have missed the signs of depression and anguish that Jesus experienced in the Garden of Gethsemane. The Bible records that "he took Peter, James, and John with him, and he began to be filled with horror and deep distress. He told them, 'My soul is crushed with grief to the point of death. Stay here and watch with me' " (Mark 14:33-34).

You probably have wrestled with some degree of depression. If you are currently experiencing depression, it is not because you are unspiritual or a bad person. Nor does depression indicate that you are an emotional basket case and ready for the "funny farm."

The fact that you are depressed does not mean that you're at the end of the road. Many people experience depression, including exceptionally spiritual people—even Jesus himself. Most of the depressed people in the Bible recovered, and they also found that God loved them during the entire process of their depression.

Causes for Depression

As you can tell from the examples we've used, depression is directly related to loss. Some of the losses were lost relationships, through death or family conflict. Others losses were physical and emotional, as with Elijah, or of lost opportunities, as with King Saul.

A VARIETY OF LOSSES

All depression has loss associated with it. If you are experiencing depression, it is extremely important for you to identify the loss that is triggering the depression.

Relational Loss. Depression can occur whenever there is a breakdown in or a termination of any interpersonal relationship—and it's all right to feel depressed. The fact that depression is normal doesn't mean we should stay depressed, but we do need time to recover.

Sometimes when a woman loses her husband through death or divorce, friends will encourage her to "cheer up." There is almost an unwritten principle—she's allowed to feel bad for about two weeks, but after that she should get hold of herself and get on with life.

We are more realistic about death or divorce if we expect a woman to experience depression for at least a year. The person must live through all the events of an entire year and readjust in each of those situations. Each new occasion brings a reminder of the loss—and depression.

Loss of Material Things. Sally and I were visiting the Tahitian Islands for our second honeymoon, in celebration of our twenty-fifth wedding anniversary. We had loaded a few things into a small outrigger canoe and were paddling from our hotel to an island about a half mile offshore. We had gone only about 150 yards when we made a slight readjustment of our weight in the canoe. To our absolute amazement, the canoe started to tip over. The outrigger pontoon, which is to keep the canoe balanced, was waterlogged and absolutely worthless. We seemed to be acting out a slow-motion movie as the outrigger pontoon slowly settled deeper and deeper into the water until finally we, and the contents of our canoe, had slipped into the Pacific.

I had a brand-new Olympus OM 1 camera with a 1:2 lens, which went straight to the bottom of seventy-five feet of salt water. Soon a ski boat came by, pulled Sally into the boat, and towed me and the disabled canoe back to shore. We later paid a diver to retrieve our shirts, tennis shoes, and other assorted items, along with my magnificent new camera.

I took the camera to our hotel room and thoroughly washed out the salt water—but it didn't work. Corrosion had already started to eat at the mechanism so that none of the metering systems functioned. I found I could easily quote a Bible verse, "All things work together for good," but it was difficult for me to shake that gnawing depression—that terrible down feeling.

If you lose something tangible that you value, you likely will feel depressed for a period of time. It's normal. It's all right to have those feelings. God has given us a full range of feelings. Feeling depressed is not wrong.

Time Loss. Repeatedly we hear from women who feel depression as they near a milestone birthday, such as thirty-five or forty. These women are experiencing the loss of life and time. You can't go back and relive the years. "And who would want to?" some women ask. Nevertheless, because of our youth-oriented culture, we often are depressed when we recognize we have moved out of the young adult era into midlife. It's depressing to feel we are losing "the best years of our lives."

Lost Opportunities. A young midlife woman asked to talk to me (Jim). She had barely gotten seated when rivulets of tears started down her cheeks. Then her story spilled out. She was a talented woman in her midthirties who felt a deep sense of remorse for a missed opportunity. She'd given up a career in business, which by now would have placed her in a vice-presidency. Instead, she chose to go to grad school for a totally different career. Now she was finding disillusionment in the new career. She could see that her former career would have been more satisfying. She asked pathetically, "Why do I feel so depressed? I feel as if I'm going crazy." Her depression was normal because she had given up a special opportunity.

Loss of Control or Choice. If we go for prolonged periods of time with too many demands without restoration, we can become depressed. When every hour of every day, day after day, is filled with obligations, we may feel dejected without realizing why. If we feel we have neither voice nor choice in decisions that affect us—we may feel depressed.

Loss, then, in any area we value, may cause feelings of depression. We must identify the sources of loss and make necessary adjustments so that the depression will lift and we can move on with living.

PROHIBITION AGAINST EXPRESSED EMOTIONS
Along with any loss we experience, we commonly have other feelings such as anger, fear, guilt, or self-pity. Whenever we refuse to allow ourselves to have these other feelings, we only intensify our depression. Sometimes women are not allowed, by others or themselves, to feel the other emotions of anger, fear, guilt, or self-pity.

For example, a woman who surrendered her personal career dream, married young, and invested all her life in her husband and children may feel guilty about grieving over her children's growing up or her husband's success. Sometimes un-thinking people make inappropriate remarks: "Why are you depressed over your husband's success?" "You should be glad your children are grow-ing up and don't need you so much anymore." "Now you will have time to play more golf, read, and do the things you want."

If your husband's success has driven a wedge into your marriage so that you feel left out, and if your children are growing independent and some-times obnoxious so that you feel like a fifth wheel, you *have* lost something. It *is* appropriate for you to grieve and perhaps experience strong anger, self-pity, and even fear about the future. But sometimes people won't let you feel those feelings.

Trying to restrain your feelings will often deepen your depression. Not only have you lost something, but now you have lost the opportunity for a normal emotional response. You are trapped, and that sense of being trapped will increase your depression.

EMOTIONAL FATIGUE

Think of your emotional capacity as a muscle—for example, a leg muscle. Now suppose you strain your muscle while riding a bike with your kids. It's sore, and you limp around for a few days until your leg finally recovers and you are able to carry on normal life.

But imagine you don't give the strained muscle those few days to rest and recover. While your muscle is still hurting, you go on a family picnic and play softball. As one of the kids hits the ball he throws the bat, which hits you on your sore leg. Now you have tremendous pain. You fall to the ground, rubbing your muscle. But at the same time, one of your other kids, who's playing on the park swing, is swinging abnormally high. There's a scream. You turn and see your child has fallen and is holding his arm. Without thinking of your leg, you jump up and run over to care for your child. It's only after you attend to your child that you realize your leg muscle has gone into a spasm. You can't put your weight down—you're immobilized.

Emotions are like that. When you're called upon to do something that drains you emotionally, you must have time for emotional recovery—or the next panic call will further deplete your emotions. Each crisis calls for expenditure of emotional energy. Dozens and dozens of such crises arise for the midlife woman. If your emotions are not allowed to recover, they will gradually become so damaged that you will go into depression. In some ways the depression is a way of insulating you from further emotional damage. It is not wrong to do what is necessary to recharge your emotional batteries.

PHYSICAL FATIGUE
If you go without sleep for a few nights in a row, your body pays a toll. Your emotions are also affected and respond in ways that are not normal for you, including feeling depressed.

Joyce, an overstressed career woman, went to her medical doctor in desperation—something was wrong. She just didn't have any drive or energy. She was irritable and had pains in her chest and abdomen.

The physician said, "I'm going to schedule a battery of tests a week from now, but in order for the tests to be effective I want you to follow my instructions completely. You are to get ten hours of sleep each night. You're not to attend any committee or board meetings or be involved in any outside obligations."

Joyce objected strenuously, but the doctor assured her that this was necessary in order for the tests to be completely effective. She came back a week later and announced to him that she felt entirely different and didn't think she would need the tests. The doctor gently explained to her that all he had done was to ensure a forced rest.

If you are continuing to overtax yourself physically, thinking that you'll catch up later, you probably *will* catch up—your body will force you to.

INCOMPLETE EMOTIONAL DEVELOPMENT

Norma had never learned how to give and receive love. She had been told repeatedly by her parents that they didn't love her, she was an accident, and they wished she had never been born. She married Rob more as an escape than for love.

Rob loved her very much, but his loving words and actions were like water running off a duck's back. His love, even though profusely poured on her, was never absorbed. She treated him with suspicion because of her incomplete emotional development.

She repeatedly complained to her husband and others that nobody loved her—even though this was not the case. Her complaining and suspicion gradually pushed everyone away. As people moved from her emotionally, she then could justly claim that nobody loved her. The growing realization that she really was no longer loved was devastating to her and sent her into deep depression.

But the problem started with her incomplete emotional development rather than from an unwillingness of her husband to love her. Women who keep growing and working on areas of emotional woundedness will be less likely to experience depression.

PRESSURE FROM ORGANIZATIONS OR INDIVIDUALS

Since the Second World War, churches (especially conservative groups) have become increasingly vocal in pushing women toward a marriage-and-mothering-only role. As we've noted earlier, these women are more likely to be depressed and may experience greater midlife trauma. Secular influences have also created stress and pressure for women by urging them to choose a career-only direction and avoid being "enslaved" as homemakers and mothers.

When a woman accepts a religious or secular movement's directions for her life, and when those ideas violate her internal sense of rightness, she is being set up for depression. If God has given you the ability, the interest, and the desire to be a mother and wife only, and if you are forced by outside pressures to engage in an outside career, you eventually may fall into depression. If, on the other hand, you follow the rigid religious teachings (which actually are based on questionable biblical interpretation) that insist a woman must be a wife and mother only, in spite of God-given desires and abilities for a career, you also are being set up for depression.

The causes for depression are many, but the key word invariably is *loss*. Therefore, in order to move out of depression, an early priority is to discover the source of loss and decide how that loss will be handled.

The Process of Depression

The first step, although not always immediately recognized, is the loss of something of value. We may then move into the first level of depression, with its normal feelings of sadness, regret, and anger, which are a response to the loss. If we continue too long in a depressed state, we may slip into a condition known as clinical depression. This can lead into a serious state of complete withdrawal from life.

YOUR PERSONAL LOSSES

To understand the process of depression and the part that loss plays, let's use an imaginary illustration. Suppose that you value yourself as a woman on the basis of your appearance and your relationship with your husband.

Now imagine that in the past few weeks, as you approach your thirty-ninth birthday, you have been startled with the discovery of gray hair, age lines on your face, your changing figure as your weight shifts to your torso, and that despicable marbleized flesh that shows on your legs when you wear a skirt or shorts. You have experienced physical loss, and because you so highly valued youth and beauty, you may not feel comfortable with yourself anymore.

A second loss might be marriage intimacy. When you and your husband got married, you promised each other you would never allow your marriage to become dull and boring—like the marriages of your parents. In spite of good intentions, your marriage has followed the same unsatisfying pattern. You both have become preoccupied with living and with meeting life's endless emergencies. You have gradually grown apart with commitments to career successes and no time for your marriage.

EMOTIONAL RESPONSES TO LOSS

Some women are unable, or will not allow themselves, to experience the emotions associated with loss. Therefore their depression tends to intensify. Let's go on with some of the possible responses to the loss in our hypothetical illustration.

When you look in the mirror and see how your body has aged, you justifiably may feel some degree of anger. It would be better to face and acknowledge your anger than to bury it and pretend it's not there. You may also feel self-pity: "I feel sorry for me because this is happening. I don't like it." In addition to self-pity, there may be fears: "What if this causes my husband to leave me? He used to comment on how he liked my figure when I was a young woman. What if he leaves me for another shapely young woman?" You may also experience guilt: "If only I had exercised, or if I hadn't always eaten so much chocolate cake, I wouldn't be in this bad shape."

It's OK for you to have these feelings, and it's better to face them. Knowing your real feelings will help you deal with loss. Sometimes unwillingness to allow your feelings to be expressed is part of a denial system that says, "I am not losing anything. I don't feel any loss."

NORMAL DEPRESSION

The next part of the depression process is the actual stage of depression itself. Normal depression is a grief process related to loss or disappointment. Some of the results you may experience are:

- A lowered self-image
- A sense of loneliness

- A degree of helplessness
- A feeling of not being loved
- A breakdown in healthy living processes of proper eating, sleeping, and exercise
- An unaccountable physical and emotional fatigue

Let's continue our example of the losses of beauty and marriage intimacy. You normally can expect to think less of yourself if these losses occur. It will be normal for you to feel lonely. You probably will sense some degree of helplessness as you realize you cannot reverse the cycles, especially those related to your physical aging. With your husband preoccupied in his business and career, you may feel unloved. This normal process of depression will probably have some effect on the way you overeat or undereat. You also may find you're sleeping less or the sleep you get is not sound and deep. You may experience an overall feeling of fatigue—some intangible force is wearing you out. That something is depression, which has been triggered by these two losses in your life—physical aging and reduced marital intimacy.

FACING THE PROBLEM
At this point most people confront their loss and decide they're going to do something about it. Other people decide to do nothing and allow themselves to slip deeper and deeper into depression.

Some people ask, "Why not stop the process of depression earlier? As soon as the event takes place, deal with it and get it out of the way." If getting it out of the way means denying that you've experienced loss—or denying that you have negative feelings—then you are not dealing with it. You are only storing up problems that will explode later.

You can, however, deal with your situation early in the process by saying, "Yes, I did lose my camera, and I do really feel crummy about it. I know I will probably feel sad about this for days or weeks. And I'm going to allow myself to feel that way. No, it isn't the end of the world, but, yes, it was a valuable camera—and, yes, there were pictures that went down with it that we'll never see."

Or, to use the imaginary illustration: Yes, you are aging. True, you don't have the physical beauty of a twenty-five-year-old. But, no, it doesn't mean that you are sexless. But it does mean you have other strengths in the place of those gifts you offered your husband as a twenty-five-year-old.

If you've had losses in your marriage, they, too, can be confronted. Talk about some of the good things you remember from the early days of marriage—consider how to get those back. Talk freely about your feelings—fear, self-pity, sometimes even anger. Confront it early, and you can reduce the depths of depression.

CLINICAL DEPRESSION

If the emotions in the earlier stages of the depression process are not dealt with, they will combine and intensify. The more anger you feel, then the more helpless, lonely, and unloved you will feel. The more these feelings and responses rage within your personality, the more they break down the healthy living process and begin to change the chemical balance in your body. Chemical imbalance in turn will cause depression and emotional stress. When the body chemistry is disturbed, you cannot handle depression and emotional stress as well. Unchecked depression wears us down and changes us chemically so that we're less able to handle the next pressures.

The cycle of clinical depression—that is, depression that keeps on feeding depression, which causes more depression—is almost impossible to break without medication and counseling therapy and perhaps hospitalization. A psychiatrist is a medical doctor who has a psychology degree in addition to his medical degree. He will look at the physical and emotional conditions and the interplay between the two.

WITHDRAWAL

The next level in the process of depression is withdrawal into a private world. If the clinically depressed person is not helped, he or she tends to retreat from reality, moves farther from confronting the loss, and withdraws into a secluded little shell. This is called an emotional breakdown. The person now becomes nonfunctioning—to some degree unable to carry on the normal activities of life such as eating, grooming, dressing, or working.

The woman who has been so affected by depression will need a great deal of care. She probably should be hospitalized to protect her from herself, to help her get physical rest and nourishment, and to receive the emotional counseling and support she needs to work through the losses of her life.

Identifying Signs of Depression

The following questions may help you identify depression symptoms, evaluate your own feelings, and seek help if you need it:

1. Have you been feeling sad, blue, hopeless, down in the dumps for more than two weeks?
2. Have your eating habits recently changed drastically?
3. Do you have trouble falling or staying asleep?
4. Do you feel fatigued, without your usual energy, and have no clear reasons for your fatigue?
5. Have you experienced an unusual loss of sexual interest?
6. Do you have difficulty concentrating or making decisions?

7. Are you feeling jumpy, unable to sit still?
8. Do you have frequent thoughts of taking your own life or wishing you were dead?
9. Are you more irritable, easily annoyed, and do you experience a great deal more anger?
10. Do you feel extremely discouraged and pessimistic about most things?
11. Do you feel guilty and worthless?
12. Are you unable to forget bad things that happened in the past?
13. Do you cry more than usual?
14. Are you constantly in need of reassurance from people?
15. Do you have new stomach and abdominal pains or severe headache or backache with no medical explanation?

As you read through this list, you probably easily identified one or several symptoms that are current in your life. This does not necessarily mean that you are depressed or that you seriously need help. The key concept is in item number one—have you felt this way for more than two weeks? If item number one is true of you and several of the other items also apply, then it would be important to seek help.

Alcohol and Drugs

Alcohol or chemical dependency may become a factor in a woman's depression. Estimates are that

4.6 million women in the United States are alcohol dependent.[7]

About half of the women admitted to institutions for alcohol problems are in the age group forty-five to sixty-four. Over half of the drug-related deaths among white women occur after age forty. Of women ages forty-five to forty-nine, 28 percent use prescription psychotherapeutic drugs, and more than one out of every three women in this age category use either prescription or over-the-counter drugs to help them deal with emotional stress.[8]

Drinking by midlife women many times is not simply a social experience but an escape. The midlife woman with a drinking problem has an emotional makeup often marked by low self-esteem, self-pity, a tendency toward self-punishment, resentment, and an inclination to project blame. She is impatient, irritable, and marked by depression and anxiety. She looks at alcohol or drugs as a means of helping her cope with life.

Allow us to be very blunt. If you need a drink to keep your world in order, or if you find you continually need a drug to enable you to handle stress, then you really ought to seek help. You need to work through the issues causing stress and depression. Identify your losses, and take positive action to reconstruct your life so losses don't eat you up.

Recovery
Someone who is clinically depressed probably will not be able to help herself nor seek help. Others

must be willing to take responsibility to refer her to competent psychiatric help. A psychiatrist may use many resources, including antidepressant drugs, which are showing great promise to bring about recovery—but these are not to be considered for lifetime use.

Let's assume, however, that you are not clinically depressed but you are concerned about working out of a lesser depression. Following is the logical progression for recovery:

1. *Identify the loss that has caused the depression.* Talk to a friend you trust—or a pastoral or community counselor. Share with that person what you've discovered, and let him or her be a mirror to reflect what he or she hears you saying—helping you to pinpoint your loss.

2. *Gather all the information you can about the loss.* Again, a friend can be very helpful. Remember, this is not a whitewash or a cover-up—you really are going to confront truth.

For example, if the loss you're experiencing is related to your youth, then confront all that involves. You can't stay up as late at night; you have some gray hair; your body weight is shifting; you've got wrinkles; you're not as athletic as you used to be. Your goal is to learn the truth about the loss you've experienced and understand the full scope of it. If you look at only a little bit, you may be leaving out some important sections that will produce depression. So, face all of the information.

Remember that some of the truth about your

loss is very positive as well as negative. You might ask, "How can there be any positive side to the fact that our marriage is not what it should be and I've lost intimacy with my husband?"

The positive side is that instead of allowing yourself to continue to slide into increased depression, you are now confronting the loss. Confronting this loss of marital intimacy now will help both of you to reorder priorities and reduce marriage stress. You will see that your unsatisfying marriage can be corrected—before it gets so bad that nobody wants to work on it.

3. *Express your feelings.* Obviously, some of your feelings will come out as you identify the loss and explore the truth about it. But at this stage deliberately ask yourself what you *feel* about this loss—not what you *think*.

Sometimes writing or talking about your feelings will help you understand them more accurately. Verbalize to another person exactly what you feel with the true intensity.

You may identify and express feelings we mentioned earlier—anger, fear, self-pity, guilt. Let them all spill out. In the process you'll have one or several good cries. Don't sweep crying under the rug with, "Well, that's just another expression of the weakness of women." An article entitled "Go Ahead, Cry Your Eyes Out!" reports from several clinics around the country that women are joining the male population in repressing their emotions. We are becoming a nation of people who do not cry. The price for these repressed emotions, according to these studies, is an early death.

The experts report that a good cry can

Help you rid your body of harmful chemical by-products of stress.

Give your vascular, circulatory, respiratory, and nervous system a workout.

Provide psychological relief. Relieve tensions.[9]

Don't believe those false comforters who try to hush you up. Express your feelings. You're going through a grief process that is necessary before you can go on to step four.

4. *Decision making is the next step.* Now that you have identified the loss, understand all the truth about it, and have expressed your feelings, what are you going to do about it? Remind yourself that you're a survivor—you're going to make decisions that will move you toward health, growth, productivity, and effectiveness. What decisions will help to move you in that positive direction?

Again, let's imagine the loss to be that of losing youth. Your decision might be to deliberately emphasize the strengths you have now as a midlife woman with insight and knowledge about life. You're not going to compete with young bodies. The bikini will not be your point of competition—you'll use your brains and experience.

If you've experienced marital loss, make decisions for reconstructing your marriage. Do whatever you can to develop true communication, meet your husband's needs, make changes in yourself, or whatever must be done to restore and enrich your relationship.

5. *Develop a climate of support and love.* Put yourself in situations where you are with groups of people who are very supportive, loving, and optimistic—and who will extend themselves to you. Cultivate people who are vulnerable so you have the emotional support you need for recovery.

Urge these people not only to hear you out as you work through this process but also to hold you accountable for any decisions you make. Groups of caring people are frequently found in churches, but look especially for people who have been touched deeply by pain and by God's love. These are the people who look at life as a great privilege and are awed by God's graciousness.

6. *Get inoculations of hope.* You need a steady diet of positive, hopeful messages. Deliberately turn away from the loss now that you have fully experienced it and completely grieved over it. Turn your face toward the future and toward God.

A helpful procedure we have often recommended is to read through the Psalms thoughtfully—with personal application. The Psalms were written by people who struggled deeply with life but who also had experienced hope.

Yes, life has many trials, but God is there to walk with you through those low valleys. "But now, O

Israel, the Lord who created you says: 'Do not be afraid, for I have ransomed you. I have called you by name; you are mine. When you go through deep waters and great trouble, I will be with you. When you go through rivers of difficulty, you will not drown! When you walk through the fire of oppression, you will not be burned up; the flames will not consume you. For I am the Lord, your God, the Holy One of Israel, your Savior' " (Isaiah 43:1-3).

Tempted to Escape

The Runaway

The crowd was leaving after the conference, but one woman remained off to the side, obviously wanting to be the last one to speak to us. When everyone had left, she asked for a few minutes to talk. In a rather deliberate, detached way, Elaine explained that her marriage was in bad shape.

She said they had had trouble for the last four years, but Tom was not willing to see a counselor. He said their problems were all her fault. If she would just quit worrying about her needs and do her job with the family business, everything would be OK.

She finally persuaded Tom to go for marriage counseling, but he resisted the whole process. Each time after they left the counselor, Tom made fun of the session and was more determined not to change or meet her needs. He would promise the counselor he would change behaviors, but afterward he would only laugh.

After the counseling experience collapsed and things were no different, Elaine decided to do something for her own sanity. Day after day she had long crying spells. She felt alone, unloved, and unneeded. Yet, she couldn't share this with her husband. He kept saying, "It's all in your head. Forget it and you'll get better." So she would never allow him to see her crying.

During these years, he had an increased need for sex. And each time, she just felt used. She would lie awake hours after having sex, crying quietly into her pillow.

As the years went by, she experienced a hardening in her emotions—she was dying inside. Something had to be done or she would die.

She was the business manager for their small business. Much of the business was done in cash, so she began secretly to skim off money into a private savings account. At the time she talked to us, she had skimmed off a little more than fifteen thousand dollars over a period of eighteen months.

Now her question to us was, "Is it wrong for me to run away? I'm secretly planning to leave as soon as the kids are out of school. I won't tell Tom or the kids. I'll just take the kids with me and go to a cottage I've located and spend the summer. We'll have a vacation, and I hope it'll drive him crazy wondering what's happened to us."

The Runaway Woman

In our culture we still believe the husband is the one who leaves the home. The runaway wife is more common today because she is more willing to admit her needs and also is better able to make it on her own. Fifty years ago women stayed in difficult marriages because there were no options. But the innumerable options for a woman today provide an easier opportunity for an unhappy woman to run.

In one sample of women we studied, approximately 78 percent of the women physically ran away from their marriage relationships for some period of time. The women in our survey were ages twenty to sixty. Those who reported they had physically run away at some time averaged 2.5 experiences of running away. The average age of the runaway woman was thirty-four; however, the runaway eras grouped around two distinct times—one in the late twenties, the second in the late thirties. Many of the midlife women felt it was their last chance.[1]

The runaway woman is a topic infrequently discussed. Yet if these statistics are a reliable indication of the situation, running away sometime during life is a very common experience in America. If it is this widespread, then we need to begin asking ourselves, "Who are these runaways? Why do they run away?" and "How can they be helped?"

Types of Runaways

There are two kinds of runaways—the ones who physically leave and others who only run in their heads. Some of the women who run physically go for brief periods of time; others plan for extended times away, as did Elaine. The emotional runaways are the dangerous ones, who verbally detach themselves from their marriages. They are silent. They say nothing—they simply die inside.

SHORT-TERM PHYSICAL RUNAWAYS

As I (Sally) was interviewing a woman for the research on this book, I asked her if she had ever run away. "Yes, I have, but it's been only for short periods of time."

I asked her, "What do you mean?"

"Oh, like once when we were driving across town to visit some friends, my husband and I were having a fight—which is very common for us. He doesn't seem to understand me, doesn't try. He's always putting me down and treats me like dirt. The same process started again. I was feeling humiliated. The more I verbally fought back, the more he smashed me with his words. We pulled up to a traffic light, and I just jumped out and started running. I cut through some yards so he couldn't find me and sat in a park for a few hours. I felt sorry for myself, yet I hated him because he knew I'd come back."

Another woman reported that after a very tense dinnertime her husband simply walked away from the table and turned on the TV while she was left to care for the children and clean up the kitchen. She grabbed the youngest child by the hand, walked out the door, and drove off. She parked the car a few blocks away and sat. Then she said pitifully, "I had no place to go." A woman may endure many stresses, but finally something happens—the straw that breaks the camel's back. She is likely a woman with a short fuse, and running away for a short time or a short distance helps her get perspective.

LONG-TERM PHYSICAL RUNAWAYS

The woman who runs away for the long term has a different need. Generally, she has been hurt over an extended period of time. Her emotional battery is dead. She feels so emotionally battered that she needs a longer period of time to recover.

Sometimes a long-term runaway woman, like Elaine, makes elaborate plans for her getaway. Occasionally the long-term runaway makes her leaving appear socially acceptable by going to live at her mother's or with another relative.

THE EMOTIONALLY EXPLOSIVE RUNAWAY

Runaway is perhaps not the correct term for this woman. She doesn't leave physically, but in very clear terms she lets her husband, and perhaps the children, know that even though she is there physically, she is not emotionally connected.

Joanne had talked to Bill repeatedly about her emotional starvation, but he was a busy contractor trying to manage a multimillion-dollar business. He kept telling her that things would get better—but they never did.

He came home one night to find that their two younger sons had been fed and were watching TV. Joanne was in the living room reading a book. He came and asked her, "Where's supper?"

She said simply and directly, "You make your own supper."

"What do you mean?" he demanded.

"I mean, from now on, I don't care for you or do

anything for you—in the same way that you don't care for me."

"What are you talking about?" Bill asked.

Joanne replied, "I mean I'm not going to ruin your reputation in front of all of your business associates and Christian friends, but I want you to know that I'm not having anything to do with you. I've put all of your clothes in the guest room. From now on, you sleep in there."

Bill went storming into the guest room to see if this was true. He came back into the living room and insisted that Joanne get up and make supper. She told him in no uncertain terms that he was on his own and if he pressed her too far, she was going to pack her bags and leave him to care for the kids. Then he could try to explain the situation to the other men who served with him on the Board of Elders.

Bill continued to fume, but he backed off. During the next several months Bill and Joanne lived in the same house while Joanne lived the role of an emotional runaway.

THE SILENT RUNAWAY

The woman who escapes by withdrawing is the most pathetic. She has chosen to coexist with the problem instead of trying to change it.

Margaret's husband was a full-time Christian worker. He held a state office in his denomination and was on several national committees for evangelism projects. He was extremely competent in evangelism but a total misfit as a husband and father. He knew how to manipulate people politically—but he did not know how to relate to people as persons. People were always just things.

Margaret had decided as a young wife that she was not going to leave the unhappy marriage. Instead, she would do her very best to help Ed be successful. Deep inside, Margaret felt she was the cause of their marital friction. If only she could be a more submissive wife—just as Ed kept telling her. Certainly their marriage would get better.

Margaret continued running away deeper inside herself until finally she was almost in another world. She would stand at the kitchen sink, peeling the same potato for fifteen minutes, carefully taking off each strip of peeling and laying it neatly beside the other strips in a row on the counter. She was consistently late with serving meals and with every household task.

Later, Ed got into an affair and felt quite justified. After all, he rationalized, he didn't have a complete woman for a wife. She was emotionally disturbed. Their problems had always been her fault.

Why Do Women Run Away?

Women gave us many different responses to the question "Why did you run away?" Many were so dissatisfied in their marriages they wanted to escape. Sometimes they ran when their husbands got involved in affairs—or when there was incest in the family.

Many responded that there was just too much

work and not enough appreciation. Some felt a sense of hopelessness—"Nobody cares about all I do." They felt constantly fatigued. Some women were very angry because they felt their husbands had left the raising of the children entirely to them. Other women reported they ran away because of physical abuse, or because they felt trapped in their insignificant roles, or to escape the derisive put-downs from their husbands.

The most common reason for running was a marriage in trouble. Sometimes the running was to punish the husband for his lack of concern. Sometimes it was a means of getting his attention, saying, in essence, "Hey, I'm serious about this. Listen to me." Other times the bad marriage relationship and running away became the beginning of a bridge to an affair.

Most of these women did not have affairs first and then run away to their lovers. They were running away out of desperation—and then affairs developed. For most of the women whom we surveyed, running was an escape. And if she didn't get help, the woman on the run was likely to be the woman who would then seek the closeness and companionship of an affair.

The Affair

Webster, in a brief few words, describes an affair as "a romantic or passionate attachment, typically of limited duration." But the dictionary in no way describes the intensity and elation, or the pain, agony, and tragedy which we have seen in the lives of people involved in affairs.

We will enlarge Webster's definition to include the word *extramarital*, meaning that one or both of the people involved in the affair is married to someone else. An affair need not have a sexual dimension, but it certainly has an emotional preoccupation, with thoughts continually drifting to the other person—while commitment shifts away from the marriage to the other person.

One woman in her early thirties tells about getting involved in an affair. She said her first contacts with the other man were very innocent. Then "his joking around with me became flirty, and eventually, he made several passes at me. I was strongly attracted to him." She decided to break it off and did not see the man for several months. But whenever she thought about him, she realized she was still in love with him.

"Then one day we saw each other again. As I was leaving, he came to me and said he missed me. Then he said it really was more than loneliness—he was in love with me. I left the room feeling confused. I was excited that someone loved me, but then I came to my senses. We could never be together."

An affair may be very casual. It may be, as in the old Alan Alda movie *Same Time Next Year*, only a yearly contact. It isn't so important to describe what happens in an affair as it is to realize you are actually involved in an affair if another man is drawing your emotions away from your husband. If you are spending energy, time, and money on a relationship with another man instead of your husband—no matter how innocent that relationship may appear—you are in an affair.

A Short-Term High

As we describe an affair, two other words are key: *infatuation* and *temporary*. Infatuation means a foolish or extravagant intense relationship. There is a sense of losing your head, losing perspective. Selling your soul for something which seems worthwhile—but in the long run really is not.

Affairs are temporary. Most affairs follow a six-month pattern. Great intensity, enthusiasm, and exhilaration, but then the pain begins to rise. Reality starts to creep in, and the woman comes down from the clouds. She realizes, "If I do live a normal life with this man, I would find he has human limitations and problems as every other man does." After all, she would just be trading one man for another—they are still men.

Affairs are like drugs. They promote a short-term high, but they do not cure the problems of your life, and when the drug wears off, you find yourself crashing again.

Why Does Popcorn Pop?

Why do people get involved in affairs?

Our world is saturated with sexual stimuli. An ad for jeans shows a young woman lying on a young man who has his shirt off. Of course, they are both wearing the jeans are being advertised—but the jeans aren't what make your juices flow. Invitations to sexual arousal are everywhere—magazine ads, television programs, commercials, plays, films, books, magazines, music, bumper stickers, jokes, clothing styles. It's as if our culture were programmed for sexual turn-on.

Besides all the visual turn-ons, we are continually bombarded with "easy sex, irresponsible sex, sex without commitment, sex to escape the pressure. At the heart of this sexual overload is the popular lie that sex is an answer for our larger human needs and pressures."[2]

Even though we are surrounded by sexual stimuli, there is a reason we respond. That reason is depravity. We are people who by nature are attracted to sin. On July 21, 1976, former President Jimmy Carter made a statement that shocked the world. It was later published in *Playboy* magazine: "I've looked on a lot of women with lust. I've committed adultery in my heart many times. This is something that God recognizes I will do—and I have done it—and God forgives me for it."[3]

The problem then is not only the bombardment of sexual stimuli but also our nature, which is attracted to it. Jimmy Carter was saying that even though he was president of the United States, he still had a sin nature that could respond with lust to sexual stimuli.

Who Will Fall?

Some people are never involved in affairs—at any time. What makes the difference? The key word is *vulnerability.* A woman becomes vulnerable through some loss in her life—physical fatigue, sickness, depression, years of singleness, divorce, or a sagging marriage. She becomes susceptible to an affair as she reaches out to solve the loss she feels.

In an article entitled "The Promiscuous Woman," Maggie Scarf says, "I have noticed in my interviews that . . . a high degree of sexual wheeling and dealing appears to exist in tandem with . . . very powerfully depressive feelings. The woman's sudden increased sexiness seems to be a kind of antidepressant maneuvering."[4]

As we noted earlier, whenever loss occurs, we experience a degree of depression. If a woman has sustained a loss in her life, she very well may feel depressed and respond by acting sexier. She is making a desperate grab to relieve the depression and loneliness. The irony is that most affairs are temporary. Even though there is exhilaration—the woman ends with another loss. She quite often feels a deepening sense of worthlessness—and more depression. Then she must also struggle with guilt.

Meaningless Marriage

A major reason for married people's getting involved in affairs is that the marriage relationship is no longer nourishing. One or both partners don't put enough into the relationship to make it a true marriage. They are still legally married, but nothing exists between them.

Lewis Smedes calls this "negative fidelity." He says, "a man or woman can be just too busy, too tired, too timid, too prudent, too hemmed-in with fear to be seriously tempted by an adulterous affair. But this same person can be a bore at home."[5]

Of the hundreds of unfaithful married people with whom we have worked, almost all had neglected their marriage—which created vulnerability for an affair. Affairs seldom start with a search for sexual involvement. Two people are vulnerable because of their unfulfilled relational needs in their marriages.

Some marriage counselors suggest that an extramarital involvement should not be criticized—it will stimulate the marriage and restore some of its lost luster. It may be true that there is good food to be found in the garbage dump, but that isn't where we choose to have our wedding anniversary dinner! A few marriages may be helped by an affair, but for every one that is helped, we see dozens—no, hundreds and thousands—that are broken, or at least severely damaged, by an affair.

The Danger Signs of an Affair

"I'm a thirty-six-year-old woman and a director of Christian education. I never dreamed of being involved in an affair, but it all began when I went to a four-week course of training without my family.

During those four weeks I often chatted with one of my classmates named Bruce. He was so easy to talk to, plus he was understanding, highly intelligent, and a very sensitive person. Sometimes, just to get away from the pressure of studies, we would take a walk and talk about philosophies and interests—but he never made a pass at me. It was beautiful, it was innocent, and it was refreshingly honest.

"At the end of the four weeks we were invited by an engaged couple to go to a movie to celebrate the completion of our course. After the movie, the four of us drove around, laughed and talked. We stopped near a lake, and the engaged couple in the backseat drifted into their own world of hugging and kissing.

"I don't even remember what I was talking about at the time, but I do remember being stopped midsentence by Bruce kissing me. He later remarked, 'I didn't know I was going to do that until I was doing it.' I was surprised and thrilled. I told Bruce it was very nice. So we did it again, several times, to the chimes of encouragement from the backseat.

"But all good things must come to an end, and the time came when we had to return to campus. Bruce let the three of us out near the dormitory, and I waited for him while he parked the car. Since there were few students, we were all housed in the same building, with men on the first two floors and women on the third. When we reached the second-floor landing, we gave each other a good-night kiss. Then another and another, with increasingly more body pressure.

" 'Chris, let's go to my room,' he proposed.

" 'We can't do that—I've got to go upstairs,' I said. Another kiss.

"Bruce insisted, 'We can't say good night now.'

" 'I know we can't, but we're going to have to anyway.' Another kiss, and he led me through the door to the hall, then into his room.

"I said, 'Let's just sit and talk awhile.' He moved in closer. 'What about Marie [his wife]?' I asked.

" 'Marie's not here.'

"I raised a couple of other objections. . . .

"I have never been loved so sweetly, tenderly, nor have I ever felt such a desire to respond—I didn't want to leave. . . .

"But the next morning, after a hug and a hand shake, we and all the other students went our separate directions. . . ."

There were obvious signs of vulnerability that each of these people was aware of—but chose to ignore. There were needs in their lives. Their marriages were unfulfilling, and each of them was using Christian ministry as a way to provide meaning in their lives and ignore the stress in their marriages.

Loneliness Breeds Rationalization

They were both lonely. Back home they had a network of friends and associates who filled the gap left by their poor marriages. But in this conference situation, away from home, they didn't have that network of friends, and they could easily be victimized by Satan. In fact, they were so deceived by Satan—they believed wrong was right. "Destruction is certain for those who say that evil is good and good is evil; that dark is light and light is dark; that bitter is sweet and sweet is bitter" (Isaiah 5:20).

Chris speaks of a later time when she and Bruce once more got together. Again, the meeting was related to church duties. This time Bruce was serving Communion. She said, "There was such love in his eyes as he offered me our Lord's body and blood that I knew beyond all else the Lord was with us and would continue to be. Never have I been so close to seeing Jesus face-to-face as I was on that evening."

Satan will attack us at our weakest point. And he comes, as the Scriptures say, as an angel of light, convincing us that what he wants for us is good—intended only for our growth and pleasure.

Another danger sign was their common interests. They could rationalize that they belonged together. They thought so much alike; they had so much in common. It was also easy for them to create opportunities to be together that appeared quite legitimate because of their common interests.

Compulsive Impulses

Another danger sign was their compulsive thought life. After they returned home to their separate cities, they couldn't quit thinking about each other. Chris continued, "One day early in September, I impulsively called him at his church office. It was then that he suggested we write to each other. Soon a letter came: 'You have no idea the explosion that took place in my solar plexus when I heard your voice on the phone. I feel like an adolescent boy must feel, and I like the feeling, even though it scares me—for all the obvious reasons as well as some I haven't even admitted.'

"Soon we were writing at least once a day and conversing on the phone twice a week. We talked of our trip around the world, fantasizing that we'd set up housekeeping on a South Sea island. Through our letters we grew to know and love each other more. We tried to limit our telephone conversations to an hour but weren't always successful!"

The compulsive thought life and addictive actions that focus on the affair partner are very obvious danger signs! These red flags should stop people.

If you wonder if you're having an affair, ask yourself some hard questions. Can I stop thinking of this person? Is there a compulsion to contact him, to be with him? Do I plan my day's activities so that our paths will cross? If you're responding yes to any of these questions—you're in trouble. You are already in an affair, whether it has become physical or not.

Small Steps—Big Changes
Still another danger sign is the small steps that soon become giant shifts in values. This couple

started with very casual talking and walking; then they moved to deeper sharing of their lives. They crossed over an emotional bridge when they responded to the invitation to go to the movie. Now they were thinking of themselves as a couple. They crossed another bridge when, with the emotional excitement of the couple necking in the backseat, he reached over and impulsively kissed her. It wasn't a big step from where they were, but it was a huge step from where they started.

The good-night kiss was another emotional bridge and another danger sign. That kiss wasn't very far from the kiss in the car, but neither was it very far from sex in his bed a few minutes later.

Listen to the danger signals! Look carefully at the signs! You may start out thinking you're going to just innocently meet a few of your needs—and you end up forgetting who you are—a child of God.

We ask, With all the obvious danger signs, why didn't they stop? The answer is that they *did* recognize the signs but they chose at each new decision point not to stop. In some part of the brain, each individual is fully aware of what's happening and how he or she urges it on, creating the conditions for its continuance—but each also seems powerless to stop.

Misconceptions about Affairs

1. *"Everyone's doing it."* Don't believe the TV or film industry—everybody is not having an affair! Studies show that spouses tend to be sexually faith-

ful to each other. Based on data from more than 1,510 husbands and a similar number of wives, 89 percent of the husbands and 91 percent of the wives reported they had been sexually faithful to their spouse during the past year.[6]

2. *"It's possible to separate sex and love."* "The argument that sex can be detached from love and marriage is simply not backed up by the biological, psychological, and anthropological evidence. As infants, we first learn to associate creature comfort and sensuous good feeling with love, and the connection is ineradicably imprinted upon us. As adults, we may be capable at times of having sexual experiences—even, indeed, powerful ones—without any emotional attachment to the partner, but this is the exception, not the rule.

"The normal tendency—and it has been true in most human societies, not just our own—is for intense sexual experiences to generate emotional ties. That's why the history of extramarital behavior is filled with stories of a mere romp turning into a great love affair that damages or destroys the marriage."[7]

3. *"An affair will meet the need caused by loneliness."* An affair may stop the loneliness in the short run, but it is still *extra*marital. It is a temporary solution.

Solving loneliness requires a deep sharing of lives through the multifaceted experiences of life. That depth of sharing cannot be accomplished by a clandestine affair. Ultimately the affair breaks up, and the woman is confronted again with her loneliness.

4. *"Affairs are fun."* Maslow says, "There's a marvelous incandescence. It blinds people to their lovers' faults and reminds them of the days when they were young and carefree.

"Then the glow wears off, and the real world starts to intrude. People appear more perfect when you don't have to get along with them daily or share the stresses of married life. If the circumstances were reversed, a spouse could easily be as exciting as a lover, and a lover as boring and predictable as a spouse."[8]

5. *"At last we have discovered the real thing."* This is *not* the real thing. It is a false world of limited scope. Anybody can get psyched up to perform well for a few minutes, or days. But the real world is living day after day in an uptight world with stress, pressure—and not enough money or time.

The affair is an artificial world that cuts you off from your friends. Have you taken this guy over to meet your mom yet? Does your Bible study group know about him? And how do you explain to your sixteen-year-old daughter, who wants to run around braless in tight tank tops, that she shouldn't do that—but it's OK for you to have an extramarital affair?

6. *"An affair will strengthen my marriage."* This distorted philosophy has been preached by many, but our observations and those of other counselors indicate that affairs do not strengthen marriage; in fact, they cause marriages to break.[9]

Prohibitions against Affairs

Why is it that Scripture is so negative about affairs? Why criticize the affair when the benefits seem so positive—relief from monotony, emptiness, loneliness, boredom, restlessness, even depression?

In many places the Bible says very simply and directly, "You shall not commit adultery." (For examples, see Exodus 20:14; Matthew 5:27; 19:18; Mark 10:19; Romans 2:22; 13:9; James 2:11.)

The biblical prohibition against adultery has a bigger meaning than simply "Thou shalt not." The commandment is intended to protect the family, to keep it united and intact. Adultery is forbidden in order to minimize the spiraling effects of insecurity caused by children whose parents are having affairs or have divorced.

In a ten-year study of children who grew up in homes where there were affairs, separation, and divorce, we found lifelong damage to these children. Many were scared by insecurity; fearful of marriage; afraid to risk, being perfectionists, controllers, sexually promiscuous, and drug and alcohol users.[10]

No Woman Is an Island

Leanne was in her first year of college when she heard that her mother had left home and was living in an apartment with another man. How could her mother do this? Leanne was filled with anger, rage, and painful disillusionment that her Christian mother would do such a thing. Her parents' marriage had seemed so good—how could this happen?

Leanne dropped out of college to keep house for her father and comfort him in his tremendous loss. The three kids chose sides. The two younger ones identified with the mother. Now there was war, not only between the parents, but also between the parents and children—and among the children.

The same conflict and turmoil was going on in the other man's home, between the husband, his wife, and their teenage children. The two having the affair had never counted on all of this disruption and pain. They thought they could just meet a few personal needs.

So Right—So Wrong

Another reason for the strong scriptural prohibitions against adultery is that the people in the affairs are themselves damaged. But how could anything so seemingly wonderful be so tremendously damaging?

Chris and Bruce, the Christian workers who had fallen in love, continued to write and call each other. Finally, they were asked by the engaged couple who had been at the four-week training seminar to participate in their marriage. Chris writes, "Bruce met my plane. We laughed and kissed. We drew smiles and stares from others in the airport, which didn't bother either of us. We drove to a motel near the church, where the wedding would take place the next day. He came around the car, opened the door for me, and said, 'I didn't ask you if I should get a double room or two singles or what,' and he kissed me. 'You didn't answer my question,' he said. Then we kissed again.

"'Yes, I did,' I said.

"And so we shared a double room. I remember little of the flight home except for a kind stewardess bringing me a cup of coffee as I sat quietly crying. Bruce told me later that the closer he got to his home, the more slowly he drove, postponing the inevitable. But it was back to work—more letters, more phone calls, and planning the next times we could be together."

The Confrontation

"Finally," Chris said, "another woman, who became aware of our affair, told us of her intention to tell Bruce's wife. At this point Bruce decided to leave his wife, and I decided to leave my family. We drove together to his home. He packed some of his personal things, left his wife and each of his children a message, and then we made the long trip to my home. By the time we arrived, his wife and son were also there. They had discovered where I lived and had chartered a plane to get there by the time we did.

"In spite of the confrontation, it did not alter our plans. We decided to drive back to his hometown so that he could care for his family. He assured me everything was all right. His son was making housing arrangements for the family since they would, of course, have to leave the parsonage. We checked into a motel and spent the afternoon discussing housing locations for ourselves and checking out possible jobs for both of us. By the time Bruce left in the early evening to meet with the church officials, he seemed very distant, and I was literally shaking with anxiety.

"When he returned to the motel a couple of hours later, my world disintegrated. 'Chris,' he said, 'you know that I love you very, very much.'

"'Of course, sweetheart, I love you, too,' I said.

"'And you know that I love God very much,' he declared.

"My reply was, 'I couldn't love you if you didn't love God.'

"Then began a rambling discourse about all the guilt he was suddenly feeling . . . maybe it was the way he was raised . . . his anguish over what he had done to both of us. On and on and on. The conclusion was that he could not fulfill his commitment to me but he intended to hole up in a room someplace and find a job. And what was I to do? I had resigned my job and left my family! I didn't know."

The Affair Falls Apart

"Thus began several months of pure hell, which I'm not sure are finished yet. The tears that began that night did not cease for ten days. They flowed like water pouring from a smashed pitcher. I took a bus back to my hometown, not so much because I wanted to go there but because I did not know what else to do. More like a zombie than a human being, I moved through the next few days until my husband and a pastor friend checked me into the psychiatric ward of a local hospital.

"I really didn't care whether I lived or died, but if I could have made a choice, it definitely would have been for death. I could neither eat nor sleep. I had staked my life on the gift God gave me in Bruce, and now that gift was no longer mine.

"The letters and phone calls continued for two months. Then Bruce experienced even more anguish as his sixteen-year-old daughter announced her pregnancy. He and his family moved to another state to help their daughter through the pregnancy, and our communication stopped. Not an hour passes when he is not on my mind with both love and pain. Meanwhile, I have no choice but to continue to go through the motions of living. . . . Indeed, life is hell."

The biblical restrictions are intended to prevent damage that spreads like the ever widening rings when a stone is dropped into a quiet pool of water. The strong prohibitions against adultery are to protect us from personal hurt and our families from disintegration. Yes, the prohibitions may seem to be going against human need at the time, but in fact, the wisdom is based on human need—long-term human need.

It's important to point out that being sexually attracted to a man is not sin—nor a violation of scriptural teaching to not commit adultery. But there are many little steps between the tempting thought that crosses your mind and the actual acts that are so damaging. Jesus warns us not to commit adultery with someone in our heart. In other words, don't think you can play the game of committing adultery in the "playground of your mind" without it's someday becoming a reality you act out.

Affair Prevention and Recovery

Affairs tend to take three different directions. There are the one-night stands, somewhat like a spontaneous eruption of sexual passion, which are later confessed—corrections are made, and the marriage continues.

The second type is the extended affair, which lasts perhaps three to six months. There is a return to the marriage, usually because the affair is seen in a more realistic light and because the married partners try to work at marriage restoration.

The third type of affair breaks the marriage. This generally involves the husband's discovering his wife's infidelity, his becoming angry, kicking her out, and suing for divorce. All of the messy custody and property-division battles are the painful result.

TIMES TO BEWARE

To help prevent affairs, we need to consider when they are most likely. We have discovered from our research that the late twenties and late thirties are the most likely times for women to get into affairs.

The following list of change events might also alert you to times to be on guard:

- Pregnancy or childbirth
- Death of family member or friend
- Accident or extended illness of a child or a mate
- A job change
- The beginning or ending of a career
- Extensive travel
- Depression because of failure or loss
- Elation because of success
- Quiet-nest time (children all in school)
- Empty-nest time (children gone from the home)

In short, any major change event that alters your psychological or spiritual balance is likely to cause you to long for deep emotional caring. If you don't receive this caring through normal legitimate channels—your mate, family, and/or friends—then you may become vulnerable to an affair.

GARBAGE IN—GARBAGE OUT
To prevent affairs you need to watch your thought life. It may sound like that old conservative line, but it's common information in the computer industry: GIGO—"garbage in, garbage out." If you put garbage into the computer, that's what you'll get back. What you put into your mind is going to come back out. We all receive hours of exposure to sexual stimuli every day. How much time do you

spend in the Scriptures and in quiet meditation with God, allowing him to counteract the sexual impact?

Affair prevention also means that you think about what really is important to you. Prioritize your goals and values so the truly significant are high on your list. Don't allow yourself to be trapped into an affair because you've not been thinking about what's important.

Get into a regular Bible study and mutual support group where people are opening themselves to God and each other. You may not feel comfortable saying to the group, "I'm really being tempted by this attractive guy in church." But you may be able to tell them, "You know, I have some special needs in my life right now—the kids are all off at school, I'm working at a job I don't like, and I don't feel I'm as close to people as I need to be." A good small group will fill some of those gaps and help to diffuse some of your vulnerability and protect you from an affair.

Commit yourself to one female friend. Ask her to pray for you and to hold you accountable. If you are especially vulnerable right now, ask this trusted friend to support you by specifically asking how you are doing: "Are you still pure? Is there some guy who tempts you? What are you doing to be strong?"

Small Steps to Start—and Stop

An affair starts with thinking only of your needs—but it ends with your forgetting who you are. Remember, affairs start with small steps. To prevent them, take the small steps of prevention. Daily make those small decisions to reduce vulnerability, to strengthen your spiritual and emotional life, and to build a strong support network. If you're married, work on your marriage relationship. Turn down the offers, innuendoes, and jokes that come your way from needy men who are testing to see if you are willing to be in an affair.

Cindy, now thirty-five, gave us the details of her story—a typical scenario of a career woman who had been involved with a married man. The affair had followed the usual skyrocket beginning, leveling off, and crashing conclusion.

She was not really able to let go until she finally prayed, *Lord, take him out of my life, and help me not to need him.* It was at that point that God began to move him away and to change her needs so that she was emotionally able to walk away.

It's not easy to pray that prayer, especially when a person seems so significant to you—but you *must!* An affair is an illegitimate relationship that is unhealthy emotionally and spiritually for everybody involved. Don't let your needs cause you to forget who you are.

The Legal Escape

Many women feel the only way to escape a troubled marriage is through divorce. However, divorce does not usually turn out to be a satisfying solution.

Morton Hunt reports, "Some years ago . . . I interviewed 200 people and conducted a questionnaire survey of nearly 400 others; since then . . . I have interviewed many hundreds more. Of them all, I can recall only a handful who did not suffer considerable pain as the result of the marital breakup; many suffered intensely, some to the point of attempting suicide."[1]

The movement toward a divorce progresses in small steps. You aren't happily married one day and then the next, without cause, decide to get divorced. Instead, as in building a brick wall, one painful problem, or brick, is put into the wall and then another and another. Many women who consider divorce have already tried an earlier stage, such as running away or an affair, to meet some of their needs.

In spite of the pain of going through a divorce,

there are still over one million divorces each year (1,194,000).[2] Most of the people who divorce seek to get married again, but the success rate with each succeeding marriage goes down.

First marriages last an average of 11 years, second marriages only 7 years, and third marriages a dismal 5 years.[3] Tragically, in the 1990s "till death do us part" averages only 7.1 years.[4]

Gain and Loss

If you're in a painful marriage, your normal human response is to want to get away. But when you think about a divorce, stop yourself and ask, "What would I gain—or lose?"

Let's look at some of the losses. One woman said, "I have learned the hard way that when I got a divorce, I not only lost my husband, I also lost a whole way of life." Divorce means a whole *change of lifestyle*. Usually, finances are reduced. Two separate family units will now try to survive on the same general income they had as one. There's also a loss of history with family, friends, and relatives— especially if you're the one who wants the divorce.

After a divorce, a chain reaction starts. Happiness suddenly gives way to second thoughts, which lead to many self-doubts and uncertainties about the wisdom of the divorce. You may even wish for a reconciliation.

When you total up the losses, be sure to include *loneliness*. You may think your present marriage is difficult, but if you file for divorce and move out, you may find yourself in a very lonely apartment with only a TV for company. (Of course, we are not suggesting that a woman should stay when there is physical abuse.)

The losses must include potential *emotional damage* to you. Loneliness can become extremely grinding. One divorced woman writes, "No, I don't miss him—but I do miss having *someone.* And there is no one. Where does one look, at my age, for intelligence, humor, and compassion? Not where I used to look. And I don't know where else to go. I believe I have grown immensely. I feel capable of a loving, loyal, dependable relationship—and yet I have not even dated in months! There *must* be someone. I can only wait and hope."[5]

Let's suppose you had a rotten marriage. Perhaps you tried leaving a couple of times, and it didn't work. Now you finally are in an affair with someone who really loves you. On the basis of that love, you have decided to get divorced. As you total up the potential losses, it's important to remember that *very few people marry the person* with whom they had an affair before they were divorced.

An affair may thrive in an intolerable marriage, but the dissolution of the marriage forces the spouse and new partner into a new intimacy, which causes a new strain.

Lynne, Henry, and Marilyn are an illustration. We knew Lynne and Henry before Henry and Marilyn began having an affair. We had little contact with Henry, but we had a friendship with

Lynne through several Christian organizations. We had never met Marilyn, but we knew she was divorced and lonely. Marilyn and Henry worked in the same office. Lynne shared her agony with us after she learned of the affair. We worked with her, trying to restore her relationship with Henry. But Henry, who was deep into his midlife crisis, resolutely divorced Lynne and married Marilyn. Neither Henry nor Marilyn knew much about our trying to help Lynne.

About eighteen months after the second wedding, we received a call from Marilyn, who had by this time learned of our work with midlife people. She felt Henry was in midlife crisis. She gave her story, unaware that we knew of it from Lynne's side. When she and Henry "fell in love," Henry had painted a miserable picture of Lynne, showing her to be incompetent, insecure, and uninterested in meeting his needs or even doing simple household tasks. He complained that she often spent the whole day in bed, not functioning at all as a wife and mother. Marilyn, who was formerly a strong, capable career woman, sobbed and said, "his behavior is driving *me* to be incompetent, insecure, and uninterested in life!"

Your Kids Suffer Too

As you total up the losses, count your children's losses. Remember, you can divorce your husband but never a child. You may temporarily or permanently lose physical contact with your children after a divorce. At first you may not notice much because you are taken up with the excitement of your new life. However, an urgency within a parent and child sooner or later erupts into a deep-seated desire to connect. Even if you have custody of the children, you have caused a deep loss for them. Your children will never have the basic family unit with their two birth parents, and they may have gigantic adjustments to make in the new situation. We have done extensive research on the negative effects for children of divorce, which are spelled out in painful detail in our book *Adult Children of Legal or Emotional Divorce.*[6]

Same Old Pattern

Originally you married to meet each other's needs. You may not have fully understood each other, but you felt a subconscious attraction to each other. The frightening thing about divorce and remarriage is that *you are likely to subconsciously choose the same type of person*—unless you have grown a great deal.

Unless you understand why you chose your first mate and how you contributed to that first marriage breakup, divorce will not remove potential emotional stresses in a new marriage. You carry yourself and your own set of needs from your first marriage. Any emotional problems you have now will probably continue to cause problems in a future marriage. Scary, huh?

Is a Midlife Divorce Necessary?

You or your husband may be going through a midlife crisis; everything may seem unstable, you feel great stress, and your marriage is not as great as when you were dating, but that does not mean you should opt for a divorce. Many midlife divorces are unnecessary. Spouses give up too quickly. If they would hang on a little longer, they could make it through this difficult time.

When a person comes for counsel, saying they want to keep the marriage, we ask, "Are you willing to put up with a great deal of stress and do a lot of personal growing over the next three to five years?" To restore a troubled midlife marriage, somebody has to be willing to commit a lot of energy and time to saving it.[7]

If you happen to be the one who wants to run from your marriage, we'd encourage you to hang on for three to five years. Don't just suffer and struggle, but grow so your marriage will change from being a drag to being a real source of strength.

Marriage Restoration

Dr. Paul Meier, of New Life Clinic, says, "Out of all the vast array of psychiatric patients that I see (ranging from childhood schizophrenics to senile patients with organic brain syndromes), marital conflict patients are the easiest to help and the most rewarding to work with."[8]

He further points out that incompatibility is too

often used as an excuse to leave the marriage. He says, "I can honestly and emphatically say that this excuse is no more than a cop-out used by couples who are too proud and lazy to work out their own hang-ups. Instead of facing them, they run away by divorcing and remarrying. Then there are four miserable people instead of just two."[9]

Les and Beverly were an attractive midlife couple whom I (Jim) had not met before. They had just seated themselves in my office when they explained in very direct terms that if I couldn't help them, they were going to get a divorce. They went on with their blunt explanation: "This is our last try."

They said they had read all of the recent marriage manuals and books and listed a dozen titles. They had been through Marriage Encounter and other weekends, plus almost a year of professional counseling—but they still couldn't stand each other.

Before they were married, they couldn't keep their hands off each other. They would do almost anything just to be with each other a few more minutes. Now when they were in bed, it was repulsive if they inadvertently bumped each other.

Their communication, sex life, and casual talking had essentially dried up. Their marriage was a day-by-day endurance contest. They said they were completely incompatible, but some Christian friends urged them to see me.

The response racing around in my mind was, *Why me? If I don't pull off a miracle and save your marriage, then it'll be my fault.* I didn't say that aloud—but I wanted to. What I did say was that I refused to take the responsibility for their marriage breakup. I further agreed to work with them only if they were willing to become active participants. They agreed to really work.

The Old Gleam

We talked about two basic matters. The first was what had attracted them to each other years before. Each one of them responded with a list. I found it interesting to see their eyes light up and see little smirks as they recalled their clandestine meetings and the magic and magnetism that had drawn them together.

Next, I had each one tell me what was irritating about the other *now*. After a trait was mentioned, the response was one of surprise. "You mean that really bothers you?" "Wow, that's such a little thing. I didn't think you ever thought about that." "I didn't realize that was important to you."

The problem was that they had forgotten what had so strongly attracted them to each other, and now they were magnifying a pile of little irritations that had become the growing wedge between them. They agreed to make some small changes in themselves and their habits and to see me again in two weeks.

Key to a Locked Door

They came back with some apprehension, but now they had experienced a few successes. They also had a number of failures, but some of the modifications were starting to work. They didn't see each other as bad as before.

During the second session I probed for more irritations, and now some of the real ones started to surface. They were little things that had been swept under the rug for so long they had become giant bumps.

I noticed that Beverly would never let Les talk for himself. If I asked Les a question, she would always respond. He never got to speak or to express his own feelings. She was always there—the helpful *mother*.

I decided to be fairly direct and told her that when I asked him a question I did not want her to answer for him. When I said that to her, suddenly Les sat up in his chair and became a new person. He came out of his shell and began to interact in ways he had not interacted for years. It was as if a key had unlocked the door of communication between them.

As the session went along, I sensed that his traveling job was more than a way to make money—it was a way to escape her. I looked at him and told him my gut reaction about his job. His face turned white. Beverly jumped in immediately and said, "You know, I've always thought that."

Now the door was ajar for communication, for rethinking his work, for building on the strengths of their past, and for eliminating some of the negatives in their current lives.

They came back two weeks later. We continued to work on the basic areas we had already covered, and then I encouraged them to begin affirming each other at least three times a day. Each was to thank and appreciate the other—not so much for what that one did as for who he or she was. If he appreciated her because she cooked a fine meal, that was something she did. If he appreciated her because she was a tender, sympathetic, and caring woman, those were qualities in her life. Both kinds of affirmation were important, but to affirm the qualities would be more enduring and basic to self-esteem than to affirm activities.

After their sixth appointment, I didn't see them again for months until we met unexpectedly in a shopping mall. They were walking with their arms around each other, acting like newlyweds who couldn't stand being apart. Grinning widely, they said, "We've fallen in love again!"

Remember, They're All Men

In Fellini's movie *Juliet of the Spirits*, Juliet is unable to allow herself to be seduced by a handsome man, and she protects herself from an affair by having a religious vision. She states her real reason by saying, "I looked around at what was available, and as far as I could see, it would only mean changing the middle-aged bore I already have for somebody else who'll be just as middle-aged and no less boring."[10]

Sally and I have helped a number of bad marriages to be renewed. Yours can experience the same kind of restoration. God wants it to work. But remember, if you do get divorced, you may not find anything better. After all—men are men.

What about Remarriage?

Some of you may be saying, "Well, that really sounds great. I wish I had had some solid marriage counseling when my marriage was falling apart. But the reality is my marriage did fall apart—I'm divorced. Now what about marrying again?"

If you're considering remarriage—listen up: *First, thoroughly understand why you married your first partner.* What were your needs that attracted you to him, and why did your former marriage fall apart? You must fully recognize your fault as well as his. He was not entirely at fault.

Sometimes people say, "Well, he had an affair, so the marriage broke up." The question still remains, "*Why* did he have an affair? What did you contribute to an atmosphere that made him vulnerable to an affair?"

Second, confess to God your part in the marriage collapse. Ask him to forgive and heal you. Ask God to help you grow so the same error will not be repeated. Suppose you've identified your fault as being a perfectionist who demands too much from people and pushes them to the edge by repeated nagging. Now you've identified your part in the marriage breakup, if that's what it was. Now ask God during the next year to help you mature so that particular problem will not taint any future marriage.

Third, allow sufficient time to elapse between your divorce and any future remarriage. You need a minimum of a year to allow for growth processes and to allow for pain to be healed. That doesn't mean you shouldn't have friendships. If you move too fast, you will probably subconsciously choose someone very similar to your first husband—and set up circumstances for a second divorce.

A side observation: If you were in an affair with someone before your marriage broke up, statistics say that relationship is probably not going to work. Our direct advice is, "If you've had an affair with someone either before your divorce or within a year after your divorce, don't marry that person."

Fourth, know that your loneliness will make you extremely vulnerable. Even though you don't feel it's necessary, expand the circle of trustworthy friends. The temptation will be to lean on only a few people and then feel guilty when you wear them out. Get into a small Bible study and sharing group. Also join a divorce recovery group. Allow those people to support you during this transition.

Fifth, remember that God loves you. You may feel very crummy, unlovable, and worthless. Christians may even try to reinforce what a "bad girl" you are—but remember, God loves you. He wants you to be restored, healed, and growing.

When you wonder whether or not he loves you, think of this promise from Psalm 89:30-34: "But if his [daughters] forsake my law and fail to walk in my ways, if they do not obey my decrees and fail to keep my commands, then I will punish their sin with the rod, and their disobedience with [a] beating. But I will never stop loving him, nor let my promise to him fail. No, I will not break my covenant; I will not take back a single word I said."

PART FIVE

Excited about Succeeding

Keeping Up
with Life's Clocks

Rebecca, who had just turned thirty-six, was crying as she shared her feelings with us about her recent miscarriage. She was six months along when she lost the baby. Once more, questions were raised. Should she try again to become a mother? Was it too late for her? Should she continue with her career? These very painful questions had been handled more than a year ago. Now they were resurrected and crying out for answers all over again.

Rebecca had gone straight through college with her sights clearly fixed on a business career. Dating was only casual for social contact. Marriage was not programmed for her life until she was in her late twenties.

She finished her degree, took a responsible position in a growing firm, and started to climb the corporate ladder. She advanced quickly. Young men her age viewed her with some degree of suspicion and jealousy—their attitudes tended to keep her socially isolated. She continued to date casually until at age twenty-nine she met Chad.

They married when she was thirty, and Chad was willing for her to continue her career. In fact, he was pleased to see her becoming successful as she moved up the business ladder.

When she became a vice-president at age thirty-four, she felt an exhilarating sense of accomplishment. Yet she began to feel a desire to slow down the frantic corporate race and to look at other values. It was then that she and Chad decided to have a child—but unfortunately, she had miscarried in the sixth month.

As we talked, the issue that kept recurring was, "I didn't know this was going to happen to me. When I was in my early twenties, I only wanted a career. I did not want children. All of my energies went toward my career through the twenties and half of my thirties. Then suddenly this change. I feel very mixed up.

"Part of me wants to press on to become president of some corporation—to make a real mark in the business world. But the other part of me, which I never recognized before, wants to be a mother and a homemaker. I don't know what it is—maybe I'm thinking about getting old. Maybe what I really want is to have children and grandchildren who will be there when I'm an old lady. Maybe I just want to leave something better in the world than success in business. Whatever it is, I didn't expect it to happen to me. I wish someone had told me."

Change? Not Me!

Hundreds of men and women have shared with us the anxiety of wishing they had been better prepared to face the midlife years. Young adults are a little curious about what might happen at midlife, but they really don't think they will change. They believe midlife adults who are wrestling with various life issues are inadequate persons who didn't have a grip on life—which they, the young adults, think they have.

What causes a woman like Rebecca, who had staunchly declared she did not plan to be a mother, to suddenly desire children? We all view life differently at different ages. An eighteen-year-old girl and a twenty-eight-year-old young woman look at dating very differently. A twenty-year-old married woman usually does not feel panic if she is not a mother; whereas a childless woman who passes thirty-five wrestles seriously with desires about mothering.

Adults are exceedingly complex, and many researchers and writers over the years have been trying to put their finger on exactly what causes these changes. Researchers such as Charlotte Bühler, from the 1930s, and later Erikson, Havighurst, Kohlberg, Neugarten, Lowenthal, Gould, Levinson, and Knox, among others, have been studying adult development. As we learn more about the *what* and *why* of changes, adults can be forewarned to prepare for various aspects of their future.

To Mature . . .

Erik Erikson's stages have been the framework around which many other researchers have worked. He proposes eight stages of development from infancy through late adulthood. Five of the stages are to be completed by adolescence. Early adulthood development then deals with "intimacy," the appropriate giving and receiving of love. Midlife adulthood settles the issue of "generativity," which is leaving something positive for the world after you are gone. Late adulthood development must handle the task of "integrity," a basic acceptance of one's life as appropriate and meaningful.[1]

As the theory of adult development progressed, it became more age related. Predictable thoughts and events were said to happen as we reach certain ages. The problem is that human beings are too complex for a simple age-specific theory. We're also finding that people do not always follow normal societal life patterns. Therefore, we feel if all adult changes are tied to age we will not account for the great variety of human experience.

Different Life Schedules

A second problem is that men have been the main focus of most adult development studies, with the assumption that women are similar. This is not true. For example, women in their forties and fifties demonstrate a great deal of assertiveness. A woman may start a new career and exert new leadership and influence, while men in that same era of life are mellowing out. She may be taking off like a rocket—while he is preparing for retirement.

With all of that as a backdrop, however, we are aware of various clocks that tick incessantly within a woman. The development of a woman is geared to several clocks. All of them are interrelated, and we should not be too simplistic when we talk about what is happening to women at midlife.

The Genetic Clock

Your genetic clock started when you were conceived. At birth you had a whole pattern of factors to influence all of your life. Your genetic inheritance determined when you would come into puberty, how difficult your monthly cycles would be, and how many years you would be fertile. The genetic clock also decides when your hair will turn gray and when those wrinkles around your eyes and mouth will begin to form.

The genetic clock is a given. To some degree you can control your weight, but not your height. Your genetic clock tells your body at what age to shift weight off your limbs toward your torso. As you progress through life, biological change will continue regardless of what you might do to slow—or alter it.

The Age Clock

On each birthday the alarm on your age clock goes off. When you were a little kid, it went off with bells and whistles. When you were a teenager, it was sirens. But as you move into midlife, you may find that your age clock is tolling slower—deep gongs, like a lonely bell in an empty churchyard.

Obviously, an interrelationship exists between the genetic clock and the age clock. As we talk about other clocks, you'll see they also are interrelated. The age clock gives each year a meaning and a history of its own. Not only does each year say something about the past, but crossing that milestone also says something about your future.

What's the difference between being thirty-nine years and 364 days old—and being forty years old? One day! You haven't changed that much biologically, but that internal age clock is saying, "You have crossed into another world."

From childhood on, you have been looking at various markers and placing a significance on them. "Wow! When I get to be five" or "When I get to be sixteen or twenty-one or thirty-two." Whatever the markers, you assign a special meaning to those particular years. When you're in the early part of life, you're looking forward to the markers because something new and exciting is going to happen. But as people think of the years after forty, they usually associate those years with losses.

I (Jim) remember that when I was about sixteen I told my dad that people over thirty were essentially brain dead, should not be trusted, and should die. As you can imagine, that attitude had a negative impact on me as I moved into my thirties. Remember the key marker years in your life. What positive or negative associations with those ages have influenced your attitudes and behaviors?

The Cultural Clock

Our culture exerts pressures on us, which could be called a cultural clock. Culture says girls at a certain age should start school, ride bikes, go to Girl Scouts, have boyfriends, learn to drive, go to college, move out of the parental home, get married, and have children. Different cultures around the world have different times for these events, and we are conditioned to live by what our cultural clock says.

The problem may come when the cultural clock is saying one thing and the genetic clock is saying something else.

For example, our oldest daughter, Barbara, did not enter puberty as early as two of her close companions. These two girls could not understand why Barbara was not interested in boys but instead enjoyed walking in the fields, finding a bird's nest, or playing with a frog along a riverbank.

One day these two girls came to our house with a big brown grocery bag. They marched up to Barbara's bedroom and took all the "junk" off her dresser—a bird's nest, some pretty rocks, a slingshot, her jackknife, and assorted other items in her collection. They put all these things into the bag and set it in the closet. In their place these friends put out perfume, nail polish, powder, lipstick, mascara—an array of makeup—and said to her, "We're going to make you into a lady!"

This produced a great deal of tension within Barbara. It was very clear that if she did not respond to the cultural clock, she would lose the friendship of these girls. But the cultural clock being enforced by these girls was out of sync with the genetic clock within Barbara.

At that time I (Jim) bought Barbara a record by Sammy Davis Jr. entitled "I've Got to Be Me." I suggested she play the record several times a day, listening carefully to the words: A person should become their own person—not what someone else expects.

Each woman will be affected differently by the cultural clock. It is not only what culture says you should do—but do you believe what they say you should do? Maybe your cultural clock said you were to marry and have children. You may have arrived at midlife, then, having listened predominantly to this clock and having ignored some of the other clocks.

The Family Clock

This clock is interrelated with the cultural clock, but it also has a unique ticking. The family clock started ticking back in your grandparents' lives. Their attitudes toward family influenced your parents—and you. Yes, the family clock is influenced by the cultural clock, but this clock tells you when to marry, the kind of person to marry, how many children to have, and how to raise those children. It also tells you if it's OK or not to mix marriage and a career—plus how to handle being an aunt, cope with the empty nest, and respond to being a grandparent.

The family clock tells you when you're "on schedule" and acting appropriately. Our family clock said to our three girls—"Go to college, get married, and combine a family with a career."

The Career Clock

Your career clock obviously is interrelated with the other clocks, but it also has a distinctive ticking. The career women who were important to you will determine how loud this ticking is. If you were strongly influenced by a woman teacher, she may have become a pattern for you. Her life schedule could be a part of your career clock. Your mother and other family members also become part of your career clock. You are living a response to your career clock—deeply involved in a career or in some combination with other life commitments.

The God Clock

Some people who do not come from a Christian background might refer to this as a morality clock. We, however, believe that God is a person who acts in us personally. Within each person is a dimension that can be satisfied only by relating to God. As one moves through life, this call of God comes at many different times and circumstances. God's calling us is like a clock inside us.

Through the years we've asked hundreds of people, "When was the first time you became aware of God in a personal way?" We've heard many interesting stories about their becoming conscious of God's seeking to penetrate their lives.

In my own life, I (Jim) can remember as a boy walking the campgrounds in Lakeside, Ohio, late at night after youth rallies. I was acutely aware that God was communicating with me. It was frightening and awesome but at the same time reassuring. It was in my late teens that I gave my life to Christ to serve and follow him all of my life.

That awareness of God's hand on my life has caused me to respond at different eras of my life in ways that cannot be accounted for just by the genetic clock, the age clock, or any of the other clocks. God is interrelated with all of these other forces, causing direction and decision in my life.

Big Trouble at Midlife

We see two types of women who struggle at midlife. The first troubled woman has responded to only one or two of her life clocks—ignoring the others. She has become unbalanced. At midlife she makes a mad dash to reorganize and stabilize her life. The second woman in trouble has too many change events piled on at once.

We have talked about the large number and variety of change events that could happen in a woman's life. Every change event (anything that happens to you) affects many of these clocks that we've talked about. In turn, all of these clocks affect your change events.

For example, if your parents were divorced because your father deserted your mother when you were a teenage girl—then you may hate men, reject marriage, and throw yourself into a competitive career, seeking to outdo men. On the other hand, some of the other forces in your life, or clocks as we're calling them, might have caused you to view that change event very differently. With strong support from your extended family, the culture around you, and a relationship to God, you may have looked at your parents' divorce and said, "Well, that's their problem. I need to move on in the right direction with my life."

Remember, each event causes you to make choices and influences your values. Your values also influence each change event. We'll speak more of this in the next chapter, "Answering Life's Questions."

Too Many Alarms

Most of the clocks tell us not only what to do but whether we're "on time" or "off time." Events that arrive "off time" can add stress to the call from other clocks in our life. But we may also experience stress from "on-time" events for which we are unprepared. Problems are also caused by the events themselves and the increased number of events—anticipated or unanticipated.

In midlife, a woman faces her own personal change events, plus her adolescent children's change events, and the potentially dangerous changes in her midlife husband. But she may also be dealing with aging parents who need her time and emotional commitment.

The overwhelming stress from events in the midlife woman is like having an alarm clock going off in every room all at once. She runs frantically from one room to the next, shutting them off as they buzz, gong, and clang. She barely gets one shut off and runs to quiet others, when the alarm she has just silenced goes off again. Then the dog starts barking, the family members all start yelling, and she feels trapped in a maze of unreasonable confusion.

But There's Hope

We both have been there. We have experienced the desperation, the confusion, and the fear of the future as each of us went through our own midlife crisis. We had a deep sense of inadequacy, and we wondered if God, or any other person, understood or cared.

We've each made it through—and you will too. God *is* alive—and cares for you. There *is* life after your midlife crisis—but you are *not* going to be the same woman. Your perception of yourself, your family, your friends, your career, and of God are going to be different. Your values are changing, and those value changes will produce a more mature, sensitive, stable, and peaceful woman—you.

Answering Life's Questions

A while ago we received a letter from a friend whom we had known well when she was a young married woman. After she gave us general news, she said, "It's good to know you are there—especially as I approach forty with phenomenal speed. My 'baby' has two years before she enters eighth grade—that's high school here. I realize there's precious little time for personal or family goals—sometimes I feel like 'I haven't done anything yet.'

"Whoever would have guessed that so many options would extract such a price of frustration over unrealistic expectations and demands. I am really not as frustrated as that sounds—especially on days when I'm free to write and chip away at my unrealized and unformed dream. My dream sits like lead inside me and I constantly run into it in the dark. Now if somebody could just tell me how to slow down the clock."

Time Runs Out

When we were children, we felt time stretched out forever. Time was vague. Time has a very different meaning at midlife. Time is now limited. We assign it a higher value. Time is worth more because we're sensing we've lived a big chunk of our lives. Time doesn't stretch endlessly before us as if we were standing on the crest of a mountain, just ready to ski down. We realize that we've skied halfway down the mountain and our ski run will come to an end all too soon.

At midlife our values come sharply under scrutiny. What should get our priority? What gets our time, money, energy, and our love? And have we been using our time (life) in the very best way?

Don't Miss Your Special Time

Reconsidering life—its values and priorities—is the most important task of your midlife passage. Don't avoid this thinking and redefinition process. You are skiing down the mountain of life. It *is* going to end, and only you can determine how to live profitably.

Some women, when confronted by change events and the incessant ticking of their life clocks, are tempted to play more tennis, exercise more, have more parties, go to more conferences, buy more clothes, or get a new hairstyle. Those activities may be helpful for your self-image and mental health. However, if they are causing you to avoid thinking about your life values and priorities, then you're fooling yourself and setting yourself up for a fall.

Now is the time to seek the truth about who you are, what you want to do, who you will love and let love you, and what mission you want to accomplish in life. The temptation will be to hush the questions—but they should not be hushed.

Jesus used an illustration common in his day as he explained the disastrous process of trying to keep new truth inside old structures. He said we can't put new wine into old wineskins. In that day wine was stored in an animal skin. As it fermented, the new skin would stretch with the expanding wine, and then the skin would harden to the new size. If you tried to reuse the skin jug, the new fermenting wine would cause the skin to crack, and all the wine would run out. The same is true of your life. The old structures, life forms, and values may not fit you now. Some of your priorities may be the same as before—but some will be discarded as you add new ones.

Midcourse Correction

Midlife is one of the times when many events force a reassessment of life. The reevaluation isn't caused only because a person turns thirty-six or forty, nor is it caused by culture, genetics, career, or family. It isn't even caused only by a stale marriage or some other traumatic loss in life. The reassessment seems to happen because of a combination of several of these factors converging at midlife.

The crucial issue is the importance of these

events in your life. When our youngest daughter, Becki, had her left leg amputated about mid-thigh at age sixteen, she responded optimistically and viewed the amputation as something God had allowed. She was convinced God was going to use the amputation for her benefit and God's glory.

Why is it that some people react positively to a difficult situation and others react negatively, with depression, with anger, or by giving up? The answer is found in their value system—in how they think of themselves, the world around them, and God. If the amputee views herself as having lost her worth and importance, she will feel depressed. If, on the other hand, as Becki said, "I'm the same person, only seventeen pounds lighter," then she will continue to be optimistic.

The way you respond to the changes at midlife will be determined by your previous values and the choices you've made all through life. In turn, the responses, choices, and decisions you make now at midlife are going to reform your value system. As new change events come, you will respond on the basis of this new system you are establishing.

Midlife Questions
Questioning at midlife is essential to the process of redefining our values and priorities. All kinds of questions will spill out.

Not only is it important to ask questions, but it's also important to decide how you will divide your energy and time among these priorities. Remember, you will experience an emotional crisis if the choices and activities are not in line with your inner value system—your life characteristics, wishes, needs, goals, feelings—your *real self.*

Midlife questions seem to group into four basic areas: the meaning of life—the choice of environment—the decisions about relationships—and the self as a person.

First are the *meaning-of-life* questions. "Why were we born? Why do we exist? What is important in life? How does it all fit together?"

My grandfather used to tell me (Jim) a story about a man digging a ditch. Someone asked the man why he was doing that. He responded, "So I can earn money."

"Why do you want to earn money?"

"So I can buy meat," the man answered.

"Why do you want meat?"

"So I can be strong."

"Why do you want to be strong?"

"So I'll be able to dig this ditch."

Do you ever feel as if your life goes around in a circle like that? There's got to be more to living than just a circle of activities.

The second group of questions is about *our world and our environment.* Reevaluate why you live in this country—with this government, in this state, this neighborhood, this house. Think about why you go to your church, shop at your supermarket, and so on. Pick the best fit in your surroundings.

The third group of questions is about *relationships*. "Whom shall I love? Whom shall I let love me? With whom shall I be friends?" Jesus had various circles of friends, three close disciples—Peter, James, and John—and then the rest of the Twelve. In addition, he had seventy disciples, and finally a large crowd who followed him. He had different levels of commitment to each circle of friends. By midlife, our friendships have often been built for political purposes or because of obligations. Our relationships may not reflect who we are—they may be out of balance.

To be healthy, you need three distinctly different types of relationships. The diagram illustrates these. The circle on the right stands for YOU with your gifts, abilities, needs, and desires—the real you. Circle One has an arrow pointing to YOU. Similar to your relationships with God, you need relationships with people who enrich you and who don't take anything in return. Obviously, this is going to be God as well as other significant people, such as a teacher, leader, pastor, counselor, or special friend or relative—someone who nourishes you.

Notice also an arrow from Circle Two toward YOU and an arrow returning from YOU toward Circle Two. This is a "peer" relationship. You build up another person emotionally and spiritu-

Significant Relationships for a Balanced Life

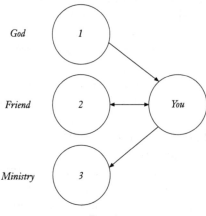

Figure 2

ally as much as that person strengthens you. It's fun to be with someone like this. You spend time talking, listening, and sharing. Yet when you leave each other, even though you have given and cared a lot, you feel nourished. In a true peer relationship, each one feels he or she has gained from the relationship. God has planned that in the sharing of two lives, each receives strength. You must have this kind of relationship to be whole and complete.

Next, notice an arrow from YOU to Circle Three. Circle Three represents your ministry. These are the people to whom you give yourself. Circle Three represents the part of the world that is enriched because of you. Ministry in other lives gives meaning beyond yourself.

When any of these relationships gets out of balance, the others will suffer. For example, if you have no peer relationships and very few relationships with significant others—such as God—then your ministry to people will become dry, sterile, a duty motivated by obligation. If you only have input from significant others, including God, and you have wonderful peer relationships but no ministry, then you are caught in a vicious cycle of "me-ism" without any life purpose outside of yourself.

The fourth group of midlife questions centers around *you as a person*. You're not the same person you were as a child, adolescent, or young adult. Who are you now? As a young adult, you may have thought you were the life of the party or a very serious person. Maybe you were a flirt or a philosopher. Did you think of yourself as a leader or a leaner? With the life experience and the growth you've had, you're not the same person—but who are you?

You may experience pain or fear as you ask the midlife questions. If you dig around too much, you might turn over a rock and find ugly bugs. What if you discover you're a hostile person—or overly sensitive to criticism? What if you're too passive, afraid to take risks—or too controlled by other people? What if you find you're aggressive, greedy, helpless, or don't really love people—just manipulate them? What if you are . . . and the list goes on and on. Remember, whatever you are has been an open secret to God all along—and he still loves you unconditionally.

A Smooth Road

All life transitions are made up of three stages. *First is the awareness stage.* Often awareness is triggered by a change event. Perhaps you feel a sense of irritation or an awareness that there is something more in life. For example, suppose you are considering returning to work. Before you decided to go back to work, there was some nagging sense of need or unfulfillment that caused you to make that decision.

The second stage is disruption. In order for you to go back to work, you have to break off the old lifestyle and start a new one. A mild-to-severe amount of disruption or confusion occurs in the process of moving to any new lifestyle or work.

The third stage is resolution. In this stage there are ups and downs. When you are comfortably adjusted to your new work experience, you will easily define yourself in both your job and your family life and capably carry out both. You feel settled again.

There are many transitions in our normal day-to-day experience that we don't even identify as transitions. For example, buying a new dress. First, there is a sense of need, a feeling of incompleteness that causes you to go through the activity of buying. Going to buy the dress is somewhat of a disruption in your schedule—and your budget. Finally there is the resolution—you are satisfied with the dress, it fits well, you look sharp, and nobody killed you for spending all that money.

Many major transitions occur in life, such as puberty, leaving home, finishing college, getting married, and having children. Major life transitions will come whether you choose them or not. You move inexorably from being a child to an adolescent—to a young adult—to a midlife adult—to a mellow adult—to an aging adult. Each of these transitions will demand a redefinition of your life structure. You have no choice about whether the transitions come, *but* the values that result from each experience *are* your decision.

Wet or Dry?

We are often asked, "What is the difference between a transition and a crisis?" A transition is a move from one settled state, through a moderate amount of disruption—to a second settled state. A crisis has greater disruption, usually including some sort of breakdown. The person in crisis is not able to function as previously.

For instance, imagine yourself standing on a dock on the edge of a beautiful little lake. There is a gentle breeze blowing, and tiny ripples cross the surface of the water. You're invited by a friend to go for a canoe ride. You've never been in a canoe before, so you are instructed by your friend to step carefully from the dock into the *exact center* of the canoe. If you step on one side or the other, the canoe will tip over immediately.

You want very much to please your friend, and it looks as if it would be fun to be out on the lake. Since you've never gone canoeing before, you decide to take the risk. Stage one in the crisis is the same as stage one in the transition—a desire for something different.

One foot is placed in the center of the canoe. Your other foot is still on the dock. You're in the middle of the transition, and everything is going along well. There is some disruption because part of your weight is in the canoe and part is yet on the solid dock. Now, if you can carefully bring your other leg into the canoe, keep your balance in the center of the canoe, and quietly sit down, you'll be all right—you've made a smooth transition.

A crisis, however, is when you have one foot in the center of the canoe, the other foot on the dock, and slowly the canoe begins to drift away from the dock. Your legs are spread ever wider. You've lost control. You make a mad grab backward for the dock—but your legs are spread too far. You fall into the lake, and in the process the canoe also tips over.

Now that's a crisis! Instead of moving from one stable position to a second stable position with only a minor disruption of fear and anxiety, you didn't make it. You went into the drink.

It's normal to experience some part of the passage as a calm transition and other parts as a severe crisis. It's possible to be having a severe identity crisis—Who am I? What am I going to accomplish in my life?—and at the same time have a very supportive and strong marriage. Or the opposite is possible. Both a crisis and a transition can be profitable because they force you to think about your value system and reorganize your priorities.

All of Life in Focus

A common human response is to avoid *pain* at the same time we are drawn toward *pleasure*. We need to add a third *p*. Our life ought to include *purpose*.

If we have purpose in our life, then we'll be able to put pain and pleasure into proper perspective. We'll be able to see the value in pain and not feel guilty about enjoying pleasure. *Purpose* gives us balance. You can't really have balance without a purpose or a reason for living. Again we're back to values.

James 1:2-4 (Conway free paraphrase) sums it up this way: "Jump for joy when a variety of trials and tests come into your life, because these very trials and tests produce stability, and this process of trials and tests, which produce stability, will bring about the ultimate result—maturity."

The point is we should be grateful when pain and trials come to our life, not for the trials themselves, but because of the growth they bring. Pain produces a strength that pleasure never can.

God Is Not a Killjoy

On the other hand, many Christian women are afraid to enjoy themselves. The more pain and hardship they have, the more effective they feel. These women imagine God to be just about as mean as Satan, only dressed in white clothes instead of red. They see him leaning over the banister of heaven, hollering down, "Aha! I saw you laughing down there. Cut that out! You're not supposed to have any fun."

The picture of God in the Bible is one of balance, with serious times of judgment *yet* the arm-around-the-shoulder type of counsel, the friend who sticks closer than a brother—and who all along loves us very deeply, who laughs and rejoices with us.

This section of the Bible always brings me a smile: "Cheer up, Zion! Don't be afraid! For the Lord your God has arrived to live among you. He is a mighty savior. He will rejoice over you with great gladness. With his love, he will calm all your fears. He will exult over you by singing a happy song. I will gather you who mourn for the appointed festivals; you will be disgraced no more" (Zephaniah 3:16-18).

God can use both a crisis and a smooth transition to bring growth in your life. He wants you to have purpose, direction, and perspective—to be able to understand what life is about, who you are, and how you fit into life.

Value Redefinition Cycle

The values you hold today—the importance you have given to each area, event, and experience in your life—are values you have built from many small choices over many years. You didn't make one choice for all time. You kept on reassessing choices and giving them more or less importance.

The following diagram should help you see how your values continue to be redefined by your decisions, by your actions, and by the events that result. In turn, those redefined values affect how you think of yourself and how you see the world around you. So, with a change event, the event not only affects you, but you interpret the event through your value system.

Suppose you wear glasses, and you're outside on a bright, sunny day. You can choose to use your sunglasses or not. The bright day influences your choice of glasses. But your choice also affects how you see the world. You are *not a victim* of your life events.

Now let's walk through the value redefinition cycle.

Notice point 1. From conception on, you have been receiving input that influenced how you will face future change events. Your relationships with your parents, relatives, and friends and your school experiences were part of your value system. This childhood value system, formed also by the small choices you made, has brought you to the early young adulthood thinking of yourself, life, and God (point 2). Let's imagine you are facing one of life's major change events—to marry or not.

Mr. Wonderful

Suppose at point 3 you met a wonderful man. You made the choice of that particular man on the basis of your values thus far in life (point 4). This change

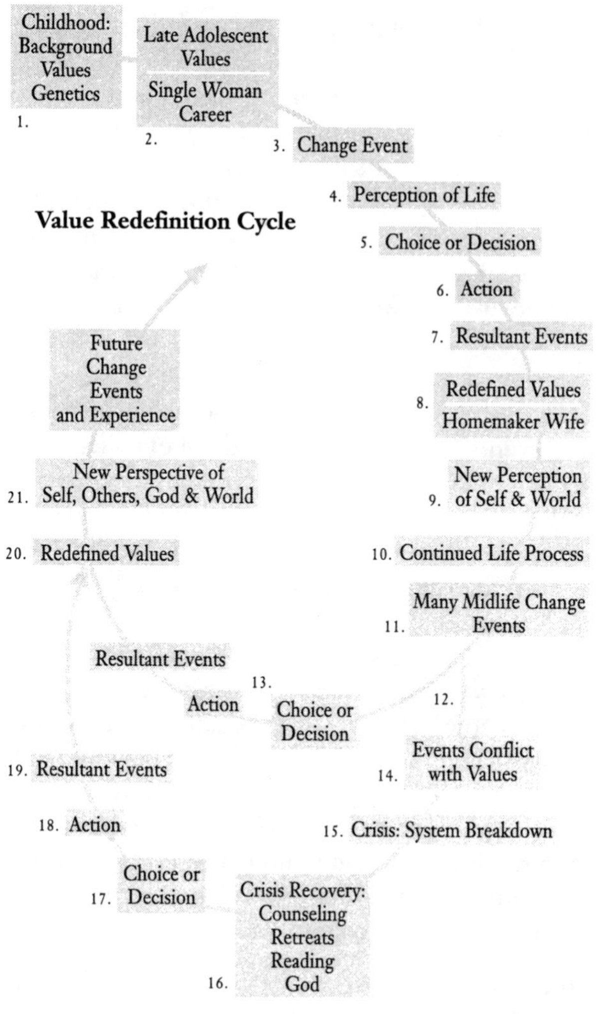

1. Childhood: Background Values Genetics

2. Late Adolescent Values / Single Woman Career

3. Change Event

4. Perception of Life

Value Redefinition Cycle

5. Choice or Decision

6. Action

7. Resultant Events

8. Redefined Values / Homemaker Wife

Future Change Events and Experience

9. New Perception of Self & World

21. New Perspective of Self, Others, God & World

20. Redefined Values

10. Continued Life Process

11. Many Midlife Change Events

Resultant Events

13. Action / Choice or Decision

12.

19. Resultant Events

14. Events Conflict with Values

18. Action

15. Crisis: System Breakdown

17. Choice or Decision

16. Crisis Recovery: Counseling Retreats Reading God

Figure 3

event will be a very powerful and life-changing event. You will never be the same. Your values influenced your selection of this man, but now your relationship with this man will also influence your value system. Here's how it works.

You made a decision to marry this man (point 5). That choice resulted in actions, events, and redefined values. You not only made a choice, but you actually married him. (See point 6.) Because of the decision you made, your actions had an impact on your values and influenced other events.

In this case we'll assume that some of the resultant events are that you dropped out of college and had your first child (point 7). The consequence was that your values were redefined (point 8). You now are a very different person with a different life perception than at point 4, which was an early young-adult view.

You see, it all started back at point 3 with a change event and your decision relating to it. That decision, the actions you took, and the resultant events all redefined your values. Look back at point 2. Your values at that point were strongly emphasizing a single woman with a career. Now your values have shifted to being a homemaker, caring for a husband and a child—you have temporarily dropped the career role.

You're Different Now

Point 9 on the cycle shows a new understanding of yourself and the world. You see yourself as a wife and mother, and you see the world as a friendly, enjoyable place to live. This view came from the positive experiences in your marriage and with your child's birth. These events redefined your values.

You continue the life process (point 10) by experiencing literally hundreds of change events. Some are rather minor, such as buying a new dress. Some are more important: a move to a larger apartment or to your first house. Some may be traumatic, such as when your first child is born and you realize the awesome responsibility of being an adequate parent.

Now we'll assume that you're in midlife (see figure 3, point 11), and several change events come at one time. Do you remember the clocks that we talked about in the earlier chapter? At midlife they all seem to go off at once. You're worried about getting older, gray-haired, and overweight. You wonder if you're losing your sexual appeal. Time is running out before you get things accomplished. Your children don't seem to need you anymore—and culture is pushing you aside. You may feel you are not quite "with it" in the career market.

Your husband may be preoccupied in his own mad dash to success, and your marriage may not be very satisfying. On top of all this, you discover your oldest daughter has been fooling around with drinking and sex, and your mother has become extremely dependent on you because of your father's recent stroke. That's enough to put anyone into stress—or a midlife crisis!

Transition or Crisis

At point 12 there are two separate paths. One arrow leads down toward a crisis, the other one follows the normal flow of choice, decision, action, and resultant events toward redefined values. The normal flow marked by point 13 indicates that even though there are many change events, they are assimilated as you pass through this transition. If you were growing and maturing in earlier life stages, then each of the earlier choices and decisions helped to prepare you for this onslaught of several events.

But look at point 14. If you have not been growing and changing in the young-adult years, then there are many change events that are *conflicting with your changing value system.* Each event is a jolting experience that sends you into confusion and crisis (point 15). (Conflict between our values and the change events results in crisis.)

Remember that any time there are multiple change events that are out of step with your previous value system, a crisis will be produced. That's why we keep emphasizing the importance of being reflective, thinking about your life, and not being afraid to wrestle with questions. It is better to face questions and life events, to redefine the events, and let the events redefine you and your value system, than to allow a crisis to build up.

Most people in a crisis don't need someone to tell them they are in a crisis. They already know their world seems to be coming apart. There are people, however, who refuse to change, hoping things will get better automatically without any thought or activity on their part.

When you get into a crisis, find the causes that triggered the crisis. Next, take one small area and work through it—ask who you are, who you want to be, and how you can accomplish the necessary changes.

For example, you may feel overly stressed by trying to meet all of the needs of your husband, children, and career. What you really want to do is run away. Try to discover the root causes. In this case, there is too much pressure and stress. You have accepted too much responsibility for other people's lives, and your reflex action is to escape.

By carefully looking at the situation, you may discover you can reduce stress by letting each family member be more accountable for himself and herself. At the same time, do restorative things for yourself, such as going for a walk, biking, skiing, window shopping, reading a good book, having coffee with a friend, or attending a retreat or special career seminar.

Warning Signs
If you are wondering about some of the early signs of crisis, look at the following list of the stress symptoms. If several apply, you probably are on the edge of a crisis. This list is from the book *Stress/Unstress*, written by Keith W. Sehnert, M.D.

- Decision making becomes difficult (both major and minor kinds).

- Excessive daydreaming or fantasizing about "getting away from it all"
- Increased use of cigarettes and/or alcohol
- Thoughts trail off while speaking or writing
- Excessive worrying about everything
- Sudden outbursts of temper and hostility
- Paranoid ideas and mistrust of friends and family
- Forgetfulness about appointments, deadlines, dates
- Reversals in usual behavior[1]

Crisis means there has been a breakdown of the system (point 15). Crisis may be indicated by negative activities or thinking—depression, involvement with alcohol, an affair, or inability to concentrate. Any abrupt life change would indicate a breaking down of your life system—your personality is trying to compensate.

Recovery—at Last
Some of the normal process in a crisis ultimately will be helpful for helping a person (point 16). For example, many people in a crisis want to be alone, to sleep or to spend time thinking. These activities can be very helpful. Extra rest can equip you to handle problems. Time away from people will give you perspective on ingredients for recovery.

Allowing God to nourish you physically and emotionally, as he did Elijah (1 Kings 19:1-18), is important. We have found that listening to music and reading Christian biographies and Scripture are rebuilding to us. Sometimes we simply leaf through several books of the Bible, reading verses about God's love and care that we've underlined in earlier years.

Crisis recovery, however, often requires more than just being alone or getting more rest. (Being in the woods or by a lake or seashore is very therapeutic for the two of us.) You must think through your values or you may not really recover from the crisis. It's helpful to talk to a trusted friend or a professional counselor or be in a group.

Times with other people should be unstressful and pleasant. You may have trouble going to some social events if they produce pressure. Understand the source of the stress and then deliberately redefine your values. At point 17 you are started back on the path again. You are now making decisions. Perhaps you decide to return to school and to work on your marriage.

Now carry out appropriate actions, such as starting a refresher course or going to a marriage enrichment retreat (point 18). At point 19 there are events that result from your action. You take a part-time job, or you spend additional time away with your husband for a weekend.

The Redefined You

When you reach point 20, you are back to redefined values. Whichever route you took, you are a different person. You still may think of yourself as a mother and wife, but perhaps now you have elevated career.

If you are single, you may have come to a fresh acceptance of your singleness, a clearer understanding of friends, and a refocusing of your career. Your redefined values now give you a different perspective of yourself, other people, God, and the world (point 21).

You have gone through a unique series of experiences, whichever route you took, and you are a unique person with a new outlook. This unique perspective will cause you to react differently from any other woman, even though you both may experience the similar future change events—deaths of your parents or your husbands.

Life is filled with thousands of change events. Our values are continually redefined, and it is our value system and the perspective we receive from our values that cause us to react uniquely.

Same but Different

Reevaluating is a normal process in life. Don't be discouraged because you're rethinking your values. Every change event causes this process to take place, and the process will continue to the moment of your death.

Perhaps a way to illustrate this might be for you to think with me (Jim) about a lake that was very important in my childhood and teen years. It is Rex Lake, near Akron, Ohio.

When I came into the world, Rex Lake was already there. As a baby and a young child, I sat on the shore looking out at the lake and its different moods and settings. There were times when the lake was very still, times when it had waves, and times when the sun made a giant path across the whole lake. I saw the lake from my viewpoint on the shore.

As I got into grade school, but before I could swim, I was allowed to walk along the shore of the lake and explore from Sandy Beach (about two hundred yards to the west of our cottage) to the channel (about two hundred yards to the east). And I was permitted to go onto the dock. I could now look at the lake from those several new vantage points.

When I learned to swim, I was then permitted to take the rowboat or the canoe out onto Rex Lake. Now I could roam anywhere I wanted around the lake. My brother, sisters, and I had great fun on hot summer days—turtle hunting, fishing, exploring the island, and checking out that mysterious "other side" of the lake. I was able to pick blueberries along the bank and apples from an abandoned apple orchard on the other side. Yes, my world was expanding. The same is true as we grow older: We continue to explore the *same values*, but we are looking at them from a *different perspective*.

Enlarged Perception

When I became a teenager, I was able to venture through the channel into the other lakes. A whole chain of lakes was there to investigate. New beaches, inlets, and coves were waiting to be explored. That's when I first saw a sailboat, and I immediately fell in love with sailing.

During those years I was also allowed to take the small motorboat and go water skiing on Rex Lake. I swam the entire mile length of Rex Lake several times each summer. It was the same lake, but now I was more a master of it. Life's value issues are the same, but as we see them from each age and each change event, we look at those values differently—and those values change us.

In my late teens the lake took on a romantic dimension, with a streak of moonlight coming across the lake to meet me while I paddled quietly in the canoe with a pretty young woman seated in front of me. I was seeing the same lake but now through different eyes. I had a deeper understanding of the lake and its meaning, just as life experience gives us a deeper understanding of our value system and the kind of people that we are becoming.

Not only was I seeing the lake differently as I grew older, but the lake also was changing me. To this day Rex Lake has caused me to feel a strong pull toward water, sailing, swimming, the sun, and enjoying the outdoors. Our value system changes us as much as we change our value system.

Mysterious yet Magnificent

John Powell in *Fully Human, Fully Alive* says, "There is no painless entrance into a new and fully human life."[2] Each transition in life can be an upsetting experience. There is a time of uncertainty, maybe even fear.

Recently I took friends to Laguna Beach, here in California. I wanted them to enjoy a good climb on the rocks, but when we got down to the shore from the grassy cliff above, the tide was high. We could not get around one of the rocky points to explore a cave I knew was just beyond that point. We discovered, however, for a moment while a wave was out, that we could go over the rocks quickly to a high spot, then wait there until the wave went out again. Then we could run across the exposed rocks to another high point. Finally we got to the mysterious little cave.

From the cave there was a magnificent view of the surf crashing against the rocks right in front of us, and the sun setting behind Catalina Island. If we had not been willing to make those dashes between the waves, we would not have experienced that special little cave and sunset. From the top of the cliff no one would know a cave existed.

Life is like that. Each change event puts us in a precarious situation, and we realize again, "There is no painless entrance into a new and fully human life."

Allow Life to Question You

Doug (real name), one of our close friends in Illinois, repeatedly asked me (Jim), "Do you enjoy what you're doing?" Or he would rephrase his question, "Why are you doing what you're doing?"

Doug was challenging my value system. He wanted me to rethink my life.

The psychiatrist Viktor Frankl said, "Let life question you."[3] Let the events of life challenge your values instead of seeing them as enemies that are disturbing your life. Change events are opportunities.

Allow yourself to be questioned by every event and person you meet. "The needy, unattractive person asks me how much I can love. The death of a dear one asks me what I really believe about death and how profitably I can confront loss and loneliness. A beautiful day or a beautiful person asks me how capable I am of enjoyment. Solitude asks me if I really like myself and enjoy my own company. A good joke asks me if I have a sense of humor. A very different type person from a background very dissimilar to my own asks me if I am capable of empathy and understanding. Success and failure ask me to define my ideas of success and failure. Suffering asks me if I really believe I can grow through adversity. Negative criticism directed to me asks me about my sensitivities and self-confidence. The devotion and commitment of another to me asks me if I will let myself be loved."[4]

My friend Doug was asking me these questions when I was a busy pastor, and my response was, "Well, these people all have needs—somebody must help them." However, it was this very distorted anxiety to meet the needs of every person who crossed my path that partially caused my own midlife crisis. Because I had not been willing to adapt as the events of life questioned me, I soon found myself in a trap with my value system out of step with many of my change events. The result was my midlife crisis.

I (Sally) feel the trauma I experienced as I began my transition into midlife also came from a mismatch of values and change events. The difference for me, however, was not that I had been *unwilling* to change but that I was *unaware* I needed to. My generation of women had little preparation for midlife. I went from year to year without a refining of my value system. When I was confronted with the need to think, I didn't even know I needed to—much less *how*.

Choosing to Grow at Midlife

You are the person you are today because of a series of events and choices you have made. The way to work through a midlife crisis is to ask what you need in your life now. Then systematically tackle each one of the troubling change events to bring about a satisfactory resolution.

The following will help you grow and change:

1. *Spend time reflecting.* Think about who you are, where you've come from, your past value system, and the events that are taking place in your life now. Then carefully think through the options before you. Reflection gives the opportunity to carefully consider your next decisions and how those decisions will redefine your values.

2. *Meet with a group of people with whom you can talk*. Other people give you an opportunity to test what you have been thinking in your personal reflection time. Talking with others also lets you ventilate feelings and allows you to hear how others react to the same change event you're going through.

3. *Get ideas from outside sources*. You need to learn about the midlife change events you are going through. Read books, attend seminars and listen to other people's experiences. Reading the Bible provides both information and perspective. Unless you get outside input, you are likely to stew in your own juices—which could lead you into depression.

4. *Allow God to be involved*. The first three ingredients will be more effective if you allow God to be the center of each one.

Suppose one sunny day you sail a boat out of Newport Harbor in California into the ocean and north along the coast. (Here's another sailing story—have you noticed I like sailing?) You enjoy sailing with the fantastic view of the coastal cities in the Los Angeles Basin, with a magnificent view of the mountains in the backdrop, a salt breeze in your face, and that deep, clear, blue ocean all around you.

About 2:30 in the afternoon you notice that Los Angeles is slipping into the distance, and you decide it's time to turn around. You also notice the wind is starting to die down. You're heading south, but by three o'clock it is dead calm. Your boat doesn't have a motor, and you're almost helpless as you wait for the wind to come up.

Later, darkness settles in, and a gentle breeze does pick up, but so does panic. It's dark out there. You can see the city lights of Los Angeles, and you know that somewhere south of there is the Newport Harbor—but where exactly? You keep sailing south. It's got to be here somewhere. If only somebody in your boat knew where the harbor was and how to get into it in the dark. Now the problem isn't the lack of wind—it's how to find the harbor.

Let us put it to you bluntly. God is the one who has created you. He's been through life with millions of people, and he's the one who can give you insights for your life at midlife—which are absolutely crucial. To use our sailing story, God wants to come on board—into your life—and he wants to steer you. Ask him to do that.

Here's a practical how-to. When you get up in the morning, say to him, "God, I'm not sure where I'm going. Use the events surrounding me, and bring people and ideas across my path to help me go in the right direction." Then, spend time reading from the Bible. If it's your first time, you might like to start your Bible reading with the Gospel of John. You don't have to read it all in one day. Take a chapter or a few verses at a time. As you read, specifically say to God, "Give me new insights that will help me to go the right way."

When you finish John, start at the beginning of the New Testament and read all the way up to the book of Revelation. Then you might like to start reading the Psalms and the Proverbs. Every day say, "God, you've helped thousands of others—give me the ideas and insights I need. Bring the people I need into my life. Help me to think the right ideas as I quietly think and reflect." What you're asking God to do is to become the manager of your life or, in sailing terms, the captain.

Sally and I have sailed at night with a gentle breeze and the moon coming across the water. There is a stillness and a beauty about night sailing that can't be duplicated in daylight—as long as you know where you're going. The difference is knowing where you are going. And God can give you that perspective—and that peace.

Preventing a Crisis

"How can I prevent a midlife crisis?" This is the most common question we are asked by young adults or early midlife people. Everyone is going to experience a midlife *transition*, but this transition can be very positive as you are forced to think about your life values for the next life stages. It's not good to suppress feelings and value questions during the midlife transition.

Following are suggestions that we've found will lessen the intensity of a midlife transition. Then your transition will become a process of easily absorbing several change events without a crisis occurring.

Discover Seed Problems

Vickie, a midthirties woman, is married with four children. Her life clearly shows the seed problems that could grow into a crisis by her late thirties.

She is a very intelligent woman who did well academically during college. She is a high achiever, somewhat of a perfectionist, and extremely adept socially. She is a warm person, committed to people and to God. She was a leader on her campus, in her sorority, and in a major Christian campus group. She was also strongly affected by the women's movement and definitely wanted to have a career.

During her last year of college in California she met a graduate student and fell deeply in love with him. They were married after her graduation. He encouraged her development as a woman and urged her to exercise her leadership ability.

They both attended graduate school. Mark earned a degree which prepared him for pastoral ministry, and Vickie earned a master's degree in developmental psychology from a state university. While Mark finished his degree, Vickie continued her career and became strongly sympathetic to biblical feminism.

UNFULFILLED-NEED SEED

After Mark's graduation, they took a position with a parachurch organization working with students. Mark and Vickie had understood that Vickie would be equally involved in ministry and thus be fulfilled in her own career direction. This was not the case. Her supervisors tended to see her more in the role of homemaker. Since she did not receive a separate salary, they saw her only as a support person to her husband.

Vickie felt a deep resentment toward this organization—and somewhat toward her husband. She wrestled hard with this frustrating career situation, trying to meet her needs with short-term, unpaid ministry opportunities.

In her late twenties Vickie had a growing desire to have a child. It may have been part of the late-twenties' assessment—wanting to get settled into life. Or it may have been a growing compensation caused by her frustration with the lack of a meaningful career. Four children were born in rapid succession, and now at age thirty-four she is pregnant again. The last three pregnancies were unplanned. She does not show signs of entering a midlife transition or a crisis—but the seeds are there.

COMPETITION SEED

More seeds of Vickie's future crisis are seen in their recent move to a church in a Texas university city where Mark is the senior pastor. He is responsible for preaching, counseling, and the direction of the church. At age thirty-seven Mark has a strong need to make this church successful, and he will give a great deal of energy to his ministry. He will divert time and energy from his family as he tries to establish a significant ministry before he is forty.

The suburban community into which they have moved is strongly affected by the local university and by financial opulence. Vickie feels that she is in competition with the young, attractive female students at the university as well as with the fashionable community women, who are able to buy expensive clothes—well beyond her meager budget.

Because she is pregnant again, she is putting on weight. She feels she is an unsuccessful competitor with the university students and the women of the town. The responsibility of caring for active children is almost overwhelming. Her husband is preoccupied with succeeding in his career. She also continues to feel the smoldering embers of her own unfulfilled career.

On top of all of this, they have decided not to have any more children—so Vickie will have a sterilization surgery after this fifth child's birth. She is experiencing unfulfillment in several areas. The sterilization is forcing a decision on her which she feels will take away part of her womanness. Other birth control measures have failed, so she knows the surgery is necessary—but she feels sad.

FATIGUE SEED

Even though Vickie does not yet show signs of a midlife crisis, she is beginning to hint in those directions with phrases such as, "It's difficult to compete with other women in this community," or "I'm tired of carrying everybody in the family—meeting all of their emotional needs. What about my career?" But it's only a few short sentences until she may be saying, "It's got to stop. I'm burned out. It's time for my needs to be met!"

If you are hoping to prevent or reduce a midlife crisis, first, recognize the potential seeds that may grow into a midlife crisis. Remember what you thought you would be—*your dreams*—from your adolescent and young-adult years. Are they being fulfilled? Dreams that are not being fulfilled will likely cause you problems unless your value system changes.

Seeds of midlife crisis can also be found as you evaluate *your stresses.* What causes you to feel burned out, abused, or exploited?

You may find midlife crisis seeds as you consider areas of *competition.* Are you competing with the younger generation or with women who are in exciting careers or with women who get to be full-time homemakers? The drive toward competition indicates an unsatisfied area.

Loss is a key word. Accumulated losses have the potential of bringing about a midlife crisis.

Communicate Your Needs

The second aspect for preventing or reducing a midlife crisis is to educate the people around you. Talk about what is happening in your life. Communicate very directly and specifically where you sense potential danger. If you're not married, talk with close, intimate friends, especially if you sense a growing urgency to be a mother and to nurture.

Friends can help you think through the concerns you're wrestling with. If you don't educate people about your need, then your bottled-up desires may become explosive. Your new longings may cause you to make panic decisions, resulting in long-term sadness and loss. Your friends will help you answer the question "Now, given this situation, what do I do?"

Compensate

Compensation is the third important aspect of lessening a midlife crisis, and it asks the question "What do I do to make up for a deficit I feel?" Look again at the illustration of Vickie, the thirty-four-year-old mentioned earlier. How can she compensate to head off a crisis?

Let's assume she's already thought about the potential seeds of her own midlife crisis. Let's also assume she has extensively reflected on which values are important. Suppose she has also started educating her husband, children, and other significant people about her needs. Now let's think of a deliberate plan to compensate—to meet her needs so she can lessen or prevent a midlife crisis.

CAREER REENTRY

Vickie might work on a plan for her career reentry. Additional continuing education or skill updating might be needed so that the reentry will be an easy transition.

Five children are going to produce a great deal of parenting responsibility. So another compensation might be for her husband, Mark, to carry more of the parenting responsibility. This request is likely to be very difficult because he is deeply committed in his own career. But if he can understand that ten years from now he will wish he had put more time into his children, he may be willing to shift some of his time priority to parenting his family—instead of just parenting the church.

TIME FOR THE MARRIAGE

Another important area to adjust is her marriage. With heavy career and parenting responsibilities, Mike and Vickie are likely ignoring their couple relationship. They need time with each other. Perhaps after the children have gone to bed they can sit with a cup of coffee and talk. Maybe once a month they could spend time together answering the question "How is our marriage doing?" They also need fun so that their marriage is not a business.

CHILDREN PITCH IN

Children can be involved in the compensation process. Teach them to assume more responsibility. The family is a team. Mom and Dad are not the servants. We all should serve each other. Sometimes children don't realize the pressure their parents are under. They don't fully understand by just being told. They may have to be put "on their own" with some responsibilities—if they don't do their tasks, then the whole family suffers. Mom and Dad are not going to jump in and do their job for them.

Grade school children can easily assume responsibility for preparing simple meals, setting the table, and cleaning up afterward. They can also do part of the housecleaning and the yard work with their parents. Older children can take more responsibility—meal preparation, laundry, taking younger children to activities, or grocery shopping.

A NEW LOOK

Vickie is feeling a strong competition with younger as well as fashionable women. Another compensation might be a spa membership to get her back in shape after the fifth child is born. If the membership is provided now, she will look forward to being in control of her life and feeling better about herself.

Compensation may also include the family budget. Perhaps a shift of funds to enable Vickie to buy one classy outfit with several changeable accessories. Then she would feel more comfortable in her role as a leader in her church and community.

SUPPORTIVE FRIENDS

Regular discussion with close women friends will help her rethink her gains and the losses. Close friends can provide stability during these potentially dangerous value redefinition years. Talking will also help to diffuse stress and give her an accountability relationship so that she doesn't feel she is experiencing life on her own.

The purpose of compensation is to bring control back into your life—to offer alternatives and to meet your needs. The common cry of women in midlife crisis is that things are out of control. Target your adjustments to restore choice and control in your life.

Balance

Strive for balance in all of your life. You were created by God as a multifaceted person. If you ignore any area, it will become the squeaking wheel that cries out for grease. For example, if you enter a career, you also must meet the other aspects of your personality. All of your energy must not be focused only on your career.

If you are a single career woman, don't ignore your living quarters. Do they really speak of who you are? Do they meet your emotional needs—are you nourished by being there? Where you live needs to be a place where you feel "at home."

Also, your career cannot substitute for your need for deep interpersonal relationships. Keep balancing your life so that friendships are continuing to develop in depth as well as in number.

ROLE BALANCE

Keep your life balanced by having a ministry with people. Aim for a ministry that is different from your work. Be creative—work with underprivileged kids, with hearing-impaired people, or at a halfway house for people who've had brain trauma.

Often women are trapped into working more hours than men do in middle or upper management. There is a terrible male chauvinism in business, which says, "Women don't really want to work—they don't really want to be in leadership." The woman in upper management has to prove her abilities and commitment by longer hours. Don't be so desperate to prove yourself that you get your total life out of balance.

An article in the *Denver Post* entitled "Women at

Midlife Shatter Stereotypes" reported a study showing that women need two basic elements in their lives. One is "mastery (feeling important and worthwhile, with a sense of self-esteem and control)," and the second is "pleasure (finding life enjoyable, measured by happiness, satisfaction and optimism)."[1]

The researchers, who evaluated three hundred midlife women, indicated that the people who showed the highest degree of satisfaction in life were the women who were married, with children, and in high-prestige jobs.[2]

LIFE-SPAN BALANCE

Living a balanced life may not always be possible. There may have been times—for example, when you were in school—when your life was unbalanced with heavy study commitments. Other times—such as with your first child—the balance of your life shifted to that child. Many choices can temporarily unbalance your life—but the goal is to get equilibrium as soon as possible.

Do you remember when you were a kid on a teeter-totter? You were OK as long as the teeter-totter was balanced and the board was going up and down smoothly. But sometimes two kids would jump on the other end of the teeter-totter, and you'd be way up in the air. Soon you'd start sliding down the board toward the middle. It's the same with life. You can tolerate being out of balance for a little while, but you must get the balance back as soon as possible, or else everything slides off the board.

Gail Sheehy surveyed sixty thousand people, evaluating, among other things, their well-being in life. Regarding women, she says, "The women in their forties and fifties who came out at the top of my well-being scale were mostly women who had made commitments to marriage, career, and motherhood, all before the end of their twenties. They did not postpone. Usually theirs were *serial commitments;* sometimes they waited to have children until they passed thirty. If there was a trade-off, it was that for the most part the highest-well-being women were not extraordinary successes in a professional sense. Few of them had gained much public recognition. Probably they had resisted devoting to their work the kind of time and absorption required to make a bigger mark."[3]

Sheehy further points out, "By contrast, the lowest-satisfaction women in this generation group had followed the more traditional path of postponing outside work until their families were fully established."[4] When we ask, "How can we prevent or reduce the intensity of a midlife crisis?" a part of the answer must be, "By living a balanced life." Remember, you don't have to do everything at one time in your life.

THE FUTURE GIVES BALANCE

Hope for the future will also help balance your life. In the past certain areas didn't go as you planned.

Now at midlife you are making necessary adjustments. Being future oriented will help you enjoy the best years of your life. You're at a powerful time in life, with physical strength, wisdom, and life experience.

Youth are slaves of their dreams, and old women often live with their past and regrets. It is the midlife woman who has all the pieces of the puzzle and whose life can make a real difference. Allow your strength and experience to give your life balance at this crucial time.

Spiritual Growth

The fifth major area for reducing or preventing a midlife crisis is your personal spiritual life. You need more than involvement with a church—you must know God in a personal way, as a friend. We will call it having a walk with God.

WALKING WITH GOD

We describe a personal relationship with God as a walk because it is an ongoing experience—not a panic confession because of a problem. Perhaps these four basic concepts will help you:

1. *Facing God.* Knowing God in a personal way means that you allow him to confront you about the way you've lived your personal life. Facing God means you confess to him the things that he brings to your attention—from your past or present life. Confession means that you say the same thing about your own errors that God says about them.

In other words, confession is agreeing with God about what was—or is—wrong. (See 1 John 1:8.)

2. *Forgiveness.* A second aspect of walking with God is to ask for forgiveness. It's simple. You say, "God, I know I was wrong. Please forgive me." (See Psalm 51.)

Sometimes women ask God for partial forgiveness about little stuff but never really face God in honesty. Or we see the other side, the repeated confessing of error but never receiving forgiveness. You need to both confess your sin frankly and then accept his forgiveness. You can walk away from your past because of God's forgiveness. He has forgotten it—as well as forgiven it. (See Psalm 103.)

The biggest sin you need to face is not some evil action from your past but the fact that you've kept God at arm's length. In essence you've said, "God, you stay up there in heaven, and I'll stay down here on earth—and we'll both do our own thing."

Face God about the distance you've allowed between yourself and him. Ask him to come into your life and to become part of all you do and think. Jesus, who is God, says very simply, "Look! Here I stand at the door and knock. If you hear me calling and open the door, I will come in, and we will share a meal as friends" (Revelation 3:20).

So, walking with God means you have faced God with your past by confessing your sins to him, and you've asked his forgiveness. Now you have given him control of your life.

3. *Communication.* Walking with God also means

you talk with him through the normal activities of your day. It is more than just spending an hour in church on Sunday morning or in your small weekly Bible study group. Communication is the moment-by-moment interaction with a friend. You share life together and are open to his promptings and leadings. "What do you think about this, God?" "OK, I'm for that! Thanks, God!"

Each day spend time reading the Bible. As you begin reading, ask God to guide you into truth (John 16:13). Jesus promises to reveal himself to those who want to obey him (John 14:21, 23). God wants to have a personal relationship with you. He will reveal himself more and more day by day as you allow this process to happen.

Some people ask, "How does God speak to you?" Think of it this way: As you read the Bible, look for ideas or phrases that jump out at you—phrases for you right now. Then try to incorporate those ideas into your life that day. God speaks to you through sections of Scripture, through impressions that he gives as you read and reflect.

4. *Trust.* Another aspect of walking with God is to rely on God. In the Psalms a beautiful phrase tells us what God wants in this relationship with us: "Trust me in your times of trouble, and I will rescue you" (Psalm 50:15). Believing in God means trusting him with our life situations. But the question always comes—*Can* I trust God? Or, even more—*Will* I trust God?

Dick, an engaged student, needed help because

his fiancée, Pam, was being harassed by her former boyfriend, Ralph. Dick was extremely distressed as he asked me (Jim) what to do. Pam had told Ralph their relationship was all over. She explained she was engaged and didn't want to talk to him anymore. Pam's family had also explained this to Ralph. He had even been confronted by other friends as well as by Dick himself. But Ralph didn't seem to catch on.

Now Dick asked, "Should I get a restraining order against Ralph? Should we move away? (Although Ralph has threatened to follow.) He's a very violent man. We're afraid of him. In the past when he has gotten drunk, he's been despondent and acts like a wild man."

I explained that a restraining order was not going to keep Ralph from harming anyone. It might make him angrier. And there was not much use in Dick's going to him again because, as Pam's fiancé, he was viewed as the enemy.

I said, "You need somebody who is a friend. Someone who can get inside of him and appeal to him." Dick assured me there was no one like that.

I told him that my suggestion might sound strange, but I would suggest he gather six or eight friends and pray for God to change this ex-boyfriend's heart. Dick looked at me incredulously. How could I suggest such a dumb, impractical thing as that with all of my counseling degrees? Wasn't there something else he could do?

I said, "Remember, you're studying to be a pastor. Not many months from now you're going to be confronted with the same kind of problem from many difficult life situations. Now is a good time to learn to believe God, to depend totally on him, to 'trust me in your times of trouble, and I will rescue you'" (Psalm 50:15).

He said, "I do believe in prayer, but this is just not going to work. You don't know this guy."

I replied, "Well, at least I'm going to be praying, and I'd encourage you to get your friends to pray."

About two weeks later Dick stopped me. "You'll never believe what happened! Ralph's mother got hold of Ralph and told him flat out the romance with Pam was over and he should stop bothering the two of them."

I asked Dick, "Who told her to do that?"

He smiled and said, "Maybe God did it in response to our prayers."

Walking with God means that in the tough times, when everything seems impossible, you believe God. It's easy for us, Jim and Sally, the married couple, to believe in God and think he is great when everything is going wonderfully well in our lives. But the real test is when we've just had a fight and we're angry with each other. When we don't feel like making up and don't want to pray together. Then the question is, "Do we really believe God now?"

Maybe you've just been passed over for a promotion because of office politics. You were the logical one to get it. In times like that, can we still believe the verse "And we know that God causes everything to work together for the good of those who love God and are called according to his purpose for them" (Romans 8:28)? In other words, to believe God is to really put our life in his hands and trust him with *whatever* happens.

5. *Let God be God.* Walking with God also means we allow God to be God. You see, Dick's problem was that he wanted to take control of the situation. We humans enjoy control.

Letting God be God means you recognize that *you are the servant* and *he is God.* Sometimes we treat God as if he were a genie in a bottle. We think if we rub the little magic bottle called prayer, God will pop out and say, "What is your wish?"

Walking with God means you allow him to be sovereign—in absolute control in your life.

LET GOD BE MYSTERIOUS
Letting God be God also means that you allow him to be mysterious or unknowable. He knows things we will never know. We are only finite human beings—he is the eternal God, the Creator, who made us and everything in the universe. It is true that God wants to reveal himself to us. The Bible says that revealing God to us was part of why Jesus came into the world: "Anyone who has seen me has seen the Father! . . . I am in the Father and the Father is in me" (John 14:9-10).

However, Scripture also says that God and men don't think or function on the same level: "My thoughts are completely different from yours," says the Lord. "And my ways are far beyond anything you could imagine. For just as the heavens are higher than the earth, so are my ways higher than your ways and my thoughts higher than your thoughts" (Isaiah 55:8-9).

When you walk with God, you acknowledge that you are the servant and he is the Lord, who knows more than you do. At the same time, you acknowledge that he is the God who loves you and wants the very best for you: "'For I know the plans I have for you,' says the Lord. 'They are plans for good and not for disaster, to give you a future and a hope'" (Jeremiah 29:11).

Whatever you may be going through now in your life, God's purpose is to use it for your maturing. He has a future and a hope for you. God is not going to abandon you. But he doesn't promise to eliminate difficulties. Remember the classic Scripture that says, "Even when I walk through the dark valley of death, I will not be afraid" (Psalm 23:4). It isn't saying that if we walk with God we don't have to go through the valley. But he promises to go through the valley with us, whatever those valleys of our lives may be.

Proverbs 31 describes a truly great woman. Some of the qualities of her life are her walk with God and her confidence in God for whatever the future holds. The Bible describes her: "She is clothed with strength and dignity, and she laughs with no fear of the future" (Proverbs 31:25).

The midlife woman who walks with God, frankly facing her past, her present, and confessing her sin, accepting his forgiveness, communicating openly, believing him, and allowing him to be sovereign in her life, will be given the qualities of "strength and dignity."

The following lines, written by a single career woman, express some of the struggles she faced in life, yet it expresses her deep sense of God's being in control of her life and her future.

> *Sometimes I feel like a stream, flowing, hidden in*
>   *the woods,*
> *beautiful if anyone would look through the trees to*
>   *see.*
> *But left alone to stumble on and on across the*
>   *rocks.*
> *But God arranged my course, set*
>   *all the stones in place, put the trees*
>   *to shelter and hide.*
> *So let me race on, sometimes still, sometimes*
>   *bubbling,*
>   *to that place where He will collect me*
>   *into the ocean of His love.*[5]

Helping a Woman
in Crisis

You can't do it on your own. God designed you to be in relationships with people. He planned that we help each other. Only as we help do we become fully human.

For a moment, think back over the issues we have been considering. None of these can be successfully handled without other people. We've talked about career, family, personal identity, and the various value questions at midlife. We've also talked about experiencing traumatic losses, depression, sagging self-esteem, and the impact of culture and physical aging. All of these require other people to be involved to help you work through these stressful times as you become a stronger, more mature you.

In many places the Scriptures urge us to be involved with each other. Sometimes we are described as stones in a building, each one fitted to the other, supporting and building on the other. But perhaps the best image of our interrelatedness—our needing each other—is that of the body. The body has many parts, yet each performs an important service for other members of the body: "Now there are different kinds of spiritual gifts . . . given to each of us as a means of helping the entire church" (1 Corinthians 12:4, 7).

This same chapter also reminds us that each part of the body is important. We can never say we don't need each other: "The eye can never say to the hand, 'I don't need you.' The head can't say to the feet, 'I don't need you.' . . . If one part suffers, all the parts suffer with it, and if one part is honored, all the parts are glad. Now all of you together are Christ's body, and each one of you is a separate and necessary part of it" (1 Corinthians 12:21, 26-27). We're not intended to make it on our own. We really do need one another.

Everyone's Always "Fine"

If we listen in on conversations at the average church, we will hear mostly positive stories of how great things are going. Here's the dialogue: "How are you?" "Fine." "How are things going?" "Great." We have all learned it's polite to say "fine." We've been convinced that church is not the place to share our problems.

Now, here's the problem: If God has given each of us abilities to help one another, how are we ever going to help if we don't know about needs? Suppose God has given me (Sally) the gifts of wisdom, discernment, and counsel. If I never know of your need, I will not have an opportunity to exercise my gifts, and you miss receiving the valuable help God intended for you.

Only as you share your struggles can others use their gifts. When you don't let people know your needs, you're cheating them out of the opportunity to use their spiritual gifts. When you share problems, you are not imposing on your fellow body members; you are giving them the opportunity to grow as Christians and practice the biblical teachings to help others.

Let people help you! Forget the excuses that keep you away from people—"They're too busy." "My problems are too big." "I don't want to be a bother." "I'll work it out myself." Instead, give the body of Christ an opportunity to use their gifts to strengthen you.

If you smash your little finger, your whole body reacts in pain. In the same way, when you're a wounded person, everyone around you suffers. When you're not emotionally healthy, you can't strengthen other people. So loosen up and let the body help you. That's the way God built us.

Now we want to focus our attention specifically on several different individuals or groups of people who can help. These next pages are also specifically targeted as coaching guides for people who will be helping the woman as she goes through midlife crisis.

The Employer Helps

The question asked by many employers is, "Why should I help a woman going through midlife crisis? I am concerned about my bottom line—profitability."

The answer is very selfish: "No man is an island." Without your employees, you can't make it. Employees provide your "profitability." If you are seen as an employer who simply chews up people and spits them out, then you have a suspicious group of employees who are not really committed to you—or your product. They are working for money. That's a dangerous group to have as employees.

Reaching out in concern for the development of your employees expresses your care. In turn, they care for you and your organization. You become a team rather than competitors.

One of our students, Mel, had an impossible boss who was always demanding blood from everyone. Mel said, "I couldn't believe one man could be so obnoxious, so self-seeking, so unwilling to give an inch."

Mel continued, "I never met a man who earned his hate so well. But sadly one day while I was talking to the boss, he told me he was a Christian. Yet commitment to Christ never showed in his attitude." He went on to say, "One Christmas all of the employees wrapped several packages with the loveliest of gift paper, bows and all, and left them anonymously on the boss's desk. The card said, 'From your crew,' but the boxes were all empty."

Employer, you can help by becoming more sensitive to the needs of your people. Provide opportunities for them to talk. Let them ventilate problems they have with the job, and talk about things they're wrestling with in their own lives.

If you have women employees in their thirties or forties, it would be helpful to give them this book, *Women in Midlife Crisis.* Giving them a fresh flower for their desks will also help, but a book or a pamphlet will probably have more impact. A book keeps saying for you, "I'm concerned for my people."

Her Friends Help

During the midlife years there's a normal shuffling of friends. Because we're changing, we outgrow people—or they outgrow us. If you're a friend of someone going through midlife crisis, realize that she is likely to shuffle you out of her life unless you really understand her and seek to meet her changing needs.

Midlife is an era when time is at a premium. You may feel you're being shuffled out of a woman's life, but in reality, she just doesn't have time for people—period.

Sometimes you feel you're being put off. This commonly happens when a person is going through traumatic changes in her value system and she's not sure how you'll react to her new values.

I (Sally) remember on one occasion saying to a midlife woman who was obviously showing midlife stress, "I'd be glad to sit down and chat with you sometime." She assured me that everything was OK. I saw her on another occasion a few weeks later, and she still seemed stressed. I said to her, "Both Jim and I have had a midlife crisis. It's not fun, but we've learned some things, and perhaps we could be of help—even if just to listen." Her response was, "Thanks a lot. It's really good to know you care, but there's really no problem."

I knew there was a problem, so I pressed again the next time we met. This time she said, "I sense that *you* have a need to talk to *me*, so let's go talk." She released some trial balloons. When she found it was OK to trust me, she began to share her inside struggles. When a friend puts you off, be caring, sensitive, gentle, and try to understand her needs—and keep coming back to help.

A study of women and their friendships concluded that "having a confidante eases major life adjustments to all ages. A confidante can support us, validate our beliefs, and act as a 'sounding board' when we need to 'let off steam.'"[1]

Being a friend to a woman going through midlife crisis is very difficult—you feel as if you're walking on eggshells all the time. You may do nothing or put off talking to her. You may say, "I don't have time," or "I don't know how to help," or "Maybe she will reject me as a friend." But please don't put off helping.

The late Billy Rose told this story: "Two sisters in their twenties were bequeathed twenty-five thousand dollars when their father died.

"After the funeral the girls began wondering what they should do. Marie, the younger one, said, 'I'd like to do some traveling and see a little of the world.' But Hortense said, 'We mustn't throw our money away foolishly.'

"So the sisters purchased a general store in their village and enlarged it. During the next few years they built it into the most popular store in the area. One day a car drove up and a couple of good-looking men came in to buy some fishing gear. They engaged in some mild flirtation with the sisters and then drove away.

"Marie studied her features in a mirror and then turned to her sister. 'Let's close the store for a couple of months this winter and visit some resorts.' But Hortense shook her head. 'People would take their business elsewhere.'

"Ten years later the sisters had accumulated enough money to take care of them the rest of their lives. 'Come on,' said Marie, 'let's sell the store and start enjoying life. Let's go to California, Mexico, or Bermuda. We might even meet a couple of fellows and get married.' But Hortense said, 'We can't sell now—nobody would pay what the store is worth.' About that time a competitor opened a store across the street, and the sisters buckled down for the next five years to run him out of business.

"But one night Marie, who was then fifty, slipped on the ice and struck her head against a fire hydrant. The following day she died. Hortense never returned to the store. She held the most elaborate funeral ever seen in the area, sold the store, and went into seclusion.

"The following spring she made an unusual request. She asked permission to move Marie's body to California. When permission was granted she had the coffin flown out and went along to supervise reburial. Then she moved into a resort hotel not far away.

"The following year she obtained another disinterment permit and this time had the coffin flown to Mexico City. A few months later she had it flown to Bermuda. In this grim manner she and her sister finally took the trips they had always planned."[2]

The story is rather bizarre, but it drives home the point. If you're really going to be a friend, take some risks *now!*

The Church Helps

People in midlife crisis are often disappointed with their church because they see it as an uncaring institution. Sadly, people in the pews are often used for fulfilling the dreams of the leaders.

When a church decides to minister to midlife people, the first step must be to *understand* the unique time of life and the special needs of midlife people. The second step flows naturally—*design programs* to meet the needs of midlife people. Plan educational classes that will face the problems common to this age group.

Classes could include the unique anxieties of the unmarried career woman, the married career woman who has chosen not to have children, the homemaker, and the "Wonder Woman" who is trying to do it all—marriage, children, and a full-time career. Classes could also cover the needs of children, how to help a husband with his career or midlife crisis, the cultural values imposed on families, or how to live with a reduced lifestyle. Whatever the topics, they can be specifically aimed at meeting the needs of midlife women.

Pastors often think only of a Sunday-morning class. But what about a luncheon meeting to discuss women's financial concerns? Why not a women's retreat for women with special concerns—never married, single-parent, married without children, married with children, divorced, or widowed. The point is, women are not just women; they are unique people with unique needs. Any program should be structured to meet those unique needs.

Churches commonly have couples' retreats. Sometimes they are heavy teaching times. Why not build them primarily for R and R to encourage couples to build their marital relationships? Make the sessions low key and yet building toward a strengthened marriage.

Perhaps the pastor needs to speak more frequently on women's concerns. Scripture is full of help for women, as well as illustrations for women to model. If women are used in a brief sharing time in the morning service, their importance to the body will be demonstrated. Their sharing can be an encouragement to other women who are struggling at midlife.

Her Extended Family Helps

In the article entitled "What Do Women Use Friends For?" the researcher reports, "Relatives were not usually considered 'best friends' by the women in this study. On the average, only 25 percent of all close friends were relatives."[3]

That's not very good news for the woman in midlife crisis—or for the extended family. In other words, extended families are not really being the support mechanism they ought to be for the midlife woman. Part of the problem is that the extended family is more spread out.

But the bigger problem is that we don't work at understanding each other. We assume that because we are blood relatives there is an automatic understanding. That's not true. Understanding requires that we listen, spend time, are nonjudgmental, kind, and open to each other. In short, understanding means we are as concerned for our extended family members as we are for other friends.

We (Jim and Sally) had always been close with some of our family, but we had many friends in the churches we served, so we really didn't feel a need for our extended family. But as we got into our middle years, there was a growing urgency to reach out to our extended family. It takes time and effort, but mostly caring.

Start by identifying members in your extended family who may be going through a midlife crisis. Drop them a note of encouragement, send an E-mail, call them on the phone, and remember them in prayer. Perhaps you can send books or articles that have been helpful to you. Rebuild bridges so that you can minister to people who are related by blood.

Children Can Help

In other parts of the book we've talked about how children can assume a greater responsibility for some of the work at the home. We think that's important, and it's one way children can express concern for their mom who may be struggling with a midlife crisis.

Another important way adolescents can help is to begin caring for their parents. Think of your ability to be concerned about your friends at school. Sometimes you cry over their problems. Now use that same care and reach out with intensity for your mom's problems.

How about this question—"How old do you think you have to be to understand your parents and help them?" In other words, at what age will you become their peer? Learning to care for your parents and being their friend will help you become a mature young adult.

Let's think for a moment about your mom's needs. How can you meet them? She is probably a little overweight, so don't make fun of her. Help her as she tries to lose weight. Maybe you can encourage her to exercise and watch what she eats.

She probably also feels insecure in her marriage. You can talk up your mom to your dad. Tell him what a great person she is. Remind him tactfully how fortunate he is to be married to her and how great they are as a couple. You can also let your mom know the good things you see in your dad. She also may need the reminder.

She may also be struggling with her career, wondering how she's going to fit it all together. Tell her how proud you are to have a mom who is really a mover, a thinker, and involved in life. Tell her you don't mind her doing less at home, and show you're willing to pitch in and help.

Another struggle—she may feel old. Encourage her by talking about how wise she is and how you wish you knew all she knows. Let her know she's at the prime of life and has it all together. Tell her you want her to teach you everything she knows.

Give your mom three compliments a day. Assure her of your regular prayers. This kind of caring will also change you—you'll grow up.

Her Husband Is the Key
Helping your wife through midlife crisis may be one of the most demanding tasks you've ever had to do. If you've thought it's been difficult to figure her out in the past, you may find it even harder now. She may have giant mood swings and obvious instability. She may express insecurity about her-

self, her values, your marriage relationship, and even life itself. If you're going to help, you've got to hang on, even though you may feel many times as if you're on a giant roller coaster.

As you help, remember that it's OK for your wife to be going through this time. It's important to understand and read about midlife crisis so that you're ready to be the supportive person she needs.

It's also crucial to realize it's all right—in fact, it's very positive—for her to spend time crying. If you're with her when she cries, touch her, put your arm around her. You don't need to say any words. Give her the warm acceptance she needs. Give her permission to cry either in front of you or privately.

Be ready to listen if she's not ready to talk now. Listening has two important purposes—to understand your wife and to help her ventilate her feelings. Be careful not to be defensive. Sometimes a cup of coffee or tea at this time will help her to be calm and will give her more objectivity as she shares her feelings.

STRONG AND GENTLE

Years ago Joyce Landorf wrote a good little book to husbands entitled *Tough and Tender*.[4] She says there are two qualities women look for in men. Women like men to be strong in themselves—to know where they're going. But they want men to be sensitive, caring, and to hurt when they hurt.

During your wife's midlife crisis you will need to

be strong in yourself. We're not talking about being macho or pumping iron. We're talking about being emotionally and spiritually strong, in touch with God, well rested, and really in tune with yourself. You need to have an emotional reserve so that you can give to your wife. You must be sure you're not so exhausted with your job that you have nothing left for her.

She needs to see you as a strong spiritual person who is walking with God. You may want to read the section on walking with God in chapter 17. Your wife needs you to be trusting God and praying for her. She needs you to be strong for her when she can't be strong for herself.

Sometimes strength will mean you help her put things into perspective, refocus her energies, and think through her values. As you help her refocus, it's important not only to be tough, but also to be tender.

NEW MARRIAGE PERSPECTIVE

The following article by Jim Sanderson is a touching example of a husband trying to reorient his wife. He does a great job. He's a little bit too gruff in the process, but he also has some soft, tender parts to him. (Jim Sanderson is a nationally syndicated newspaper columnist and the author of the book *How to Raise Your Kids to Stand on Their Own Two Feet*.)[5]

> The morning after the wedding she found herself standing in her nightgown in the doorway

of her daughter's room experiencing the void. I almost feel as if she's died, the woman thought wryly. Stop it. She's on her honeymoon, surely some of the happiest days of her life.

But, later, as she packed away some childhood artifacts to be put in the attic for the grandchildren, the hollowness returned. Her daughter was not planning any babies right away. It would be a long time before she might need a grandmother's help.

The woman heard the questions echoing in her head again: Of what use am I, really? What's my function now? She became angry at herself for permitting the question, in this form, and the anger diffused toward her husband.

Riding home in the car after the wedding, they'd had the worst fight in their marriage. "You're actually glad they're all gone," she had cried out.

"Of course. It's over. We've done our job," he had said.

"What's over?" she had flared. "You sound as if you're planning to cut our children right out of your life." She had known at the time that she was overstating; obviously he loved the kids.

But finally he had said those bitter words: "You became a different woman with the first baby. All those years you were a mother first and a wife second. Sometimes I felt I was at the bottom of your list, right after the dog."

Outrageous and cruel. Not true. Not true at all. He'd had too much champagne, and now suddenly he was like a wounded little boy: "You never had time for me. Your mind was always somewhere else. If a child sneezed, you were out of my arms in a flash, like a mother bear defending her cubs in mortal danger."

Sex, that was it. "Yes, that is it," he had said. "But also when we were talking, or not talking. Or trying to do something together as adults, just the two of us. Evenings out, we'd talk about the kids. I couldn't get you off it. And we never took a vacation on our own."

"I thought you loved our family vacations," she had cried.

"I did. I do," he had groaned. "What's the use? A man can't ever fight Motherhood—all that virtue."

"What do you want from me?" she had finally asked in a small, tight voice.

"I want us to be lovers again, the way we were before the kids came. There's only the two of us now. We've got the rest of our lives to live together, alone, and it's got to get better than it has been—or else."

Suddenly now, just thinking about that brutal threat, she became weak and had to sit down. Yet, it happened all the time: Men and their midlife crises. Looking for young bodies, young women to flatter their egos.

And, yes, in all those frenzied months of the

wedding preparations, he had become distant. Maybe he already had a mistress. She tried to think when they had last made love. Was it possible that something terrible was about to happen to her?

No, surely not. Surely he knew how much she loved and respected him. He'd looked so sad that morning when he'd left for work, so tired. He wasn't a young man anymore. But he's right, she thought, I can be a better wife to him. If it isn't too late.

At the bottom of her despair that morning in the kitchen she unscrewed her jar of instant coffee and found inside his scrawled note: "Dear Wife, grow old with me. The best is yet to be, the last of life, for which the first was made. —Robert Browning and Your Husband"

She read it again and again. Then, when she had exhausted her tears, she reached eagerly for the phone to begin her new life."

The Game Plan
Perhaps these coaching tips might help you to work more effectively with your wife during her midlife crisis. These ideas are in brief form. More extensive information is given in some of our other books, listed in the notes at the end of this book.[6] We have been working with thousands of women with stresses similar to what your wife is experiencing. You can make a difference in your wife's life,

your life, and your marriage. Think through these tips:

1. *Understand midlife crisis.* Connect to your wife's feelings and the causes behind them. Understand the confusion she feels. Midlife is a short segment of life—it won't go on forever. Understand what you can do to help her through this time.

If you've read only this section of this book, we encourage you to read the whole book so that you get a good understanding of a woman's midlife crisis.

2. *Your wife needs space.* She needs time to be alone—but at other times she needs to be dragged out of those low periods of depression. Look for a balance in your relationship with her. Give her time to be reflective—to go on walks by herself, to ride a bike, or to wander through the shopping mall. But there are times when the two of you need to be together. In those together times, don't push her with words such as, "Now, let's be reasonable; let's be logical." Instead, ask, "What are you feeling?" or say, "Talk to me about your confusion."

3. *Build her self-image.* All of the suggestions we made earlier in this chapter to your children could also be used by you. Think of positive ways to meet her special needs at this time. At least three times each day verbally express appreciation to her. Congratulate her and thank her for who she is. Be careful not to thank her only for the things she does. Thank her for the *quality of person* she is.

If you say thanks for doing the laundry, that's important, but you could hire that out. When you say thank you for being a kind and sensitive person who cares for hurting people, that's something you can't buy. That's a quality of her person—that's what you want to reinforce.

4. *Be attractive to her.* How about getting rid of that extra twenty pounds you've put on since you were married? Maybe you could work on muscle tone. Remember that male bodies are going to be more important to her now, especially if she's wondering if she has any sexual appeal.

Dress attractively. Wear the style of clothes she likes to see you in. You can also be attractive to her by doing unusual stuff together that might not be part of your normal routine. Plan special weekends. Surprise her with special gifts. Be sexy. Flirt with her. Make some passes at her. Start touching her more often. Look for creative ways to warm her heart. Remember the flowers—before you push for quickie sex. Look for creative ways to have sex. Build your attractiveness in the same areas that drew you together at first. If you need ideas, look at a practical book with hundreds of ideas—*Love to Love You.* You'll be transformed into a great lover overnight.[7]

5. *Encourage her blooming.* The next chapter, "Blooming at Midlife," should become your guidebook for practical ways to help her during this time.

You are the most important person to help her

through this midlife crisis. She will either love you because you care and understand—or want to be away from you because you "blew it."

Understand her needs, and adapt to meet those needs. Don't wait, because tomorrow you might not have a marriage. Your wife might be singing the Laura Branigan song "Solitaire." This song is the story of a guy who was always gone, leaving his wife home alone to play solitaire. She needed him and tried so hard to please him—but he didn't need her. He just did what he wanted—he didn't care.

Now life has turned. He wants her, but she's on the run. It had taken some time, but she had become accustomed to living without him. Now he finds he loves her, but "it's a little too late."

The song ends as she defiantly sings the pathetic words "Don't wait up, babe, because I won't be there."[8]

Blooming at Midlife

≈

"Is it not possible that middle-age can be looked upon as a period of second flowering, second growth, even a kind of second adolescence?"[1]

Midlife reevaluation should be extremely positive for a woman. Realigning her values and priorities can cause her to bloom and be productive for her next season. She has new freedoms and life experience; she's ready for a fresh surge of productivity. Her success will depend largely on whether she emphasizes her assets—or her liabilities.

A Tale of Three Women

There are three kinds of women at midlife. The first is marked by "despair and disgust." She feels tremendously sorry for herself. Life seems to have handed her a pile of difficulties. Listening to her story, you agree—her life has been very hard.

The woman in despair feels helpless, without hope. Tragically she is determined to live her sour, withdrawn life. She's like a rosebud that has come to full size but started too late in the season. The cold, early winter winds never allow the bud to open and blossom.

The difference between the late-season rosebud and a midlife woman is that the woman has a choice—to stay in the pit of despair or to bloom. Other people have also had difficult experiences yet have bloomed in spite of their stresses. If you're one of those people caught in despair, you can bloom—you *must* bloom!

The second kind of woman is the one who has decided to "grin and bear it." She is not lost in despair, but she believes she will never really come to her flowering. This woman says, "I'm stuck with a job I hate, a marriage that doesn't satisfy, and kids who don't need me." When she's asked if she has given up, she'll say no. Ask if she believes it can be any better: "No, it will always be the same."

If you're trying to hold out until you die, take hope. You can bloom—you *must* bloom!

The third woman has chosen to "bloom at midlife." Her decision doesn't mean she didn't accomplish anything in her adolescence or young adulthood. This woman sees each era of life as a crucial time to grow and mature. She looks back on the past and says, "That was good" or "That was bad," but she goes on to ask, "How can I make the most of what I have?" She is more than a survivor—she is creating a whole new future.

Creative Risking

Our daughters have a real gift from God, or maybe it's from poverty. They are able to take junk and make it look great in a room. When we say "junk," we're not talking about antiques; we're talking about *junk*. They mix together old burlap bags, rusty cans, growing plants, used chairs, wooden crates, things scavenged from old barns, with special handmade things they've created. The result is a warm, homey living environment that says to everyone entering the room, "You're welcome."

The growing midlife woman is not held back by obstacles such as a poor marriage, a job that isn't right, little money, limited education, an imperfect body, or by thinking it's too late in life. Instead, she asks, "What can I do with what I have now?" She makes something good even out of the junk of her life. Blooming means something that was not there will now appear. It means leaving the safe places of the past. Even if the past was uncomfortable, at least it was familiar. Now you're going to launch into something very different.

Blooming, launching, or creating something new is always frightening—but it's also frightening to stay where you are. Remember the times you've been afraid—perhaps when you left grade school, or puberty, your first date, your first job, or the first time someone close to you died. Life is filled with frightening experiences. If we face the challenge, we grow. Later we look back and are grateful.

If a sailboat stays in the harbor, it's very safe. There's no risk. But sailboats were not made to stay in harbors. There's no risk if you stay in the old personality of the young adult woman, but you'll miss the flowering. You'll miss the emerging of the new midlife butterfly—a new, more complete you.

Forces That Cause Midlife Blooming

Several factors will help you to bloom at midlife. Most of these forces will exert pressure for your growth without your conscious effort.

THE COMMAND GENERATION

The middle generation in the United States holds the control over power, wealth, and prestige. The people in the middle generation are the decision makers. Even though society reveres youth, society is controlled by midlife people.

By the time a woman reaches forty, she has twice as much life experience as a twenty-year-old woman. Remember when you were a young woman and walked into a room full of strangers? You wished you could just disappear into the wall. Or remember how you had difficulty looking people in the eye—especially persons in authority or who were attractive to you? Think about when you applied for your first summer job or when you wished for courage to talk to a teacher about your low grade. Remember when you needed to confront the boss when it was time for a raise and you just let it go by? Twenty years of life experience helps you to look at life differently and handle the issues more gracefully than when you were twenty years old.

Being a more experienced person and part of the command generation will be part of the push helping you to bloom and flower. You sense that you are in charge, that you can do it, that you've got the experience, the background. Now you're ready to take off and become a more fully developed midlife woman.

ASSERTIVENESS

There is a natural assertiveness that grows in women at midlife. After midlife, men tend to become more mellow, less authoritative, less domineering, less aggressive, and less interested in conquering the world. Women, on the other hand, become more aggressive and more assertive than when they were young. They are less likely to conform and more likely to dominate. Carl Jung observed, "Woman . . . allows her unused supply of masculinity to become active."[2]

A fascinating study done some years ago explored this idea of the shifting characteristics in men and women. Over a hundred people were asked to make up a story about a picture showing a younger couple and an older couple. They were asked to assign an age to each of the four people, to give a general description of each, and to describe what they thought the figures in the picture were feeling about each other.

"Most striking was the fact that, with increasing age of respondents, the old man and the old woman reversed roles in regard to authority in the family. For the younger men and women . . . the old man was seen as the authority figure. For older men and women . . . the old woman was in the dominant role, and the old man, no matter what other qualities were ascribed to him, was seen as submissive."[3]

You probably know more older women than men who are assertive. Or if you know their history, you know how they've changed. The men are now more affiliative and the women more assertive than when they were younger.

This quality of assertiveness is going to help you flower and bloom. It doesn't mean you have to become aggressive or obnoxious, but it does mean that God has built into you an urgency that will help you to develop into a more expansive person at midlife.

LIFE EXPERIENCES

Every experience you have in life is like being given another crayon of a different color to use in creating a picture. Each new color allows you to expand the shading, the tone, the richness.

The career midlife woman knows a lot about being a career woman. She not only has skills, but she also knows the games, the politics, the times to be quiet, the times to make suggestions. She has learned how to plant ideas in people's minds, how to ask for raises, how to handle men with sex on the brain and arms like octopus tentacles.

If she chose the mother direction, she knows about being up all night with a child running a high fever. She has learned to sing quietly at bedtime and cheer wildly at games. She has learned how to say no, and she has learned to listen as she sits on her child's bed late at night while the sad or happy stories pour out.

After all these years of managing a family, she has administration and coordination skills galore. She knows how to balance budgets and meals. She is a travel agent, scorekeeper, public relations agent, and still keeps clean clothes in everyone's drawers.

The midlife woman has it all over the girl at age twenty. Yes, the twenty-year-old has a firmer body but not a firm life. She doesn't have the life experience to make her as indispensable as you. All that life experience helps you blossom, grow, and become that great midlife woman God wants you to be.

MIDLIFE PRESSURES

Midlife pressures and problems that have caused you to think and reevaluate are giving you a great opportunity. Reassessment can be either the "Renaissance" or the "Dark Ages." It can become a time of growth—or a time of retreating.

Think of people you know in their sixties or seventies. Now pick out the ones who are optimistic and growing—who seem to enjoy life. You want to be around them. We both have relatives like that. Our girls have always looked forward to being with them. These people made choices to bloom all through their lives.

We also have relatives and friends who are just

the opposite. They are depressing to be around. They crab and complain about everything in life. We often think, *If we're miserable just being around them, think how miserable they must be living with themselves.*

I (Sally) have an aunt named Marie (real name). She's not had an easy life, but she's made life nicer for those who know her.

She was the oldest daughter in a family of seven children. After graduation from high school, she taught in country schools. She lost her money in the depression and didn't get to go to college. She has fought a chronic, life-threatening disease all her life.

She married a kind, loving man, but they were poor. Yet they always seemed to have fun. My aunt could "make something out of nothing," whether it was a meal or a new pair of drapes.

She was told by doctors not to have children because of her health, but she had two sons anyway. They grew to be men worthy of the pride she had for them. But one was suddenly snatched by death when his military plane crashed.

In a few short years her husband died a painful death from cancer. His business partner maneuvered in such a way that there was nothing left in the estate for my aunt. She was in her late fifties, nearly broke, without a "trade," and her only surviving son was married and living with his family several hundred miles away.

Those are some of the facts about Aunt Marie.

More of the facts are that after my uncle's death, she went to college and received a degree in library science. She taught in city schools and then, because of an unfortunate political situation, was not rehired. Where does a woman somewhere around age seventy go to apply for a new teaching position?

She didn't find a teaching job that year, so guess what she did. She managed an airport! After age fifty-five she had taken flying lessons and had become a pilot. She also had the skill to manage a small town's air terminal. Then she taught several more years at a rural school in sparsely populated western Nebraska. I can tell you, those kids are some of the best educated in the nation.

Her son finally convinced her to move from the sand, cactus, and winter snows to be nearer to his family. She moved to her own home and garden in a Denver suburb. Did she retire? No. Besides motherly and grandmotherly roles with her nearby family, she spent several hours a week tutoring adults in English and collaborating with her son in a writing venture.

Aunt Marie is a delight to be around. She is loved by all who know her and is a model of courage and optimism. My memories of her cheer and uplift me. She made choices at every point in her life that caused her to be a woman people enjoy.

You have the opportunity at midlife to decide what the rest of your life will be. Are you going to end up being a grouchy old lady, making yourself and everyone else miserable from now until you die? Or are you going to use this midlife crisis to become more positive? Will you discard the bad stuff from your past and add positive things for your future? Your midlife crisis can be a force to cause blooming in your life.

ENOUGH IS ENOUGH

It is usually by late midlife that people begin to say, "That's enough. I'll let go of it. I'll quit pushing. I have enough success. I am rich enough or thin enough. I've achieved enough."

When we're able to say, "That's enough," it means we're willing to let go. We're willing to shift our priorities. At midlife the woman is able to say, "I've had enough of being the little girl, even the young adult girl; I'm ready to be the midlife woman—mature, poised, knowing who I am and where I'm going."

Midlife is also the time to say, "That's enough exploitation. I'm through allowing others to take advantage of me. It's time for me to look at myself in a different light. Enough is enough!" Being able to say, "Enough," perhaps for the first time, enables you to start your new blooming and flowering.

ABILITY TO SYNTHESIZE

Certain parts of your intellectual capacity, such as your memory, started going downhill at about age seventeen. But there are other dimensions of your intellect, such as your ability to synthesize—to make sense out of the pieces of life—that increase through your late fifties. If you try to survive on just the memory part of your intellect, you'll fight a losing battle—just as you'll fight a losing battle trying to keep your body looking young, your hair from turning gray, or your face from wrinkles. Emphasize your strengths, not what you are losing.

It always looks as if the girls' basketball coach is just sitting on the bench. The girls are the ones playing the game. That's not true. The girls on the court are the players being directed by the coach. The coach, in a sense, is really playing the game. She has learned to go with her brains and wisdom—she doesn't have to play the game with her muscles anymore.

As you come to midlife, God has given you the ability to make sense out of life. The young adult is able to understand only separate pieces of life—she doesn't understand how the pieces connect. As a midlife woman, you're no longer asking the question "What is it worth?" You're asking, "What is worthy?" You're able to pull the pieces together to give worthy directions to your life.

You're growing in wisdom that you've accumulated from life experience, your growing assertiveness, your midlife crisis, and your ability to say that enough is enough. Wisdom is a gift from God that you didn't have when you were twenty. God uses wisdom to help you bloom.

Take advantage of all that God has poured into you. Then you'll respond the same way the apostle Paul did: "But whatever I am now, it is all because

God poured out his special favor on me—and not without results. . . . God was working through me by his grace" (1 Corinthians 15:10).

Attitudes for Blooming

Cathy was an attractive midlife woman. She sat on the rock wall with her legs crossed and her toe bouncing up and down nervously. "I just don't like what's happening to me," she said to us. "I don't like what's happening to Duane. I saw this same ugly thing happen with my parents.

"I remember when I was thirteen, my parents fought a lot. I don't mean hitting, just words. It wasn't that I was afraid they were going to leave each other—but I just wanted them to love each other. Now it's happening to us.

"The big thing, I guess, is that Duane is following his dad's pattern. He just keeps getting pushed for more work—he keeps doing what they want him to do. He's like a puppet on a string, or maybe like a donkey following a carrot—a little more time, a little more sacrifice, and you'll get the next promotion.

"We've already had five major moves, and each time I've had to give up friends. This last time, I told Duane I wasn't going to move again. I didn't like what was happening to me. I was afraid to make friends for fear I'd lose them—yet I need people.

"I told Duane I didn't like what was happening between us. We never had any time to talk—no time for fun. I didn't like the way our marriage was going.

"I told him it was time for me. I'd followed him all over the country for *his job* and *his promotion*. But now it was time for me! Time for me to finish my education, to work on my career. I told him, I want to do things before I die—I don't like living in this lousy, dry marriage and being dragged all over the country losing friends."

All the midlife forces were at work in Cathy, causing her to take a hard look at her life and future.

Cathy was asking the question "How can I bloom? How can I make it happen?" Perhaps you also wonder how you can move from where you are to become that mature midlife woman who has it all together. You'll need several attitudes to move to a new level of maturity.

Think of riding a bike up a hill on a country road. At the top, you stop for a moment to catch your breath and look back over where you've been. It was a hard climb. It's a great view backward, but you also look forward to where you're going—both views are crucial.

Cathy was reflecting on where her marriage had been. She compared it to her parents' marriage. She looked at her goals, aspirations, and dreams of her twenties—she hadn't arrived. Now was the time for Cathy to reset goals and change priorities—Duane's company would not control their lives! Cathy was determined to follow the pattern we outlined.

We suggested:

- *Evaluate.* Jot down your growing experiences, as well as events and relationships that were crummy. Include your dreams not yet fulfilled.
- *Refocus.* Focus less on your body and more on the mature wisdom God has given you—your life experiences. Stop competing with young adult women. The twenty-year-old is often socially inept, feels awkward, and doesn't have skills for a career, for mothering, for being a wife. She has a long way to go to learn as much about life as you already know.
- *Shed the past.* Walk away from attitudes of the past. Paul said in the Bible, "No, dear friends, I am still not all I should be, but I am focusing all my energies on this one thing: Forgetting the past and looking forward to what lies ahead" (Philippians 3:13).

So you've made some bad choices. You're ashamed—you wish you could change some things—but you can't. Confess very simply and directly to God. Then walk away from your past failures, because he has forgiven you. Accept it! Also don't live off of past successes. Yes, you were the homecoming queen, but you must live in the "now"—now!

Before you were born, you were safe and secure

inside your mother. But you could never grow into a mature, complete person, develop to your full size, until you were born. Becoming a midlife adult may be as difficult as passing through the birth canal. As you shed that past world, take the good stuff with you—God and all you've learned.

Anne Morrow Lindbergh said, "Perhaps middle age is, or should be, a period of shedding shells; the shell of ambition, the shell of material accumulation and possessions, the shell of the ego. Perhaps one can shed at this stage of life, as one sheds in beach-living, one's pride, one's false ambitions, one's mask, one's armor.

"Was that armor not put on to protect one from the competitive world? If one ceases to compete, does one need it? Perhaps one can, at last, in middle age, if not earlier, be completely oneself? And what a liberation that would be!"[4]

- *Choose to Bloom.* It demands bravery. Blooming includes risk and instability, but always—*always*, the result is growth!
  Sometimes it appears that people are forced to choose, but ultimately it's their decision. It is a privilege to have a choice. Choose to grow. Choose to bloom.

Actions for Blooming

Your new attitudes are going to change your actions. Reinforce your new attitudes by taking on new behaviors. As you act out new directions, you will stabilize the new attitudes. Each strengthens the other.

DREAM, DREAM, DREAM
First, encourage daydreaming. Set aside quiet time for reflection. Daydreaming is an activity that creative people use to form new ideas and directions.

Daydreaming allows your mind to think about putting things together in different combinations, various alternatives, and new possibilities. Think-tank sessions, or brainstorming, are forms of active daydreaming. Any thought that comes up in the session is allowed to be considered. None is rejected at the beginning. The attitude of being open helps you to get a better perspective on the past—and on your future—with dozens of different possibilities.

In spiritual terms, meditation with God is a form of daydreaming. You reflect with God about who you are, what the Scriptures mean to you, and how you should fit into life. Encourage daydreaming every day. Find time to do so as you go for a little walk, ride your bike, sit quietly in the house, or drop off to sleep.

ACCENTUATE THE POSITIVE
Second, identify your gifts and abilities. What are the things you do well? What are your talents? Make a list. After you've made the list, rank the items so that you can see which are your strongest abilities and gifts.

When you reflect on your spiritual gifts and abilities, ask God to help you focus on people-helping directions to make a difference in the world. Your blooming will never be complete unless you use your abilities, under God's guidance, to help people and change the world.

Ruth (real name) was a normal midlife, middle-class white woman sitting in a typical evangelical church. She was not much aware of the great social issues swirling in the seventies. During a morning message, God challenged her to consider her own personal ministry. What could she do to make a difference in the world? She began to ask God specifically to guide her.

God gave her a deep burden for the poor African American people in her community. She began by taking food and clothes to them. Then she listened to their accounts of poverty and injustice. She heard stories about slumlords who didn't care and about rents that were higher than in nearby middle-class communities. She saw families with several children sleeping in one room and with no running water. She also became acquainted with women who didn't know how to read, write, or care for their families.

Now she understood God's calling in her life. She began to mobilize other people to pray with her for these forgotten people living only a few blocks from her home. Soon people were bringing canned and boxed food to the church every week. One room of the church became a storehouse from which used clothes were distributed. She also found kitchen appliances and furniture for these families.

She, her husband, and their task force started confronting landlords and appealing to the city council. They began to make waves. Ruth's mission was making a difference—people were starting to care and help.

Whenever anyone took food, clothes, or other help to a home, they were to sit, listen, learn, and share in the family's lives. Ruth started classes for the women—a combination of Bible study, reading, and homemaking skills. Soon there were several groups. Ruth then saw a need to include husbands. She began discipling couples to teach other couples. Some of those couples became staff members of local African American churches.

God was laying the burden on other people through Ruth's prayer and concern so that other churches and organizations became involved. Today many needs are being met in the African American community because of one woman's obedience to her mission.

You're at a crucial time in your life now. Ask God to give you a special ministry that will change the world around you. We have often asked ourselves what would happen if every Christian had a ministry as effective as Ruth's. Wow! Our world would be different.

WHERE'S THE TARGET?

Third, set goals. Goals may be short, just for today, but also set long-range goals. Goals should be very specific, but be tolerant with yourself for any miscalculations. General goals are harder to measure for success, so be specific.

Ruth's first goal was to obey God and to seek his wisdom for what her ministry should be. Then her goals began to flow out of the insight God was giving her. You don't have to call them goals if you don't want to. I don't think Ruth ever set out "goals" as such. She just said, "This is what I want to do for people. This is what I think we ought to do as a church. And here's how I'd like to get people helping themselves."

When we had a missions conference in our Urbana church, the youth group asked us (Jim and Sally) to talk about some of our overseas travels. They were a typically bored teen group, preoccupied with their own self-image struggles. Could they be challenged?

We talked about the needs of the world in specific places where we'd been. Then I (Jim) said, "You teens know more about the Bible than many of the people who are serving as pastors overseas." That blew them away. Then I threw out the challenge: "Why don't you take a summer off and go overseas and teach people? Why not go door-to-door and share your faith? How about helping missionaries with work projects?"

The questions flew. Was it possible? Could they

really do it? "Yes! You can do almost anything if you plan what to do and then bite off small pieces toward accomplishing your goal."

They took the bait and spent a year and a half in preparation. They studied the reasons why we were Christians so that they could answer questions. They learned how to share their faith. They listened about how to work with missionaries and identified their special needs. They read about Venezuela, the country chosen for the mission. They learned to speak and sing in Spanish. They learned to sing as a group and to play the guitar. They wrote a drama and memorized it in English and Spanish. They prayed, raised money—and believed God.

We spent a month in Venezuela. In two of the several towns we visited we went to every home, door-to-door, sharing the gospel. Bible study groups sprang up. In some towns we went door-to-door in high-rise apartment buildings. Again, ministries grew. We sang in the public plazas, gave the drama, and showed Christian movies. Venezuelan young people were always teamed with our teens.

Missionary lives, as well as Venezuelan lives, were changed. One missionary said, "I've been a missionary for twelve years, but I've never led another person to Christ. Kevin [real name] was talking to a young Venezuelan. But because he couldn't speak Spanish very well, he couldn't go any farther than explaining the Four Spiritual Laws. He turned to me [the missionary] and said,

'You do it.' Believe it or not, I led that young man and two others with him to the Lord."

The outcome was that about a hundred people made decisions for Christ. Small Bible study groups were started. At two different sites all the interior walls in large Bible institutes were painted. The biggest benefit was the spiritual growth in the lives of our church teens. Without goals it never would have happened.

Growth and change will not happen unless you set goals. A good way to start is to ask, "If I could do anything to minister to people, what would I do?" Other good questions are, "What do I feel strongly about? What is it that really disgusts me? What would I like to change? What would I really like to do for other people?" Your responses to these questions should give you insight. Then set goals that will put feet on your insight.

As you keep acting on your goals, you will change. Life is made up of many small choices. Each choice brings new change events into your life—and changes you.

NEW ADVENTURES

A fourth new action to help your blooming is to try new adventures. Why not . . .

- Develop your painting or pencil sketching
- Write a book
- Learn to play a musical instrument
- Attend a live performance of a symphony
- Visit Niagara Falls

- Take up serious photography
- Ride a donkey to the bottom of the Grand Canyon
- Learn to fly
- Go to a live, major-league sports event
- Attend a church service very different from yours
- Learn to scuba dive
- Take a canoe or backpacking trip
- Dig for clams
- Learn to sail
- Visit a coal mine
- Sleep out overnight
- Visit a seminary
- Work at a school for the blind
- Invite a missionary to stay in your house for a week
- Serve on a jury
- Ride in a police car with a policewoman
- Write a letter to your congressman
- Visit a halfway house for alcoholics
- Invite your neighbors who've never visited your home
- Visit a retirement home

The list is endless. Do something different. Expose yourself to people and lifestyles that are not common to you. Get to know people from different countries and different cultures who live in our country. Talk with someone who is a more mature Christian than you are. Talk to an atheist.

Remember, every change event in your life changes you and influences your value system. All these new adventures will help your process of becoming a mature midlife woman. Who knows? Out of all of your new adventures, God may lead you to a special ministry that's going to change your world—as well as you.

CRACK THOSE BOOKS

A fifth major action is to go back to school. All kinds of educational opportunities are offered by high schools, community colleges, and four-year colleges and universities. Classes are offered in the evening, grouped on weekends, or held during intensive one-week sessions, which fit the busy schedule of the midlife adult.

Some women return to school to improve their skills and abilities so that they can be more effective in their career. Others want to learn new skills. Perhaps you'd like to learn tailoring, home repair, car maintenance, sculpturing, painting, weaving, playing an instrument, singing, acting, or dancing.

Other people take continuing-education courses to improve their inner selves. Most churches have small Bible study groups where people meet to help each other grow. Other organizations such as a local hospital or mental health clinic offer marriage-enrichment or divorce-prevention seminars.

Added to all of the seminars that are available,

there is media. If you would listen, for example, to Chuck Swindoll's program, *Insight for Living*, and study along in the guidebooks, you would find yourself growing at a faster pace than you believed possible. He will lead you in a very warm, human way through important sections of Scripture and apply them to everyday life. Or, listen to Dr. James Dobson's *Focus on the Family* as a regular diet to stimulate the growth in your personal and family life.

Perhaps the educational side of you can be expanded by a trip to your local bookstore. Ask for suggestions about the most important books they have in the area in which you want to grow. If you read six to eight pages a day, you can cover an average book in a month. Think of the difference in your life from reading twelve outstanding books in a year. (In the chapter notes we suggest a few).[5]

THE PHYSICAL PACKAGE

Sixth, give special attention to your body. You are a package with three parts: physical, psychological, and spiritual. If you allow your body to get run down, you are going to be affected psychologically and spiritually.

Sleep. Each woman requires a different amount of sleep—but get enough. Sometimes women are so busy during their twenties and early thirties that they try to save time by sleeping less. Try getting an extra half hour of sleep a day. If there's an improvement in your overall outlook in life, it's a good indication your body needs that extra half hour.

If you have trouble dropping off to sleep at night, try a warm cup of cocoa. The chocolate will turn on your happiness juices, and the milk produces chemicals that will somewhat tranquilize you.

Dr. Joyce Brothers recommends an occasional extended period of time when the body can dictate how much sleep to get. Every four or five months, she plans to stay in bed for about thirty-six hours. Friday night she gets everything around her bed, such as the radio, TV, telephone, and lots of reading materials. The refrigerator is stocked with yogurt, fruit, cottage cheese, and lots of juices. Then she just does whatever her body wants her to. If she feels like reading, watching TV, or sleeping, she does. She says, "I sleep and wake and don't worry about whether I'm awake in the middle of the night or asleep in the middle of the day. I just relax and do nothing."[6]

We can hear you laughing, "If only I had that luxury!" With a little bit of planning, you can do it too. You have to plan ahead. Eliminate all other obligations. If you have children, arrange for them to have a little vacation with friends. If you're married, you might want to do the resting time as a couple. You don't even have to leave home. Just put the car in the garage, pull down all the blinds, turn off your telephone, and put an old newspaper in the driveway so it looks as if nobody's home.

Eat. Another ingredient for caring for your physical body is to eat correctly. Many times the midlife woman, in her determination to lose weight, eats an unbalanced diet. A poor diet can result in physical and emotional fatigue, depression, and lack of motivation.

It is important to learn how to stay healthy and feel well through a proper diet. Many books are available, and each seems to have a particular emphasis, a pet slogan, or an out-and-out gimmick. As we have checked them, we believe it's best to choose a book with general information and then use your common sense and willpower about correct eating. Avoid fads and strange, unproved procedures. But do get excited about eating right to feel right.

Exercise. Try to work physical exercise into your daily routine. The fact that you're tired at the end of the day after work, or from caring for your home and family, does not mean you've had good exercise.

"A nine-year study of 575 paired brothers, one of whom had stayed in Ireland and the other had emigrated to the United States, showed the rate of heart attack to be higher in the United States. The research sought to discover what differences might account for this. By using brothers, the factors of constitutional differences were minimized. Every possible fact was considered—nutrition, activity, types of work, degree of tension, living arrangements, etc. . . . . Only one factor had been found to be consistently different, namely, the amount of exercise."[7]

Twenty minutes of activity to force your heart and lungs to work hard is good exercise. It means stressing as many of your muscle groups and moving as many joints as possible. Whatever exercise will accomplish that for you three times a week is good exercise.

You'll exercise more easily if you choose an activity that's fun. Maybe biking, jogging, swimming, or working out with an exercise video on your own or in a class. A good brisk walk—or an enthusiastic sexual experience with your husband—can provide exercise your body desperately needs.

Exercise will help to keep your muscles in tone so that your weight is not the flab around your middle. Exercise increases your capacity to endure physical stress. You'll be able to go longer without that sagging feeling. Exercise also changes your body chemistry so that you can handle emotional stress better. It helps break the cycle of depression.

When we think of all the positive aspects of exercise, we wonder why we don't do more. Our usual response is, "We're too busy." That's why it's so crucial to try to build exercise into our normal routine. As we mentioned before, for many years Sally and I walked almost daily. We exercise and talk about what's happening in us. We do other fun things for exercise, but some of them are none of your business!

RELATE

Another activity to enable you to bloom is to build personal relationships. The stimulation of meaningful friendships is essential for growth.

In *Pathfinders* Gail Sheehy tells of interviewing 106 professional or managerial women. She asked them to draw three lines on a graph. The first was to graph their achievement from age five through fifty in five-year increments. The second portrayed their friendships over the same period of time. Positive, close, harmonious relationships were to be charted as highs, and the negative, isolated times as the lows on the graph. The third line was to show their overall life satisfaction.

Sheehy commented, "A statistical analysis of the 106 charts from this group was startling. The achievement line was consistently high for these professional woman. But it was their affiliation [friendship] line that was closer by a significant degree to their overall life satisfaction line. Although most of their efforts were being directed toward achievement, their zest for life was much more profoundly affected by their relationships with people."[8]

These women found significance in achievement, *but* their life satisfaction was measured by their relationships. Be careful that you don't think of your blooming as only achievement focused.

Real blooming—deep life satisfaction—must be tied to satisfying interpersonal relationships. Deepen your friendships and also increase their number.

Sometimes because of the busyness of the late twenties and early thirties, women have few and only surface relationships. Your full development as a mature midlife woman needs deep interpersonal relationships. In the opening chapters of the book of Genesis, God says, in essence, "I created mankind with needs." People need each other. Mankind was designed incomplete, needing companionship. We are basically lonely creatures who need the psychological warmth of interpersonal associations.

Friendships take time and energy, but they can't be put off for some other day. Think of two or three people with whom you really hit it off. How can those relationships be deepened? Take concrete steps to make it happen.

Some women renew letter correspondence with women friends from the past. Other women determine to spend more time with their maturing adolescent children—helping that relationship to be a peer friendship. Some spend more time with their husbands or other relatives. Others join small Bible study groups. Other blooming activities, such as education, will put you into contact with people who may become significant friends.

Putting It All Together
We started the book by telling you a little bit about Sally's midlife crisis. We don't want to leave you

wondering what happened to her. I (Jim) want you to see the blooming that has taken place in her life.

The years of her midlife crisis were difficult years for me as well as for Sally. I felt, somehow, I was failing her. We had no clear direction about how to work through her midlife crisis. In fact, we didn't know there was such a thing. But I saw Sally emerging as a very different, more confident, witty, and insightful woman who has had a large impact on thousands of people across the United States and around the world.

An outgrowth of her midlife crisis was that she returned to finish the last two years of college—before it was commonly accepted for women her age to do so. She was in the minority. On one occasion students were waiting outside the classroom for the first day of class. When Sally walked up, all the students moved to the door—assuming she was the teacher.

During those two years, God expanded her interest in writing as she took writing courses and became a witty writer. One piece, written in jest, was a letter to the chancellor of the University of Illinois. During that era students were activists, and minority groups were often pressing their demands. Sally facetiously demanded equal rights for the 141 (out of a total of 35,000) minority students—undergraduate students over age thirty-five.

She asked, first of all, that the university population over thirty-five be increased to equal the same percentage as the population in the state of Illinois (a demand often made by other minority groups).

She also demanded that courses such as "How to Live with Your Teenager 101," "Caring for Your Aging Parents 216," "Coping with Menopause 263," and "Planning for Retirement 333," be added to the curriculum.

She further demanded elevators in all buildings, motorized sidewalks, reserved at-the-door parking spaces, upholstered seats with footrests in all classrooms, and telephones at each seat so these people could keep in touch with families. Among other requests, she also asked for lounges equipped with corn-pad and Poly•Grip vending machines. We all enjoyed this humorous blossoming in Sally.

Sally graduated with her bachelor's degree the same spring that our oldest daughter graduated from high school. We all went to Sally's graduation and waved proudly as she stood in her cap and gown. Her degree was in elementary education, but her focus was on helping children with reading disabilities.

She took a job as a reading specialist in a local school. She taught kids how to read, but she also helped them to develop positive self-images. Some kids continue to write letters at Christmas thanking her for the contribution to their lives.

Sally has been deeply involved in all the articles I have written and in all of our books. In 1981, in response to hundreds of letters from wives of midlife men, she wrote her first major book, *Your Husband's Midlife Crisis.*

Sally was soon thrust into speaking at workshops and conferences all over the country. She was on radio and television talk shows. God was enlarging her communication skills to reach far beyond our local community. The same year her book came out, she returned to the university to work on a master's degree in human development.

When we moved to California, Sally was invited to be an adjunct professor at Biola University, Talbot Theological Seminary, where she taught at both the master's and the doctoral level. She enjoyed teaching graduate men and women preparing for full-time ministry. She had a strong burden for pastors' wives and families because of her twenty-five years as a pastor's wife.

We also started *Midlife Dimensions,* our counseling ministry, and started a daily radio program on two hundred stations, as well as started counseling people all over the world through letters, by phone, and via E-mail. We have written fourteen books to date and have a Web site on the Internet (www.midlife.com).

She delighted in the role of being a mother who helped our three daughters to blossom as leaders in their own fields. "Gramma" Sally enjoyed training and coaching another generation.

Sally's midlife crisis changed her. She became more assertive and more goal oriented. At the same time, she became more keenly aware of people's hurts. She was more sensitive, and more easily jumped to rescue people who were exploited or misunderstood.

Her walk with God was fostered day by day in a quiet time alone with him. She didn't have a childish faith—but a faith of a mature woman who wrestled with life's unanswerable questions and found God walking with her. Most of all Sally developed a great strength and a deep, supportive love that helped me through my midlife crisis.

Additionally, she was a tower of strength as we went through the trauma of our daughter Becki's losing her leg to cancer at age sixteen, and through the anguish of years of recovering from our daughter's sexual molestation by a trusted relative.

Finally, her walk with God gave both of us strength in our seven-year battle with Sally's breast cancer—which we both lost.

Sally stepped out of her body and into eternity on May 27, 1997.

Sally was truly the fulfillment of the Proverbs 31 woman. As a young man I received from God a very special gift. God knew my dysfunctional home background and my insecurities, so he gave me Sally—a woman of great intellect, sacrificial love, creativity, courage, and spiritual insight, plus exceptional beauty.

I am who I am because of the grace of God (1 Cor. 15:10)—and God's gift of Sally.

Sally Ann Christon Conway
1934–1997

NOTES

Chapter 1: Collision of Expectations and Reality

1. Helen Passwater, unpublished poem, printed with permission.
2. Bill and Pam Farrel, *Marriage in the Whirlwind* (Downers Grove, Ill.: InterVarsity Press, 1996), 99.
3. Joan Israel, "Confessions of a 45-Year-Old Feminist," in *Looking Ahead*, ed. Lillian E. Troll et al. (Englewood Cliffs, N.J.: Prentice-Hall, 1977), 65.
4. Israel, "Confessions," 66.
5. Israel, "Confessions," 67.
6. Israel, "Confessions," 68.
7. Jim Conway, "Women in Midlife Crisis" (Ph.D. diss., University of Illinois, 1986).
8. Thomas A. Desmond, "America's Unknown Middle-Agers," *New York Times* magazine, 29 July 1956.
9. Gail Sheehy, *Passages* (New York: Dutton, 1976), 378–383.
10. Abraham Maslow et al., "A Clinically-Derived Test for Measuring Psychological Security-Insecurity," *Journal of General Psychology* 33 (July 1945): 24–41.
11. Janet Harris, *The Prime of Ms. America* (New York: New American Library, 1976), 11, 14.
12. Jules Henry, "Forty-Year-Old Jitters in Married Urban Women," in *The Challenge to Women*, ed. Seymour M. Farber and Roger H. I. Wilson (New York: Basic Books, 1966), 152.
13. Henry, "Forty-Year-Old Jitters," 153.
14. Henry, "Forty-Year-Old Jitters," 163.
15. Iris Sangiuliano, *In Her Time* (New York: Morrow, 1978), 130–132.
16. Joel and Lois Davitz, *Making It from Forty to Fifty* (New York: Random House, 1976), xvi.

Chapter 2: The Homemaker Runs Dry

1. Jim Conway, *Men in Midlife Crisis* (Elgin, Ill.: David C. Cook, 1978, 1997).

2. Anne W. Simon, *The New Years: A New Middle Age* (New York: Knopf, 1968), 183.

3. Anne Statham Macke, George W. Bohrnstedt, and Ilene N. Bernstein, "Housewives' Self-Esteem and Their Husbands' Success: The Myth of Vicarious Involvement," *Journal of Marriage and the Family*, (February 1979): 52, 54.

4. Laura Shapiro, "No Place Like Work," *Newsweek* 129 (28 April 1997): 64.

5. Joel and Lois Davitz, *Making It from Forty to Fifty* (New York: Random House, 1976), xvi, 210–211.

6. Gail Sheehy, *Passages* (New York: Dutton, 1976), 382–383.

7. Sonya Rhodes with Josleen Wilson, "'I'm Sick of Being Supermom!' The Story of a Woman's Revolt," *Woman's Day*, 10 February 1981, 65. (Excerpted from the book *Surviving Family Life*, Putnam, 1981)

8. Rhodes with Wilson, "Woman's Revolt," 90.

9. Rhodes with Wilson, "Woman's Revolt."

10. Judith Abelew Birnbaum, "Life Patterns and Self-Esteem in Gifted Family-Oriented and Career-Committed Women," in *Women and Achievement*, ed. Martha Tamara Shuch Mednick, Sandra Schwartz Tangri, and Lois Wladis Hoffman (New York: John Wiley and Sons, 1975), 418.

11. Birnbaum, "Life Patterns."

Chapter 3: The Professional Shifts Dreams

1. Carl Jung, *Modern Man in Search of a Soul* (New York: Harcourt, Brace, and World, Inc., 1933), 108.

2. Betty Friedan, "The Myth," *Family Weekly*, 8 November 1981, 10–11.

3. Friedan, "The Myth."

4. Kari Torjesen Malcolm, *Women at the Crossroads* (Downers Grove, Ill.: InterVarsity Press, 1982), 85–133, 209–212.

5. Paul Tournier, *The Gift of Feeling* (Atlanta: John Knox Press, 1981).

6. Friedan, "The Myth."

7. Friedan, "The Myth."

8. M. Kuhn, "How Mates Are Sorted," in *Family, Marriage, and Parenthood*, ed. H. Becker and R. Hill (Boston: D. C. Heath and Co., 1955).

9. Sherri Dalphonse, "To Have or Have Not?" *Washingtonian* 32 (February 1997): 48–53.

10. *Ladies' Home Journal*, 21 July 1961.

11. Cynthia King, "Childless by Choice," *Harper's Bazaar*, June 1996, 134–135.

12. Barbara Ehrenreich and Deirdre English, *For Her Own Good* (Garden City, N.Y.: Anchor Press/Doubleday, 1979), 294.

13. Erik Erikson, *Adulthood* (New York: W. W. Norton, 1978).

14. Christy Casamassima, "Battle of the Bucks," *Psychology Today* 28, no. 2, (March/April 1995): 44–46.

15. Casamassima, "Battle of the Bucks."

Chapter 4: Wonder Woman Tries It All

1. Victoria Secunda, "Mothering instead of Career: Was It Worth It?" *New Choices for Retirement Living* 35 (5 April 1995).

2. Arlene Hershman and Amy Aronson, "Are Women Really Leaving the Working Force?" *Working Woman*, October 1994, 14.

3. Women's Bureau of the Federal Department of Labor, quoted in Patricia Ward and Martha Stout, *Christian Women at Work* (Grand Rapids, Mich.: Zondervan, 1981), 11. Bureau of Labor Statistics, quoted in Caroline Bird, *The Two-Paycheck Marriage* (New York:

Pocket Books, 1979), 4–6. *Information Please Atlas and Year Book*, 36th ed. (New York: Simon and Schuster, 1982), 54.

4. Barbara Hetzer, "The Second Income: Is It Worth It?" *Business Week*, August 1997, 192

5. Helen Gurley Brown, *Having It All* (New York: Pocket Books, 1985).

6. Barbara Ehrenreich and Deirdre English, *For Her Own Good* (Garden City, N.Y.: Anchor Press/Doubleday, 1979), 8–9.

7. Eda J. LeShan, *The Wonderful Crisis of Middle Age* (New York: Warner Books, 1985), 47.

8. Patricia Gundry, *The Complete Woman* (Grand Rapids, Mich.: Suitcase Books, 1995).

9. Sally Squires, "Is Work Healthy?" *Ladies' Home Journal* 109 (June 1992): 50.

10. Debra Kent, "The Psychological Payoff," *Working Mother* 17 (December 1994): 30.

11. Caroline Bird, *The Two-Paycheck Marriage*, (New York: Pocket Books, 1979), 43.

12. *Ladies' Home Journal*, 113 (October 1996): 87.

Chapter 5: Culture's Creation

1. *Ladies' Home Journal*, August 1919.

2. *Ladies' Home Journal*, August 1919.

3. Janet Harris, *The Prime of Ms. America* (New York: New American Library, 1976), 43.

4. U.S. Bureau of the Census of Population: *Urban and Rural Population*, 1990.

5. Wallace Denton, *What's Happening to Our Families?* (Philadelphia: Westminster Press, 1963).

6. James Servin, "Ask Her Age," *Harper's Bazaar*, March 1994, 116.

7. Phil Pastoret, Newspaper Enterprise Association in *Reader's Digest* 11, no. 668 (December 1977): 122.

8. Anne Newman, "The Risks of Racing the Reproductive Clock," *Business Week*, May 1997, 96–98.

9. Jim and Sally Conway, *Traits of a Lasting Marriage* (Downers Grove, Ill.: InterVarsity Press, 1991). Sally Conway and Jim Conway, *When a Mate Wants Out: Secrets for Saving a Marriage* (Grand Rapids, MI: Zondervan, 1992). M. Abrioux and H. W. Zingle, "An Exploration of the Marital and Life Satisfactions of Middle-Aged Husbands and Wives," *Canadian Counselor* 13, no. 2 (January 1979): 85–93. R. O. Blood and D. M. Wolfe, *Husbands and Wives: The Dynamics of Married Living* (Glencoe, Ill.: Free Press, 1960). J. J. Locke and K. M. Wallace, "Short Marital-Adjustment and Prediction Tests: Their Reliability and Validity," *Journal of Marriage and the Family* 28 (February 1966): 44–48. B. C. Rollins and K. L. Cannon, "Marital Satisfaction over the Family Life Cycle: A Reevaluation," *Journal of Marriage and the Family* (May 1974): 271–82.

10. Bill and Pam Farrel and Jim and Sally Conway, *Pure Pleasure: Making Your Marriage a Great Affair*, (Downers Grove, Ill.: InterVarsity Press, 1994). Jim and Sally Conway, *Traits of a Lasting Marriage* (Downers Grove, Ill.: InterVarsity Press, 1991).

11. Eda J. LeShan, *The Wonderful Crisis of Middle Age* (New York: Warner Books, 1985), 51–52.

12. LeShan, *The Wonderful Crisis of Middle Age*, 43–46.

Chapter 6: A Stale Marriage

1. B. C. Rollins and K. L. Cannon, "Marital Satisfaction over the Family Life Cycle: A Reevaluation," *Journal of Marriage and the Family* (May 1974): 271.

2. Jim and Sally Conway, *Traits of a Lasting Marriage* (Downers Grove, Ill.: InterVarsity Press, 1991).

3. Morton Hunt, *The Affair* (New York: New American Library, 1969), 60–61.

4. Jeannine Amber, "Young and Abused," *Essence* 2 (January 1997): 66.

5. Elizabeth Mehren, "Shattering Myths of Sanctity of Home," *Los Angeles Times*, part 4, 26 January 1983.

6. Mehren, "Shattering Myths of Sanctity of Home."

7. Jack London, "In a Far Country," *Great Short Works* (New York: Harper and Row, 1965).

8. Barbara L. Fisher, Paul R. Giblin, and Margaret H. Hoopes, "Healthy Family Functioning: What Therapists Say and What Families Want," *Journal of Marriage and Family Therapy* (July 1982): 273–274.

9. Jerry and Barbara Cook, *Choosing to Love* (Ventura, Calif.: Regal Books, 1982), 57. Used by permission.

10. Cook, *Choosing to Love*, 66–68.

Chapter 7: Her Husband's Own Crisis

1. Avery Corman, "The Old Neighborhood," *Flightime* magazine, January 1981, 15.

2. Quoted in Peter Chew, *The Inner World of the Middle-Aged Man* (New York: Macmillan, 1976), 113

3. Edmond Bergler, *The Revolt of the Middle-Aged Man* (New York: A. A. Wyn, 1954).

4. Barbara R. Fried, *The Middle-Age Crisis* (New York: Harper and Row, 1967), 15.

5. Daniel Levinson et al., *The Seasons of a Man's Life* (New York: Ballantine, 1986), 8, 199.

6. Cheryl Russell, "The Baby Boom Turns 50," *American Demographics* 17 (December 1995): 22–23.

7. Jim Conway, *Men in Midlife Crisis* (Colorado Springs, Colo.: Chariot Victor, 1997).

8. Conway, *Men in Midlife Crisis*.

9. Conway, *Men in Midlife Crisis*, 71–74.

10. Iris Sangiuliano, *In Her Time* (New York: Morrow, 1978), 119–120.

11. We have written extensively on restoring a marriage

and recovering from an affair. Jim and Sally Conway, *When a Mate Wants Out* (Grand Rapids, Mich.: Zondervan, 1992). Farrel and Conway, *Pure Pleasure* (Downers Grove, Ill.: InterVarsity Press, 1994), 15–25. Jim and Sally Conway, *Traits of a Lasting Marriage*, (Downers Grove, Ill.: InterVarsity Press, 1991), 25.

12. Quoted in Peter Chew, *The Inner World of the Middle-Aged Man* (New York: Macmillan, 1976), 72.

Chapter 8: The Pain of Parenting

1. Jim Conway, *Men in Midlife Crisis*, (Colorado Springs, Colo., Chariot Victor, 1997), 271, 275. Neugarten, Abrioux, and Zingle. Margorie Lowenthal and David Chiriboga, "Transition to the Empty Nest: Crisis, Challenge, or Relief?" *Archives of General Psychiatry* (26 January 1972): 8–14.

2. Eda J. LeShan, *The Wonderful Crisis of Middle Age* (New York: Warner Books, 1985), 15–16.

3. Margie Patlak, "Medical Report: Postponing Motherhood: What are the Risks?" *Glamour* 88 (March 1990): 68–70.

4. Bickley Townsend, "Room at the Top for Women," *American Demographics* 18, (June 1996): 28–33.

5. Frank F. Furstenberg Jr., "The Future of Marriage," *American Demographics* 18 (June 1996): 34–37.

6. Barbara R. Fried, *The Middle-Age Crisis* (New York: Harper and Row, 1967), 75.

7. Anne W. Simon, *The New Years: A New Middle Age* (New York: Knopf, 1968), 6–7.

8. Becki Conway Sanders, Jim and Sally Conway, *What God Gives When Life Takes* (1989). *Trusting God in a Family Crisis* (1992), (Downers Grove, Ill.: InterVarsity Press).

9. Quoted in Peter Chew, *The Inner World of the Middle-Aged Man* (New York: Macmillan, 1976), 77.

10. Quoted in Edmond Bergler, *The Revolt of the Middle-Aged Man* (New York: A. A. Wyn, 1954), 281.

11. Quoted in Peter Chew, 83.
12. Ross Campbell, *How to Really Love Your Children* (New York: Arrowhead Press, 1996).
13. Gail Sheehy, *Pathfinders* (New York: Bantam, 1982), 424.
14. Joel and Lois Davitz, *Making It from Forty to Fifty* (New York: Random House, 1976), 188.

Chapter 9: Too Much Too Fast

1. Carol B. Aslanian and Henry B. Brickell, *Americans in Transition* (New York: College Entrance Examination Board, 1980).
2. Bernice Neugarten, "Dynamics of Transition of Old Age," *Journal of Geriatric Psychiatry* (1970): 86.
3. Roger L. Gould, "Phases of Adult Life," *American Journal of Psychiatry* 129, no. 5 (November 1972): 528.
4. Becki Conway Sanders, Jim and Sally Conway, *What God Gives When Life Takes* (1989). *Trusting God in a Family Crisis* (1992), (Downers Grove, Ill.: InterVarsity Press).
5. Josh Greenfield, "A Dramatic Sense of Age . . . A Sudden Sniff of Death," *Today's Health*, March 1973, 46.
6. U.S. Bureau of the Census, "Marital Status and Living Arrangement: March 1977" (Washington, D.C.: GPO, 1977).
7. Nick Gillespie, "Child-Proofing the World," *Reason* 29, no. 2 (June 1997): 20–27.
8. David A. Chiriboga, "Adaptation to Marital Separation in Later and Earlier Life," *Journal of Gerontology* 37, no. 1 (1982): 11.
9. Judith S. Wallerstein and Joan B. Kelly, "California's Children of Divorce," *Psychology Today*, January 1980, 67.
10. Jim Conway, *Adult Children of Legal or Emotional Divorce*

(Downers Grove, Ill.: InterVarsity Press, 1990). Judith S. Wallerstein and Joan B. Kelly, *Surviving the Breakup: How Children and Parents Cope with Divorce* (New York: HarperCollins, 1996), 74–75.

11. E. O. Fisher, "A Guide to Divorce Counseling," *The Family Coordinator* 22, no. 1 (1973): 55.

Chapter 10: The Marks of Time

1. Barbara R. Fried, *The Middle-Age Crisis* (New York: Harper and Row, 1967), 81.
2. Lillian E. Troll, *Early and Middle Adulthood: The Best Is Yet to Be—Maybe* (Monterey, Calif.: Brooks/Cole, 1975), 20–23.
3. Susan Sontag, "The Double Standard of Aging," *Saturday Review of the Society*, September 23, 1972.
4. Anne W. Simon, *The New Years: A New Middle Age* (New York: Knopf, 1968), 35.
5. Joyce Brothers, *Better than Ever* (New York: Simon and Schuster, 1975), 19–20.
6. Troll, *Early and Middle Adulthood*, 22–23.
7. Leslie Aldridge Westoff, *Breaking Out of the Middle-Age Trap* (New York: New American Library, 1980), 42.
8. Nancy Stahl, Universal Press Syndicate in *Reader's Digest* 111, no. 668 (December 1977): 122.
9. Troll, *Early and Middle Adulthood*, 22–23.
10. Brothers, *Better than Ever*, 29.
11. Ruth Weg, "More than Wrinkles," in *Looking Ahead*, ed. Lillian E. Troll et al. (Englewood Cliffs, N.J.: Prentice-Hall, 1977), 32.
12. Bruno Hans Geba, *Vitality Training for Older Adults: A Positive Approach to Growing Old* (New York: Random House, 1974), 9.
13. Jim Conway, *Men in Midlife Crisis*, (Colorado Springs, Colo.: Chariot Victor, 1997), 230–231. Jim and Sally Conway, *Sexual Harassment No More*, (Downers Grove, Ill.: InterVarsity Press, 1993), 38–42. Ollie Pocs et al.,

"Is There Sex After 40?" *Psychology Today*, 11 (June 1997): 54.

14. Sally Conway, *Menopause* (Grand Rapids, Mich.: Pyranee Books, Zondervan, 1990).

15. Carol A. Nowak, "Does Youthfulness Equal Attractiveness?" in *Looking Ahead*, ed. Lillian E. Troll et al. (Englewood Cliffs, N.J.: Prentice-Hall, 1977), 59.

16. Alice Lake, "An Honest Report on Breast Cancer," *Reader's Digest*, September 1982.

17. Jane Haas, "History of Cancer Haunts Orange County Family," *Orange County Register*, September 1997. (www.ocregister.com/news/1997/0997/092497/breast.html).

18. Nowak, "Does Youthfulness Equal Attractiveness?" 63.

19. Eda J. LeShan, *The Wonderful Crisis of Middle Age* (New York: Warner Books, 1985), 63–64.

Chapter 11: Defeated by a Sagging Self-Esteem

1. Iris Sangiuliano, *In Her Time* (New York: Morrow, 1978), 238.

2. N. Mischel, "Sex Bias in the Evaluation of Professional Achievements," *Journal of Educational Psychology* 66 (1974): 157–166.

3. Archibald Hart, *Dark Clouds, Silver Linings* (Colorado Springs, Colo.: Focus on the Family, 1993).

4. Denise Mann, "Women Must Become More Involved in Treating Midlife Depression," (http://www.thriveonline.com).

5. James Dobson, *Hide or Seek* (Old Tappan, N.J.: Revell, 1974).

6. Archibald Hart, *Feeling Free* (Old Tappan, N.J.: Revell, 1979).

7. David A. Seamands, "Perfectionism: Fraught with Fruits of Self-Destruction," *Psychology Today*, 10 April 1981, 24.

8. Helen Haiman Joseph poem, "The Mask."

9. Joyce Brothers, *Better than Ever* (New York: Simon and Schuster, 1975), 27–159.

10. Alan B. Knox, *Adult Development and Learning* (San Francisco: Jossey-Bass, 1977), 489.

11. Cecil G. Osborne, *The Art of Learning to Love Yourself* (Grand Rapids, Mich.: Zondervan, 1976), 99–123.

12. Ardis Whitman, "The Awesome Power to Be Ourselves," *Reader's Digest*, January 1983, 80.

13. David D. Burns, "The Perfectionist's Script for Self-Defeat," *Psychology Today*, November 1980, 38.

14. Burns, "The Perfectionist's Script," *Psychology Today*, 46.

15. Burns, "The Perfectionist's Script."

16. Burns, "The Perfectionist's Script."

17. Burns, "The Perfectionist's Script."

18. Burns, "The Perfectionist's Script."

19. Edwin Robertson, ed., *Dietrich Bonhoeffer: Selected Writings*, (London, England: Fount Paperbacks, 1995).

Chapter 12: Trapped by Depression

1. Phyllis Chesler, *Women and Madness* (San Diego: Harcourt Brace, 1989), 39–40.

2. Archibald Hart, *Dark Clouds, Silver Linings* (Colorado Springs, Colo.: Focus on the Family, 1993), ix.

3. Maggie Scarf, "The Promiscuous Woman," *Psychology Today*, July 1980, 2.

4. Thomas G. Whittle, Jan Thorpe, "News: The Selling of Depression," *Freedom* 26, no. 2 (November 1996): 16–21.

5. World Health Organization, "Mental Health of Women," *WHO Press* no. 68 (October 1996): 1–2.

6. Margaret Williams Crockett, "Depression in Middle-Aged Women," *The Journal of Pastoral Care* 31, no. 1 (March 1977): 48.

7. Stephen E. Kauffman, Paula Silver, and John Poulin, "Gender Differences in Attitudes toward Alcohol,

Tobacco, and Other Drugs," *Social Work* 42 (May 1997): 231–241.

8. Robert N. Butler, "Prospects for Middle-Aged Women," in *Women in Midlife—Security and Fulfillment* (part 1), a compendium of papers submitted to the Select Committee on Aging and the Subcommittee on Retirement Income and Employment, U.S. House of Representatives, 95th Congress, 2d sess., December 1978, Comm. Pub. No. 95-170, 330.

9. Susan Seliger, "Go Ahead, Cry Your Eyes Out!" *Orange County Register*, January 1982, D1.

Chapter 13: Tempted to Escape

1. Jim Conway, "Women in Midlife Crisis," (Ph.D. diss., University of Illinois, 1986).

2. Mel White, *Lust: The Other Side of Love* (Old Tappan, N.J.: Revell, 1978), 18–19.

3. *Playboy*, September 20, 1976.

4. Maggie Scarf, "The Promiscuous Woman," *Psychology Today*, July 1980, 83.

5. Lewis Smedes, *Sex for Christians* (Grand Rapids, Mich.: Eerdmans, 1994), 168–169.

6. P. Blumstein and P. Schwartz, "Intimate Relationships and the Creation of Sexuality," in *Homosexuality/Hetero-sexuality: Concepts of Sexual Orientation*, ed. David P. McWhirter, Stephanie A. Sanders, and June M. Reinish, (New York: Oxford University Press, 1990), 307–320. Tom W. Smith, "Adult Sexual Behavior in 1989: Number of Partners, Frequency of Intercourse and Risk of AIDS," *Family Planning Perspective*, (1991), 23, 102–107.

7. Morton Hunt, *The Affair* (New York: New American Library, 1969), 93–94.

8. As quoted by Alice Fleming in "Six Myths about Extramarital Affairs," *Reader's Digest*, October 1982, 67.

9. Alan Loy McGinnis, *The Romance Factor* (San Francisco: Harper and Row, 1990), 153–155. Bill and Pam Farrel and Jim and Sally Conway, *Pure Pleasure: Making Your Marriage a Great Affair* (Downers Grove, Ill.: InterVarsity Press, 1994). Jim Conway, Sally Conway, *Moving On after He Moves Out* (Downers Grove, Ill.: InterVarsity Press, 1995). Jim Conway, *Men in Midlife Crisis.* (Elgin, Ill.: David C. Cook, 1978, 1997).
10. Jim Conway, *Adult Children of Legal or Emotional Divorce* (Downers Grove, Ill.: InterVarsity Press, 1990).

Chapter 14: The Legal Escape

1. Morton Hunt, *The Affair*, (New York: New American Library, 1969), 186.
2. National Center for Health Statistics, Advance report, final divorce statistics, 1987, monthly vital statistics report, vol. 38, no. 12, suppl. 2. Hyattsville, Md.: Public Health Service, 1990.
3. National Center for Health Statistics, Advance report of final mortality statistics, 1990, monthly vital statistics report, vol. 41, no. 7, Hyattsville, Md.: Public Health Service, 1993b.
4. Bureau of the Census, Statistical Abstract of the United States: 1993, 113th ed. (Washington, D.C.: U.S. Bureau of the Census, 1993).
5. Morton Hunt, *The Affair* (New York: New American Library, 1969), 253.
6. Jim Conway, *Adult Children of Legal or Emotional Divorce* (Downers Grove, Ill.: InterVarsity Press, 1990).
7. Sally Conway and Jim Conway, *When a Mate Wants Out* (Grand Rapids, Mich.: Zondervan, 1992).
8. Paul D. Meier, "Is Divorce Ever Necessary?" *Christian Medical Society Journal* 7, no. 1 (winter 1976): 4.
9. Meier, "Is Divorce Ever Necessary?"
10. As quoted in Barbara R. Fried, *The Middle-Age Crisis* (New York: Harper and Row, 1967), 40–41.

Chapter 15: Keeping Up with Life's Clocks

1. Erik Erikson, *Childhood and Society* (New York: W. W. Norton, 1950).
   For Further Reading about Adult Development:
   Bühler, Charlotte. "The Curve of Life as Studied in Biographies." *Journal of Applied Psychology.* 1935, 405–409.

   Chiriboga, D., Lowenthal, M. F., Thurnher, M. et al. *Four Stages of Life: A Comparative Study of Women and Men Facing Transitions.* San Francisco: Jossey-Bass, 1975.

   Commons, Michael, Jack Demick, and Carl Goldberg. *Clinical Approaches to Adult Development.* Norwood, N.J.: Ablex, 1996.

   Conway, Jim. *Adult Children of Legal or Emotional Divorce.* Downers Grove, Ill.: InterVarsity Press, 1990.

   Conway, Jim. *Men in Midlife Crisis.* Colorado Springs, Colo.: Chariot Victor, 1997.

   Gruen, Walter. "Adult Personality: An Empirical Study of Erikson's Theory of Ego Development." In B. Neugarten, ed. *Personality in Middle and Late Life: Empirical Studies.* New York: Atherton, 1964.

   Knox, Alan B. *Adult Development and Learning.* San Francisco: Jossey-Bass, 1977.

   Levenson, Michael R. and Cheryl A. Crumpler. "Three Models of Adult Development." *University of California Human Development and Family Studies.* David, Calif.: *Human Development.* 39, no. 3 (May–June 1996), 135–149.

   Levinson, Daniel. *Seasons of a Man's Life.* New York: Knopf, 1978.

Chapter 16: Answering Life's Questions

1. Keith W. Sehnert, *Stress-Unstress* (Minneapolis: Augsburg, 1981), 74–75.

2. John Powell, *Fully Human, Fully Alive* (Allen: Resources for Christian Living, 1995), 87.
3. Quoted in John Powell, *Fully Human, Fully Alive*, 90.
4. Powell, *Fully Human, Fully Alive*, 92.

Chapter 17: Preventing a Crisis

1. Linda Matchan, "Women at Midlife Shatter Stereotypes," the *Denver Post*, 22 February 1983, 2-E.
2. Matchan, "Women at Midlife Shatter Stereotypes."
3. Gail Sheehy, *Pathfinders* (New York: Bantam, 1982), 165.
4. Sheehy, *Pathfinders*.
5. Unpublished poem used by permission.

Chapter 18: Helping a Woman in Crisis

1. Sandra E. Gibbs Candy, "What Do Women Use Friends For?" *Looking Ahead*, ed. Lillian E. Troll et al. (Englewood Cliffs, N.J.: Prentice-Hall, 1977), 108.
2. Robert Peterson, *New Life Begins at Forty* (New York: Trident Press, 1967), 135–136.
3. Gibbs Candy, "What Do Women Use Friends For?" 107.
4. Joyce Landorf, *Tough and Tender* (Old Tappan, N.J.: Revell, 1975).
5. Jim Sanderson, "Now That the Kids Have Grown," *Los Angeles Times*, 15 December 1982, V-8. This column reprinted through the courtesy of Sun Features, Inc., 1992. All rights reserved.
6. Sally Conway, *Menopause* (Grand Rapids, Mich.: Pyranee Books, Zondervan, 1990). Jim and Sally Conway, *Traits of a Lasting Marriage* (Downers Grove, Ill.: InterVarsity Press, 1991). Jim and Sally Conway, *When a Mate Wants Out* (Grand Rapids, Mich.: Zondervan, 1992). Bill and Pam Farrel and Jim and Sally Conway, *Pure Pleasure* (Downers Grove, Ill.: InterVarsity Press, 1994).

7. Bill and Pam Farrel, *Love to Love You* (Eugene, Ore.: Harvest House, 1997).

8. Laura Branigan, "Solitaire," *Branigan 2* album, Atlantic Recording Corporation, 75 Rockefeller Plaza, New York, NY 10019.

Chapter 19: Blooming at Midlife

1. Barbara R. Fried, *The Middle-Age Crisis* (New York: Harper and Row, 1967), 8.

2. Quoted in Peter Chew, *The Inner World of the Middle-Aged Man* (New York: Macmillan, 1976), 10.

3. Bernice L. Neugarten and David L. Gutmann, "Age-Sex Roles and Personality in Middle Age: A Thematic Apperception Study," in *Middle Age and Aging*, ed. Bernice L. Neugarten (Chicago: University of Chicago Press, 1974), 71. Henry Grunebaum, "Middle Age and Marriage: Affiliative Men and Assertive Women," *The American Journal of Family Therapy* 7, no. 3 (fall 1979): 46–50.

4. Anne Morrow Lindbergh, *Gift from the Sea* (New York: Knopf, 1995), 84–85.

5. Anne Ortlund, *Disciplines of the Beautiful Woman*. Dallas: Word, 1996. Swindoll, Charles R. *Strike the Original Match*. Portland, Ore.: Zondervan, 1993. Schaeffer, Edith. *What Is a Family?* Ada, Mich.: Baker, 1993. Richard Bolles. *The Three Boxes of Life*. Berkeley, Calif.: Ten Speed Press, 1978. Richard Bolles. *What Color Is Your Parachute?* San Francisco: Ten Speed Press, 1997.

6. Joyce Brothers, *Better than Ever* (New York: Simon and Schuster, 1975), 118.

7. Eda J. LeShan, *The Wonderful Crisis of Middle Age* (New York: Warner Books, 1985), 102–103.

8. Gail Sheehy, *Pathfinders* (New York: Bantam, 1982), 150.

*Jim and Sally Conway cofounded Midlife
Dimensions, a ministry of Christian Living
Resources, Inc. The organization's purpose is
"strengthening and healing midlife marriages."
Midlife Dimensions works worldwide through
letter counseling, radio and TV programs, a Web
site, and conferences. If you would like more
information about conferences, publications,
media, or counseling, contact:*

Midlife Dimensions
P.O. Box 3790
Fullerton, CA 92834
E-mail: conway@midlife.com
Web site: www.midlife. com